9071O 000 468 562

D16Z7536

Beyond Bad

Also by Chris Paley:

Unthink (2014)

Beyond Bad

How obsolete morals are holding us back

CHRIS PALEY

CORONET

First published in Great Britain in 2021 by Coronet
An Imprint of Hodder & Stoughton
An Hachette UK company

1

Copyright © Chris Paley 2021

The right of Chris Paley to be identified
as the Author of the Work has been asserted by him in accordance
with the Copyright, Designs and Patents Act 1988.

A CIP catalogue record for this title is available from the British Library

Hardback ISBN 9781529327090
eBook ISBN 9781529327106

Typeset by Palimpsest Book Production Limited, Falkirk, Stirlingshire
Printed and bound in Great Britain by Clays Ltd, Elcograf S.p.A.

Hodder & Stoughton policy is to use papers that are natural, renewable and
recyclable products and made from wood grown in sustainable forests. The logging
and manufacturing processes are expected to conform to the environmental
regulations of the country of origin.

Hodder & Stoughton Ltd
Carmelite House
50 Victoria Embankment
London EC4Y 0DZ

www.hodder.co.uk

For my family, by far the most important of
the groups I belong to.

CONTENTS

Morality's what we're doing when we shout at the TV, gossip about our boss or leave comments online. It's held empires together, kept soldiers marching under fire, fed the hungry, passed laws, built walls, welcomed immigrants, destroyed careers and governed our sex lives.

But morality is meaningless rubbish. It's a malfunctioning relic of our evolutionary past. Philosophically flawed, psychologically bizarre, morality's a diseased appendix of the mind. Belief in vice and virtue, good and evil, rights, responsibilities, duties and moral codes should be put aside along with faith in the sun god and flat-earth physics.

This is a science book. It's about how we work rather than how we imagine we work. It's about how people gain moral values rather than how they think they gain moral values.

Some of you will find this hard to stomach. You'll have a nagging feeling that somewhere out there, if only we could discover them, there are deep moral truths that are absolute and indisputable. Things we ought and oughtn't do. Moral values, or virtues, or duties, that we all ought to obey. The first chapter is to set your mind at rest. Philosophers have given the search their best shot, and they have failed because there are no such things.

Some of you may be here because you want to improve yourself. You want to have more and be more. Before you dive into the details, you want some promise that getting rid of your morals isn't merely the right thing to do, it's the thing that will get you what you want. The second chapter is for you; it will tell you what you want to hear. You'll be more successful if you ditch your morals.

There's plenty of hard evidence that society's most successful already see morals as baggage for the little people. The wealthiest, and those highest up the social ladder, are more willing to break the rules. And it's not just your bank balance that will benefit from casting off your constraints: immorality and creativity go hand-in-hand. Ethics don't just constrain our actions, they act as a block on the types of things we are able to think. But if morals aren't reasoned truths, and people with fewer of them do better in today's society, why do we have them in the first place? In chapter three, I'll argue that humans have the mental machinery to moralise because it was in our ancestors' genes' interests. We'll see that humans imposed morality on each other: not because it was the 'right' thing to do, but because the costs to our DNA of not joining in were too great.

In chapter four, we'll find that these morals aren't about deep philosophical reflection or knotted arguments. They're about what we read into people's minds, about the impression we have of them, and the stories we tell about them.

People judge you based not on what you have done, but on what they think went on in your brain when you did it. Since they can't see inside your skull, or track the messages flicking between neurons, they have to invent a mind for you. We'll find out how they do that, what sorts of things they use when deciding what to put in that mind, and how to ensure that the mind they invent for you is the mind you want them to invent for you.

If, as I propose to show, we have morals to avoid punishment and gain the trust of other humans, and if other humans choose

2

how to act towards us based on the minds they read in us, then the evolutionary pressure on our ancestors wasn't to *be* good, it was to *seem* good. In chapters five and six, we'll see that these are very different things.

We are naturally adept at shaping what other people read in our minds. At giving off signals of good intentions even when we don't have them. What's more, and stranger, is that we often do this without realizing, fooling ourselves about why we do what we do.

But if our brains are excellent at changing what other people think and how they behave, then the science of morality creates dangers for those who take others' and their own intentions at face value. Those who unthinkingly follow their consciences make themselves targets, vulnerable to the machinations of people who are thinking about these matters.

Once you can predict something, you may well be able to manipulate it. This is as true of others' morals, judgements and actions as it is of the electrons in your phone or the bullet in a gun. Big business, PR agencies and advertisers are already in the game, and we'll see how their tactics work.

Our morals also get in the way of us accomplishing things. Morality constrains us, biases us and pushes us in the wrong direction because we fail to understand what it is for.

Morals made cooperation possible for our ancestors; they bound them into effective groups. But, as we'll find in chapters seven and eight, the point of cooperation was competition: tribes, families, armies, teams and companies all coordinate their behaviour to outdo other groups. Morality needs a 'them' and 'us' to function: it's what it's for.

We might imagine our morals are fair, universalisable, group-blind. But behind the scenes, out of conscious awareness, our moral brains are busy bending our behaviour to their ends. All the greatest evil today and in history is the result of good people following their consciences: the coordinated action behind it wouldn't have been possible otherwise. The Russian gulags, the Spanish Inquisition, slavery – all were carried out by people who had as much reason to think they were 'doing the right thing' as we do.

Understanding, overcoming and discarding morality is urgent. The biggest challenges our species faces, whether global warming, nuclear proliferation or the rise of the robots, are pan-human. They are beyond what our moral minds were designed to cope with. You can't build smartphones with stone-age axes, and you can't solve modern humanity's problems with tools that are designed to create primitive, competitive groups.

We need rid of morality, for our own sake and for that of the world. This won't be easy, but reading this book will help: understanding morality is the first step in losing it, and research shows that books on ethics are more likely to be stolen.[1] So make paying for this book your last ethical act.

ONE:
Morality can't be what we imagine it is

What is morality? It seems sensible that a book on the topic should start with a clear definition up front.

However, scientists usually prefer to understand things *before* they define them. It was only after they'd found that negative electric charges arose in discrete chunks that they coined the term 'electron'. As they blasted these charges through gratings and span them around in particle accelerators, they learnt more about them: and the definition of the electron we now use was formulated. An electron is what it has to be in order to explain the results of their experiments.

This is a book on the science of humans, with an emphasis on evolutionary psychology. It's about how they have gained beliefs that they describe as 'moral'. About when they act on those beliefs and when they don't. It's about what people do when they think they're alone, what they do when they know they're being watched and what they do in groups. It's about what people say they believe and what they say they'll do, and how these change when they're in different situations. It's about how people judge and trust, and how both of these affect their behaviour. These things are all measurable. You can study them experimentally.

This book asks the question: what has to be true about morality and human behaviour in order for us to explain the experimental findings that scientists around the world are unearthing?

We'll discover that what is true about 'morality' is so far from what we mean when we usually use the term that it's question-able whether we should call them the same thing. We'll see that if 'morality' were what people think of it as being, then morality doesn't exist – except perhaps as a figment of our imagination, a bizarre flat-earth story of how people behave and how they ought to behave.

As I say, some of you will find this hard to stomach. You possibly believe that if scientists think they can tell us about morality, then they simply haven't understood what it is. Your definition, and that of most people, seems to you self-evident and impervious to anything that might be found in a lab: it's common sense, you may say.

You may think that 'you oughtn't keep slaves' is a true state-ment whatever any scientist has to say on the matter, and that good people recognise such truths and act upon them. You probably also have a firm idea of what morality is *for*. It improves the well-being of humans. It's altruistic. It involves putting others' interests before your own. Isn't that what philosophers say?

Furthermore, if you accept that there are university professors with a deeper understanding than you of what is right and what is wrong, of what you ought and oughtn't to do, you may well imagine that they sit not in science labs but among their books in philosophy departments.

The aim of this chapter is to clear away some of those miscon-ceptions so that you can approach the rest of the book with a more open mind. The common-sense understanding of morality falls apart with only the slightest prodding. Philosophers have had the field for thousands of years, and their endeavours have failed. Spectacularly.

I've written this book to show that it's time to give science a go. Even if that means letting go of much of what we thought we knew about morals, and about ourselves. Even if it means *giving up on morals themselves.*

Pure thought is for idiots

Armchairs are worn out as philosophers think deeply about ethics. They've been at it for three thousand years. Socrates, Plato, Aristotle, Hobbes, Spinoza, Kant, Hegel, Mill are names to conjure with: some of them are almost synonymous with rational thought and scholarly might.

What is the crowning glory of this multiepochal, multicultural, multilingual monumental project? Is it a set of rules all agree we ought to follow? A universal consensus on virtues to be cultivated? Duties to uphold? Rights to bestow? Perhaps something more modest: an agreed definition of 'ought' or an explanation of how moral obligations arise?

Unfortunately not. Philosophers are still squabbling and scribbling after all this time not because they're making great leaps of progress, but because they can't even settle the basics. By the standards of any other discipline, philosophical ethics has been a spectacular flop.

We can have sympathy for the poor pipe-puffers. They are in good company. Watch day-time TV and you'll see moral arguments that are as passionate as those between Plato and his pupils, and about as productive.

When Amber objects to her sister sleeping with her husband, she has no doubt at all that she oughtn't to have. It's not a tentative opinion. When her sister Chloe argues that the aggrieved party doesn't satisfy said husband and deserves to lose him, she's not advancing a hypothesis that she will readily drop.

When the audience tires of Amber and Chloe, there are plenty of other topics to open the phone lines for. The politician's sex scandal; the Olympic drug cheat; the Arab revolution; the *Love Island* liar; gun laws in the US; the death penalty; paedophile vigilantes; city-centre housing shortages; global warming; bankers' bonuses; your colleague's promotion; immigration; the Iraq war; taxation; torture of terrorists; bending the truth on your CV; sick leave when it's sunny; statutory rape; marijuana decriminalisation; faking orgasm; your husband leaving the toilet seat up; internet porn; swearing at the ref; liver transplants for alcoholics; standing for the national anthem; tobacco advertising; nuclear disarmament; assisted dying; inheritance; nepotism; wearing fur; eating beef; the minimum wage; elephants in circuses; charity skydiving; designer babies; Frankenstein food.

All of these involve questions of what *ought* to happen; how people *ought* to behave. What is right and what is wrong. You probably have a view, and you probably imagine you can tell me why you hold that view and why all others are wrong.

We moralise at home, at school, at work and for pleasure. The simplest spy thriller delivers its pay-off through morality: the bad guy getting justice. The more sophisticated question just who the bad guy is; what ends justify what means. Every story worth your time, from *Cinderella* to *Crime and Punishment*, from *Macbeth* to *Breaking Bad*, insists you make moral judgements.

However bright or stupid we are, this instinct that moral statements can be true or false and that we have the capabilities to work out which they are doesn't go away. We might be poor at maths, but we're certain we can reason morally.

If reasoning can do anything, you'd think it could settle arguments. Yet moral differences don't disappear.

Is this book a scream of despair that progress can't be made? Thankfully not. In the last few decades, more progress has been made in understanding why we moralise, how we moralise, how moralising affects our behaviour and the sorts of errors we make than in the preceding three thousand years.

This is because scientists have got involved. They may not all be as smart as Plato or Hegel, but they do have techniques that work.[3]

Moral facts are magic. Magic doesn't exist. Therefore, moral facts don't exist

You can't reason out of nothing. At the base of all logic is an axiom, a postulate, a premise, an assumption. Take the argument: 'All men are mortal. Socrates is a man. Therefore, Socrates is mortal.' As a piece of logic, it's a classic. Indisputable. But for it to be useful, for the conclusion to hold, we have to accept as axioms that all men are mortal and that Socrates is a man. As I say, in logic as in life, you don't get something for nothing. How might we establish the facts used in the above argument? We can define 'man' in some way, and then pull up Socrates' toga and check that he meets the definition. We then have to convince ourselves that all creatures meeting the definition are mortal.

In principle, this is nearly impossible. What we would need is a mad woman to take herself up in a rocket, and blow up the Earth. Provided that all the men died, she could be satisfied that all men were mortal.

This method's a little drastic. If, instead, we select a hundred men at random, and find that they all stop breathing when we

6

slit their throats, we are *reasonably* confident of our statement that 'all men are mortal'.[4] In practice, most of us settle for the third-best observation that there aren't any two-hundred-year-old men wandering about.

Science, unlike moral philosophy, has a spectacular track record. Observing the world, poking it, heating it up, setting it on fire, stretching it and blasting it through gratings has given us tremendously powerful rules for predicting how it will work. We have great confidence that our aeroplanes will stay in the sky, that apples will fall to the ground and that men will die. It gives us facts we can usefully reason with.

The problem with philosophical ethics isn't the *reasoning* itself. It's the 'facts' that go into the reasoning. These are nothing like those that scientists use and reason with so successfully.

Let's take an example to see what's wrong with them. You are laying the foundations of a building, and working hard to keep to time. You notice a drunk collapse into the path of the cement you are laying. Nobody's looking, so you could keep on, the boozer would be squelched under the building and you'd collect your bonus for completing the job.

Your conscience is working with you. 'You ought to stop,' it whines in that wheedling voice that consciences have. 'Why?' you reply, keeping on. 'If you don't, you'll kill him.' 'So?' 'You oughtn't kill people.' 'Why?'

The reasoning continues. Your conscience might argue that you oughtn't kill because you oughtn't harm others. Perhaps you oughtn't harm others because you ought to treat others as you'd like to be treated yourself. But at some stage it has to stop at a fact, a premise, an assumption. Something that isn't supported by yet another logical step. There has to be a foundation to the tower of reasoning.

What sort of fact is it and how can you get hold of it? We're going to see now just how jolly odd the facts underlying moral reasoning are, and how different to anything else.[5] Let's list some of the properties that moral statements are supposed to have before we examine whether they are plausible:

1. Moral rules ought to be obeyed whether we recognise them or not. If you say, 'I don't accept there's any reason to treat others as I'd like to be treated myself,' does that mean you do nothing wrong in cementing the drunk into your new building? Or do the rules apply to you regardless? If a Nazi sincerely believes that extirpating gays is a good thing, does he do wrong in killing them? If he does, then moral rules aren't just a matter of our own feelings or thoughts: they are external to us.

2. Moral facts seem to be objective. The fact that a few hundred years ago most (white) people might have thought slavery was fine and now they don't doesn't affect whether or not it is. The statement 'you oughtn't keep slaves' is true or it is false.

3. Moral facts *seem* to provide a reason for doing things. I know that cola contains sugar. That doesn't in itself give me a reason to drink it or not to drink it. But if I have a desire[6] to lose weight, that desire coupled with the knowledge that the cola contains sugar does give me a reason not to do so. And if I value the taste more than the slim-fit trousers then I'm free to drink it. The external, objective fact of cola containing sugar isn't enough: I also need a desire to give it some oomph, to give me a *reason* to act one way or the other. The same apparently isn't true of morals. If you, as the builder, were to say 'yes, I acknowledge that killing the poor soak is wrong, but that changes nothing' we'd question whether you understood what 'wrong' meant.

There are no other facts like this in the world: objective, external and yet motivating to those who are aware of them. In every other context, motivation is internal and subjective. It comes from neurons and chemicals in the actor. But we're supposed to believe that moral facts are something else: they come from without and yet carry an impulse, a command, a reason to behave in a particular way. So how do we come by these very odd facts?

If you're religious, you could ask God or commune with the spirits. Later in this chapter, we'll have a look at the claim that the faithful have a separate and solid basis for their moral commitments. But if you're not religious, then just how do you get them? Is there something special in us that allows humans to intuit them if we try hard enough? What does it mean to intuit a fact; what knowledge could we possibly be accessing?

Are they magic particles, philosophical photons whizzing through space? Maybe they were transmitted at the big bang. Is our nervous system really an antenna allowing us to pick them up?[7]

Yet even if these fantastical rays or particles existed, why should we have evolved to detect them? As we will see, our genes don't care about such profundities: evolution selects those genes that are good at sticking around, not those that make us *good*.

There's also the difficulty of the diversity of sincerely held ethical beliefs, which runs counter to the second property that moral facts are supposed to have. There are women who want their daughters' genitals slicing off. Men who think it their duty to avenge the slaying of a family member by hunting down male relatives of the murderer. In history there have been pederasts, slavers and destroyers of cities who slept comfortably at night and were admired within their communities.[8]

Perhaps philosophers haven't tracked down the source of objective moral truth because, as I've intimated, *there isn't one*.

But let's begin to examine the science of morality. We are going to see that understanding the way we have come to these odd, impossible-to-justify beliefs, and the real causes of our moral behaviour, is a particularly hard task. This is partly because we seem to be built to believe things about ourselves that aren't true. To study morality, we have to use our brains to overcome what our brains are designed to do. It's difficult, but I hope to show it's doable.

That we can reason doesn't make us reasonable

I said earlier that moral philosophy has been a spectacular failure, but you might wonder what the philosophers are up to. If they haven't thrown in the towel and got proper jobs, they must think they're on to something.*

A few philosophers are clever, very clever. But in the end, they are only playing with words.[10] At some point, when wrestling with definitions before you have facts, you lose sight of what is important.

It is sad when any group of highly trained individuals become obsolete, whether they are coal miners, footmen, Ptolemaic cosmologists or switchboard operators. There could be pathos in the moral philosopher continuing, like the redundant footman

---

* In the endnotes, there's a brief discussion of their hapless attempt to save their discipline.[9]

who dons his livery at the weekends and sets out the cutlery in his one-bedroom flat. But moral philosophers are in a privileged position. Our universities still churn them out by the thousand, and as long as they can convince eighteen-year-olds that their subject is worth studying, vice-chancellors have no reason to cull this very cheap department. I think we'll always have moral philosophers, in the same way that we still have astrologers, clairvoyants and theologians.

What morality and religion share

Philosophers aren't the only non-scientists who claim some understanding of moral behaviour. There are bearded men sitting in caves, bearded men in ashrams, bearded men in synagogues, bearded men in mosques, bearded men in temples and bearded men handing down commandments from the clouds. There are also non-bearded men in orange robes or dog collars, and a smattering of typically non-bearded ladies.

Religion, power and morality have always gone together. They are the three main ways of creating coordinated action among human beings. Power means you will be hit over the head if you don't do what you're told; religion means you will be hit over the head for all eternity if you don't do what you're told; morality means you will hit yourself over the head if you don't do what you're told.

So it shouldn't be any surprise that those with power have traditionally sought religious and moral authority or vice-versa. The Queen of England is also the head of the Church of England; the Emperor of Japan is descended from a sun-goddess and is the highest authority in Shinto; the Iranian president is a Muslim cleric.

Today, the three are becoming unbundled. CEOs write high-minded missives to their staff deploring terrorist atrocities and supporting initiatives ranging from gay marriage to sexual equality. Prime ministers speak of what is *right* for the nation. But the religious thread in the plait is fraying.

The number of atheists is rising. They are still a minority, but they are very influential. In Europe at least, few think that moral questions can be settled by determining what God would want.

This change has been dramatic, and it has happened in living memory. What is perhaps surprising is that morality hasn't disappeared to the degree that religion has. The moral rules have changed a little bit, particularly in relation to sex and sexuality. But people still believe in right and wrong; they give money to charity and march for people's rights.

It's not obvious that it should be so. Back when Plato thought that ethics could be reasoned, he knew that most people weren't up to the task. He proposed that the unwashed masses were given religion, and even stipulated that anybody who tried to take it from them should be executed. He couldn't see how you could behave morally without either an exacting ethical (i.e. philosophical) education or a belief in higher powers.[11]

Today, many have neither. They know that no god gives them access to moral facts, or provides a reason for acting on those facts, and yet they still believe they have access to moral facts and ought to follow them. It's not clear that they know something Plato didn't.

In the main varieties of religion, and certainly in Christianity, the variety that is dwindling fastest in the West, there is an afterlife and an all-seeing and just God. Alicia believes in this God. She believes with certainty that she should care for her neighbour: God has told her to do so. She also believes that if she does so she will be granted eternal bliss as a reward.

Bertha doesn't believe in any god. If she cares for her neighbour, there are no direct positive consequences for her (other than perhaps a warm and fuzzy feeling).

It can't be rational for Alicia and Bertha to behave in the same way if either certainty of belief or self-interest have any bearing on our behaviour. Of course, Bertha might argue that Alicia just isn't rational: her belief in the man in the sky is ample evidence for this. Alicia might counter that whether Bertha believes in God or not, God still loves her and guides her.

But if Bertha wants to maintain that she is rational when she bungs a fiver in the homeless charity collection tin, she clearly has more explaining to do than Alicia. Alicia has made a leap of faith that she's aware of; Bertha has made one without realising.

I don't think that science has done away with religion. That we evolved by natural selection doesn't disprove the existence of any creator god. Indeed, if I was a god, I'd think it a jolly clever way of doing things.[12]

But the difference between science and religion is why we're going to reject the latter for the purposes of this book. Science uses observations as factual inputs; the religious can use facts derived from faith.

The problem with religious facts, of course, is the same problem we have identified with moral facts: we can't agree on what they are. Even within a tradition, there are sects and cults. Christians disagree on the virgin birth, purgatory, original sin and the utility of the sacraments. Muslims slaughter more of each other over doctrinal differences than they kill infidels in the West. Every religion of any importance has this same problem: if the facts are knowable, the elect are few.

This is hugely different to science. Experiments are repeatable.

Theories are testable. We can agree on a starting point from which to do our reasoning.

Studying morality is subversive

We've looked at how difficult it is to justify morality with philosophy. We've claimed that science has the tools to make a better stab at it, even if using those tools may be difficult. In this section, I'll argue that precisely because scientists might achieve what they set out to achieve it could be dangerous too.

During the Cold War, the curiosity of nuclear physicists was channelled into the making of a device that could exterminate all humans. Scientists don't always realise where they're headed. When Rutherford split the atom, or Einstein equated mass with energy, I doubt either of them envisioned a nuclear holocaust or feared for the citizens of Hiroshima.

We can have some sympathy for the early nuclear physicists. Before they did their work, it was impossible to know where it might lead. Learning how particles are glued together didn't *necessarily* have any practical implications.

But scientists who investigate morality can't, or shouldn't, be so innocent. Morality glues us together; it affects how we act towards other people. Even rules around flag burning or standing during the national anthem exist to shape how people perceive their duty and their loyalties, to modify how they behave towards each other.

Questioning morality might undermine such behaviours. Without trust that others will behave in a certain way – that they will behave morally – society isn't possible. Power itself isn't strong enough to coordinate human behaviour. As I see it, there are three obvious dangers in getting to the bottom of how morality works.

The first danger is the danger inherent in all science. The better you understand nature, the more easily you can manipulate it. We will look at experiments which show how morals can be used to manipulate people, including by those who intend to harm and exploit.

Is it beyond imagining that Mark Zuckerberg, Larry Page, Rupert Murdoch or Vladimir Putin might want society to be a bit different? A little more in line with their self-interest or how they think it ought to be? Studying the science of morality could, and perhaps already does, make it more than a little easier for them.

The second danger in trying to get to the bottom of morals is that we find things we don't like. We have already seen that morality and society have altered dramatically since history began. Old men oughtn't bugger children; slaves oughtn't be kept, let alone tortured; peasants aren't hanged for stealing sheep.

Do we think that a scientific study will one day conclude that the particular form of society we now live in, the conception of morality we hold, the list of ought and oughtn'ts, will turn out to be just the right one? Who are we kidding? We already know that it won't. Studying morals, therefore, can lead to pessimism or even nihilism.

But the third is the greatest danger. Humans are not particles; they don't do what they do regardless of what scientists find out about them. Knowing how we work and why we work the way we do will in itself affect how we work in ways that could potentially be extremely alarming.

It's not news to us that people believe false things, that believing them changes their behaviour, or even that their errors sometimes serve a useful purpose. Believing in the bogeyman keeps children out of the dangerous forest; Santa Claus keeps them well behaved at Christmas. Jupiter motivated the Roman troops, and the fear of Ammit kept the Egyptians in line.

But once we stop believing the myth, its power fades. I don't believe in Santa, and I'm no longer extra-good in December.

The scientific study of morality doesn't just question the content of morality – the prohibition on stealing or the duty to pay your taxes, say – it questions its very structure. I intend to show that morality relies on us believing in facts that don't exist, arguing about reasons that aren't reasons and behaving in particular, irrational ways for motives we're unaware of.

It might well turn out that some of these myths are essential for society to function. That explaining what glues us together damages the binding.

This is already worrying some thinkers. Moral error theory is the technical term for the recognition that moral 'facts' of the sort we've looked at in this chapter can't be true; that we are in error when we talk of them. In an academic book[13], Richard Joyce, a moral philosopher, considers whether the knowledge ought to be kept under lock and key. 'Some people may be "in the know" about the moral error theory while, for the greater good, keeping it quiet and encouraging the hoi polloi to continue with their sincere (false) moral beliefs'.

Joyce doesn't like the idea ('manipulative lies'). He prefers an approach called 'moral fictionalism': that we act as though we still believe in moral truths even though we don't. Others think we should try and cram the genie back into the bottle: to find some way, any way, to justify normative discourse before the idea gets out.

I like the sound of moral fictionalism; I think it's cute. Unfortunately, I don't think that people are designed like that.

Pretending to believe something isn't the same as believing it, and it doesn't have the same impact on our behaviour. I'd like to believe I can fly. I can pretend to do so. But there's no way you're getting me to jump off the roof.

On the alternative – cramming the genie back into the bottle – I think it's too late. The genie has granted too many wishes, dispensed too much wisdom. Morality is in the hands of scientists now and it can't be returned safely to the philosophers. By pussyfooting around with the subject for so long, they've done humanity a great service: greater than they know or intended. But their tenure is over.

TWO:
Being bad

Questioning your morals is, as we've just seen, a big step. A scary step. During the course of this book, we'll see just how big a part of you, and your social life, morals are.

You might have an emotional reaction to even contemplating the possibility that morals as you think of them aren't doing what you think they're doing. You might ask what about Hitler? Pederasty? Murder? Rape? The implications of ditching right and wrong are just too big.

This is a little like the mum who, on learning that her daughter has renounced her faith, asks 'Does this mean you don't believe Grandma is in heaven?' Yes, that is a consequence. But wanting Grandma to be in heaven doesn't conjure paradise into being; it's not a sensible reason to believe, even for the faithful or a child.

We can't study morality without taking the risk that what we believe is wrong. Bertrand Russell wrote:

The pursuit of truth, when it is wholehearted, must ignore moral considerations; we cannot know in advance that the truth will turn out to be what is thought edifying in a given society . . . One of the defects of all philosophers since Plato is that their enquiries into ethics proceed on the assumption that they already know the conclusions to be reached.[14]

Wanting something to be so doesn't make it so. And, in the case of morals, we shouldn't want it to be so. I hope to show that the more you learn about how morals really work, the more you'll want to be rid of them.

In later chapters, we will find that the reason we can moralise (even if moralising isn't quite what we imagine it to be) is because doing so granted a benefit to our ancestors' genes. We will also discover that the social environment that led to morality's evolution has disappeared: we no longer live in tribes, or know everybody we interact with. What benefitted our forebears imposes an irrational cost on us, and makes modern humanity's problems worse.

This chapter is a foretaste of those discoveries and revelations.

Modern common-sense morality is supposed to include sharing, following the rules, doing things for others. Believing that others' good is at least as important as your own. But we will see now that the most successful people in modern society do less of all of these. We'll find:

- Rich people carry around less moral baggage.
- Less ethical people are more creative.
- Knowing when to appear good, and when not to, can improve your sex life.
- Moreover, people don't regret their unethical actions nearly as much as they expect; instead, they tend to worry about the opportunities they missed out on.

I'd like to believe that all readers are here out of sheer curiosity. But if science tells us how morality works, and if, when we get there, that's a good reason for casting it off, this research also gives a simpler argument for ditching your morals.

As hinted at in the last chapter, morals are for suckers. They hold you back. They stop you doing what you want to, and make you want to do things that aren't in your interests. They diminish you. They constrain your behaviour to match the expectations of the time and culture and place you live in.

The rich are different to the poor: they have fewer morals

It's hard to become rich without prioritising the acquisition of money over other things. It's hard to stay rich if you give your money to those who need it more. But you might expect the wealthy to come into their own in respect for the rules. After all, the system works pretty well for them.

Property rights depend on laws, for instance; cash can be safely stashed away in the bank only due to government support and regulation; the police protect them from the envious while the rich swan around in cashmere coats or Jimmy Choos. International trade, markets, the force of contracts, inheritance: all of the things the wealthy feed off are only possible due to laws and people's willingness to follow them. If people stopped doing what the statutes said they were supposed to do, the rich would lose most. Whether rules and regulations are morality codified or a replacement for it, the well-heeled are their greatest beneficiary and they know it, surely?

Scientists in the US weren't so certain. The researchers set up at a busy junction in California and played traffic cops for the day. They kept track of which vehicles illegally cut in front of others. They counted the drivers who refused to stop for pedestrians at a crossing.

They also graded the cars. The sleek Aston Martin of a

23

hedge-fund manager or an early Facebook investor was classed as a '5' in their system. The type of old banger my mum ferried me to school in was a '1'.

This is a neat experiment. It doesn't rely on asking people what they would do in such-and-such a hypothetical situation. It doesn't test how smoothly volunteers lie, or what they think researchers want to hear. It measures how people actually behave when they don't know anyone is watching.

Not all rich people drive flash cars. But if you're whizzing around in a Tesla you're not scrubbing floors or serving coffees. So, were affluent drivers more likely to be careful because they respected the rule of law or because they didn't want the blood and brains of poor people messing up their paintwork?

Neither. The fancier the wheels, the less care the driver took of others. Nearly half of drivers in the most expensive two grades of vehicle hurtled past the pedestrian at the crossing versus about one in four of those in the ropiest two classes. Grade '5' drivers were four times as likely to cut in front of other cars as those in the rust buckets. When the rubber hits the road, the affluent know that the rules are for the little people.[15]

The rich have more, take more and give less

The car experiment's nice. But perhaps there's something about sitting in a leather seat with a prancing stallion on your steering wheel that frees you from the rules. If you'd put Mother Theresa into a sports car, maybe she'd have cut up the traffic too. It could conceivably be the motor driving the behaviour rather than the person.

But you probably don't believe that, and you're right not to. Research shows that the bad behaviour is driven by the rich individuals. There are plenty of studies showing that the most successful people in society share less and take more. They're more comfortable accepting amoral motives, and don't empathise with others so well.

- Experimenters quizzed students on their background and how they thought their social and economic status compared to others. A week later, the students took part in a game. They were given ten points and asked how many they wished to share with a partner in the game, who had none. The greater people perceived their status, the less they were willing to share.[16]
- Researchers gave adult participants twenty photographs of faces and asked them to identify which of a list of emotions were expressed. The more education people had, the less accurate they were at judging emotions in the pictures.[17] (Those who have a college education are worse at it than those who only finished school by almost as much as women are better than men.)
- Those who thought their social class was higher took more sweets from a jar which they believed was intended for distribution among children at a nearby lab.[18] Such people are also more willing to admit that greed is good, and to cheat for money.

Wealth, education and status are all comparative things. An ancient king would be astonished at how many of our poor have central heating and running water. A medieval monk, spending his life in a library, couldn't comprehend the theories of Darwin and Newton, let alone believe that we teach them to even our stupidest teenagers. Which suggests that if you want someone to do you a favour, you shouldn't remind her how well off she is, or how lucky.

Indeed, this is what researchers find. When they ask volunteers to compare themselves to the worst off in society – reflecting on how their income, jobs and education are better – the volunteers afterwards believe they should donate *less* of their own money to charity than those who have compared themselves to the wealthiest.[19]

Nobody ever called the wealthy the salt of the earth

Some psychologists[20] have seen moral understanding as something that develops in the course of a lifetime. Young children think being good is doing what mum tells them to. As we progress, we think that being good is doing the things others approve of; we follow rules and do our duty. Then we believe in laws and maintaining the social order for its own sake. Finally, as fully formed adults, we move on to universalisable ethical principles, human rights and respect for individuals' dignity.

There is even a questionnaire which purports to measure your level of moral maturity. According to this particular questionnaire and theory of development, liberals score highest. Conservatives are stuck somewhere in late adolescence.

But this theory is tosh. It's tosh because the difference between liberal and conservatives isn't a matter of development. When conservatives are asked to 'think like a radical', their performance on the moral maturity questionnaire balloons. They are quite capable of passing the test: they have all the cognitive maturity; they just believe different things.[21]

The hypothesis is suspect from the outset. It tends to be the wealthy and the better-educated who are liberal, and poorer people who hold conservative moral beliefs.[22]

Who imagines they have more need of society, and recognises that their life depends on other people behaving ethically? The trust-fund kid at Harvard who worries that exposure to second-hand smoke might knock a few seconds off his privileged life? As we've already seen, the system works pretty well for the rich.

Or is it the poverty-stricken cleaner in an inner-city slum who recognises his reliance on morality? Who will put me up if my git of a boss sacks me and I can't pay the rent? Who will look after my children if I'm caught in the crossfire of a drugs deal without insurance? Who will cover for me when I'm ill?

Money is important. It's weird and it's horrible and it's imaginary and it distorts the way we treat other people. And so does lack of money.

Poverty takes its toll early. Experimenters read ambiguous scenarios to schoolchildren.[23] For example, 'You raise your hand in class and are called on. Immediately after making a comment, you hear a classmate of yours begin to laugh'.

The poorer the parents of the child, the less likely they were to assume a funny story or a dirty picture was doing the round, and the more likely they were to jump to the conclusion that they were the butt of the joke.

Poorer children also have a greater physiological reaction (increased heart rate and so on) to stressful events. From an early age, they know that bad things can happen to them. We'll see later that morality historically played a role in forming groups and protecting us from aggressors. When people are frightened, they're more likely to stick to the rules.

Morals are bad for rich and poor alike. But if morality causes poverty, it's also possible that poverty is responsible for the stronger ethics of the poor. Morality preys on those with little, and leaves them with little.

The more you have, the more you think you're worth it

It might seem surprising that having cash in the bank can have a profound effect on our morals, our respect for the law and even how relaxed we are. But the wealthy have a secret. They're not merely rich; they *deserve* to be rich. We live in a just world, and people of their ilk couldn't do anything but succeed.

The caste system of India, in one form or another, is three thousand years old. Traditionally, Indians were strictly categorised into one of four *varna*. Your varna influenced your social standing, what job you did and who you could marry. The Brahmin formed a priestly class at the top of the heap; the Dalits were so far underneath that they fell out of the classification system altogether. Since Independence, caste has been a fraught political issue. In spite of government action to reserve jobs for the previously 'untouchable' groups, Brahmins on average have substantially greater income and more education than Dalits.[24]

Is this persistent difference due to some intrinsic property of the different stocks: is an Indian's caste linked to innate character and abilities which will always shine through? Or have millennia of oppression taken away the aspirations and opportunities of those at the bottom of the pile? A researcher, Ramaswami Mahalingam, asked this question of both groups.[25] He told them of a swap at birth: in a muddle at the hospital, a Dalit baby went home with a Brahmin couple, and a Brahmin baby was given to Dalit parents. How would the kids get on?

Brahmins believed that a Brahmin child would act like a Brahmin whoever brought it up, and a Dalit child would revert to type even in a Brahmin household. Dalits, on the other hand, thought that opportunity and social connections mattered more: a Dalit in a Brahmin family would do as well as any Brahmin, and a Brahmin transplanted into their own household would suffer the consequences.

In the US, they're not supposed to have classes, never mind castes. But the divide between the haves and have nots is at least as stark. And the greater a person's income and education, and the higher up the social ladder they perceive themselves, the more likely they are to believe that somebody's class is determined by their genes.[26]

To be creative is to think different; to think different is to be immoral

Einstein's affairs. Hemingway's womanising. Steve Jobs' egomania and paternity denial. John Galliano's anti-Semitic outburst. Thomas Edison's invention of the electric chair.

We could make an argument that the most creative people in any field are missing a moral compass. But to do so with a list like this is perhaps not the most reliable way to go about it. The errant, if not evil, genius could well be biased by a desire to make a provocative, attention-seeking point. Does Hemingway seem more of a genius, more inspired, because of his womanising?

Nevertheless, the evidence is that there *is* something in this stereotype. In advertising, there are creative people and not so creative people. There are suits who schmooze clients and take orders, and there are oddballs who realise that you can sell beer with videos of white horses in the sea.

Experimenters at Harvard and Duke gave moral dilemmas to employees in a large agency.[27] They also asked managers which of the employees did the funky stuff and which were in accounts. Results showed that the more creative the job, the less ethical the responses.

Still, we might not be convinced. Do other motives come into play? Maybe the imaginative types had, like Hemingway, bought into the myth: they thought they were expected to be a little dodgy. So the same scientists gave other volunteers some standard tests of creativity – and the chance to cheat for money. Again, the more creative the person, the greater the willingness to break the rules.

Why should this be so? Does imagination lead to immorality, or is it the other way around? Is it the ability to have great ideas, or the success that comes with them, that mangles our morality? Before Jobs hit on his great idea, was he a charming young man?

It turns out that when we contemplate iffy behaviour, there's a predictable brain signal (the N400) that spurts under the crown of your head about half a second later.[28] Nobody's quite sure what it does, but it seems to act as some sort of inhibitor. Think that clapping at a funeral's OK? Woah no, the signal says. Thinking of kissing the handsome doctor at the hospital? Stop that.

The signal's stronger in some people than others. It might not surprise you that, in general, it flares up more energetically in poorer people's skulls or that of those who believe their culture is superior (i.e. those who endorse statements such as 'Our people are not perfect, but our culture is superior to others'). But it's also the case that the more imaginative you are, the weaker this signal.

So it's not an accident that creative geniuses are weird loners, that they fail to get on with other people or that they get away with what they can get away with.

Morality's about doing what other people do; creativity's about doing what other people don't.

You only need to be good if you want to be good

A friend asked me recently, 'Why are there no good men anymore?' I think she was talking about men in general rather than me specifically, and I don't believe she expected a serious answer. That her gran spoils her with tales from a mythical era, when knights took a break from killing dragons only to deliver flowers to maidens, rescue kittens from trees and serve in the soup kitchen, doesn't mean it was ever so. Yet if the anecdotal evidence has a kernel of truth, and men are crummier than they used to be, there might be a reason.

Researchers created short descriptions of eight men.[29] Some of the men were brave: they liked rock-climbing and free-fall parachuting. Some of them were altruistic: they manned the lifeboats voluntarily, or did odd jobs for elderly neighbours. Some of them sounded deathly dull. Henry worked in a supermarket, played golf and enjoyed surfing the internet.

They asked female volunteers to rate the men. How attractive did they seem for a short affair, or to live and start a family with?

Whether the women were looking for a one-night stand or something more permanent, bravery was enticing. Killing dragons is a plus point on a Tinder profile.

Men know this, explicitly or implicitly. If their genes want to pass into the next generation, there's a trade-off between risking getting killed in a motorcycle accident and finding someone attractive to be with. It seems the risk is worth taking.[30] Young men drive faster, consume more drugs, take hairier financial decisions and compete in more dangerous sports. Between the ages of fifteen and thirty-nine, men are more than seven times as likely to drown as women. (From there, the ratio drops but only slowly: in their seventies, men still die in the water at twice the rate of elderly ladies.)

Spending time helping others also increased potential mates' attractiveness, but only when the women were seeking a life partner. When they were thinking of short-term thrills, altruism lost its allure; being kind and caring did nothing for them.

If you're a man looking for a long-term relationship, if you want to settle down and produce heirs, then bunging some change in a collection tin might be a decent investment. But if you just want some fun between the sheets, save your money for the hotel bill.

If men's behaviour has changed over the years, it might be because women's has too. When our grandmas were dating, women had much worse jobs and they frequently lost them when they fell pregnant. Short-term flings were dangerous. It's well known that the contraceptive pill causes breast cancer and mood swings. Another side-effect could be that men really aren't as good as they used to be.

You'll only regret having nothing to regret

Amorality will lead you to worldly success. But what if, in your dotage, your morals come back? You perhaps imagine yourself wracked with unbearable guilt, your last days blighted. Could it possibly be worth it, and what does psychological research have to say about it?

Regrets are inevitable whatever you do. The life not lived can be more vivid than the life we do live. What if I'd married Katie or Suzie instead of Charlotte? What if I'd studied economics rather than science? Taken this job rather than that?

We dream about the lost us: we may wake up in a sweat wondering whether we're on the right track; regret all the things we did and the things we didn't. The sins we committed and the sins we didn't.

Some claim to be philosophic. '*Je ne regrette rien*,' sang Edith Piaf. 'Regrets, I've had a few, but then again, too few to mention': Frank Sinatra (who said he hated the song and perhaps he regretted singing it; but he went on singing it and cashing the cheques).

Some of us are also haunted by the spectre of *future* regrets. The Fear Of Missing Out (FOMO) may well dog our risky investment decisions, our optimistic property purchases and our craziest choices. Why do marketers spam us with messages that the sale closes in three days? 'Don't miss out.' As if not buying that fridge magnet which says 'Keep Calm And Eat Cupcakes' is going to haunt our dreams.

So, what *do* we regret in life? Scientists have interviewed thousands, and one thing is clear. We regret what we didn't do rather than what we did.[31] It's true of both intellectually gifted and normal people; it's true whether we're American, British, Chinese, Japanese or Russian.

This isn't so surprising. The things we didn't do, the grand risks we didn't take, can fill our imagination more readily than the things we did do: the consequences of which tend to be drearily real.

But more surprising, perhaps, are the *types* of things that we regret. Researchers classed these into two groups. The first are our moral regrets: our failure to do what we ought to do. The second are more egotistical. They're our failure to live up to what we could be, to follow our dreams and be a star.

It's supposed to be common knowledge that the first are the more poignant. On our death beds, we won't regret time not spent with our boss or dollars not earned. Instead, we'll be filled with remorse for the evenings we didn't spend with our families, for the kind words that we didn't give, for the good deeds we didn't do.

Technically, the studies of over six hundred people by researchers in New York can't tell us what we'll feel when we're dying. The researchers didn't interrogate the mortally ill. But across six studies, they asked everybody from students to the middle-aged what their biggest regrets in life were.

And overwhelmingly, people's biggest regret wasn't an ethical mistake. Instead it was a failure to try and have what they wanted to have. So perhaps the footballer George Best was sincerer than Piaf or Sinatra. 'I spent a lot of money on booze, birds and fast cars. The rest I just squandered.'

Not all amoralists are good amoralists

So, morality's not just irrational as we saw in chapter one. In this chapter, we've seen that it holds you back. But whatever the benefits of plumping for amorality, there's a chance you still feel queasy about making the leap. I want to suggest now that, in part, this might be due to the reputation of others who have done so.

Two amoralists[32] in particular have queered the pitch. One real, the other fictional. Niccolo Machiavelli and Hannibal Lecter. Feared, revered, but not to be emulated.

Let's take Machiavelli first. Why is this Renaissance man of letters a favourite of ambitious shoe-shop managers?

It's not that he advocates aiming to succeed and to hell with the rest. That's surely not a big enough idea to sustain a man's reputation for five hundred years, and nor is it especially original.

His infamy, and the reason that he is still read, rests on only a few pages. Machiavelli discusses what makes a ruler praise-worthy: mercy, trustworthiness, religious devotion and so on. He finds that truly cultivating such virtues can be harmful, causing the leader to act in ways that run counter to maintaining his grip on power. But if a leader 'need not actually possess all the above-mentioned qualities . . . he must certainly seem to.'[33]

Machiavelli describes how a prince might avoid hatred and contempt. He explains when a ruler should be generous and when to hold onto his resources; he gives examples of leaders who have broken promises and yet kept their reputation. He tells his eager readers how to feign morality, or at least how to gain its benefits.

Hannibal Lecter isn't one of the great literary characters because of his evildoing. He's far from being the most prolific killer. He's not even the cruellest, and he has no designs on world domination. It's his use of morality to get what he wants that mesmerises.

'Quid pro quo,' he tells Clarice. I'll give you something if you give me something; a distillation of one of the most famous ethical rules. When a fellow prisoner insults Clarice, he tempts the beast to suicide. Hannibal is able to make himself trust-worthy. But if he can use ethics, he doesn't believe in them; they don't hamstring him.

Lecter's heart rate doesn't rise as he bites the face from a nurse. He takes pleasure in a recording of the Goldberg Variations while dismembering a prison guard. He gives a soaring academic lecture on the connection between avarice and hanging, greed and suicide, before pushing a policeman out the window with a flex around his neck.

Hannibal chills because we cannot infer from his expressions or his behaviour what is in his mind. If we met him, we would not know what he was until it was too late. The Hell's Angel and the punk with tattoos on his face are signalling what they are; Lecter uses our expectations to signal something else.

Sophisticated as they were, neither Niccolo nor Hannibal are our models. We shudder at them because they let the mask slip. Lecter was caught. Machiavelli, the idiot, published his ideas under his own name. We found out what was in their minds.

I suspect you are less ambitious than Machiavelli or Lecter. Few readers will have any desire to butcher other humans and fry their sweetmeats. Running an Italian city state sounds a lot of hard work.

But there are surely things you want. Perhaps you aspire to move from running a shoe shop to head office. I, like Lecter, simply hope to be amused.

To get what we want, we need the help of other people.[34] To get people's help, we need to use morality, according to both Machiavelli and Lecter.

Society forces us to dissimulate. If you are transported to ancient Inca, and want to get ahead, you'd better worship the sun god. If you have private doubts that child sacrifices will prevent earthquakes, it's probably in your best interests to keep them to yourself.

So even if we consider Machiavelli and Lecter as fellow

travellers in jest, there's a serious point to be made. Common-sense morality, we'll find, is nonsense. It doesn't work in the way moralists think it does, and it doesn't achieve the ends that most people imagine. But they are very attached to it. Telling them that they are wrong has a social cost attached to it, and we'll see in later chapters why it isn't a small one.

This isn't a book to 'like' on Facebook. If you're going to read it on the way to work, you should cover the jacket. It might well be that, even once you know the truth, it's better to pretend not to.

THREE

Punishing genes – how humans got their morals

Why don't you go on that killing spree you've been dreaming about? Why pay for your new computer when you could take it? Why not sleep with your boss's obviously bored, but rather attractive, partner?

It seems there's a fly in our ointment. We live among people who have moral beliefs and act upon them, and we'll see in this chapter that not only do they punish people who fail to conform, many of them *enjoy* doing so.

How come? In this chapter, we'll see that humans created, among themselves, a unique evolutionary niche. In this niche, genes that caused our ancestors to be perceived as good spread faster than genes that didn't.

Genes don't have minds

Genes and morals have different PR advisers. Genes are weaselly little creatures, selfishly doing what they need to do to make more copies in the future. Theirs is the law of the jungle or of the large corporation: do what works and to hell with everything else.

Morals, on the other hand, are glorious, selfless, beneficent, civilised, *good*. They are the very opposite of genes. For them, helping others rates above helping the self, and making the world a better place above being more prevalent in the world.

It's perhaps possible, we might imagine, for morals to run counter to genetic interest because we see no reason to believe that morals are genetically determined. Support for slavery didn't diminish because some new mutation spread rapidly. Take twins and put them in different societies and they'll hold different principles, fight for different causes, worship different gods and act accordingly. Ethical systems vary too much across the world and change too fast to be determined by the design information in our nuclei.

Ethics, it seems, are cultural. We'll see in more detail later how beliefs spread through word of mouth and seeing how others behave. We'll find that we do what others do and come to believe that what we do is right.[35]

However, this isn't the whole story. I can only reason morally because my genes enable me to do so. I only pick up the ethics of my culture because those devilish little strands of twisted nucleic acids make me do so. *My mind is there because of my genes.*

Humans have morals, talk about morals and act morally because genes for doing these things have done better in the past than genes for not doing these things.

This statement is mind-bogglingly counterintuitive. It's important to understand how this works: morals lead us to help other people who aren't related to us at an apparent cost to ourselves, so why would genes that make us do such a thing be successful? On the face of it, this looks unlikely. Every human that we aid is a competitor fighting for the things that would help us to pass on our DNA.

There's no greater conflict of interest than that between two animals of the same kind. Sure, the fox and the farmer will be forever at war: the fox wants to eat what the farmer wants to sell. But the fox doesn't compete with the farmer for school places; he doesn't bid against him for a new plot of land; his son won't later compete for lasses with the farmer's.

All else being equal, an animal's genes aren't indifferent to other animals of the same species: they want them to fail. The fewer competitors, the more of whatever it is – food, mates, territory – that enables the gene to go on replicating.

Consequently, the animal kingdom is full of fierce battles between con-specifics. When a lion takes over a pride, he doesn't just kill the other fellow, he kills his children too*. Even the friendly garden robin is territorial: he attacks other redbreasts who stray on to his turf.[37]

You might think of exceptions; instances of animals living reasonably harmoniously in cooperative groups. Chimpanzee troops, wolf packs, lion prides or beehives are common examples. But dig deeper, and these small groups are generally composed of brothers, sisters or other close kin, i.e. they are genetically related.

Humans are the *only* species that have stumbled upon a way to properly manage the conflicts of interests and cooperate within groups that *aren't* genetically related. To understand how we did this, we've got to keep an eye at all times on what's happening to the genes: what's in it for them? Or, more precisely, why did this gene spread and not some other gene which instructed the humans it inhabited to do something else?

---

* Human children living with a stepparent are seventy times more likely to be killed, and forty times more likely to suffer abuse, than children in a home with two genetic parents.[36] However, the base rate is so low that even with stepparents the vast majority survive, in contrast with lion cubs.

Genes aren't there to make us happy

When I was a boy, I had a book which told me what humans will look like in the future. We'll have long, pointy noses. A tall domed head to fit all our brains in. And we'll be bald as eggs.

This is an addlepated fairy tale that assumes evolution has some directional arrow that will persist forever. On this premise, giraffes will one day be a hundred feet tall. Cheetahs will break the sound barrier. Millipedes will really have a thousand legs.

Things don't work like that. Evolutionary incentives change. Today, and for at least the past hundred years, British people with higher education bear, on average, fewer children.[38] One of the arguments put forward for educating girls in developing countries is the evidence that the longer they stay in school, the fewer offspring they will have.

Our genes aren't those that did best in *today's* world. Clearly, there has been a time when being a little smarter than your peers was advantageous to your genes. We wouldn't have these enormous, energy-hungry, vaginal-tearing brains if it wasn't so.

Nowadays, that benefit has gone away: from your genes' perspective, being smarter is a disadvantage.[39] This seems an odd thing to say. Every parent wants their child to do well at school. Those who do end up richer, have higher status and gain more interesting jobs.

So the second point is that your interests and those of your genes aren't necessarily aligned. The genes that spread are those that are effective at making copies of themselves, not necessarily those that make you smarter, prettier or even happier.

41

Genes can't see into the future

If we think about what morals do for us, perhaps we can get to why genes that made them possible have spread. We might observe that morals make coordinated action possible. They bind us into cooperating groups with other humans who aren't our family. It isn't hard to see why that's beneficial.

Let's do a little thought experiment (if there are any philosophers still reading, they'll be pleased). In this experiment, there are no morals. Civilization hasn't happened. Humans are running around the savannah in family-oriented little groups. They hunt and forage and try to keep out of each other's way. Occasionally they fail and a little war ensues, just as happens between chimp troops today.

From time to time, the families get too big. The head honcho of the family doesn't have too many genes in common with his wife's cousin twice removed. There's a conflict of interest. Sensibly, the distant relations sneak off in the night and form a new group somewhere else.

Each family has perhaps a hundred people within it. The total human population is measured in thousands rather than billions.

Then imagine a few of these families banding together with a moral code. This super-group, working together, eliminates all comers. It takes the best territory. It expands still further.

People in the super-group are better off. And so are their genes. People without the moral gene are being slaughtered mercilessly by the good guys; people within the super-group are living off the fat of the land and having babies.

Could this be how morals evolved? If you think the story is plausible, you're in good company. This seductive tale – moral groups outperform amoral groups, and so the genes within moral groups do better – has appealed to many a thinker since Darwin.

But it's wrong. One evening, in this super-group, a boy is born. We'll call him Damien. By our utopian standard, he's a little defective. When his mother's egg was being formed, the genes within it didn't copy quite correctly; the do-gooder gene, which causes those with it to cooperate within the group, was corrupted.

When others within his group are slaying competitors and conquering territory, he hangs back. He's a little less likely to die in battle, but he takes his share of the spoils. When the moralists are dancing round a tree singing 'Kumbaya', he's raping their wives. Without the do-gooder gene to reign him in, his other genes are ensuring that they are replicating as fast as they can.

Before long, there are lots of little boys and girls of Damien's ilk. Utopia hasn't lasted long.

The story's too simple. Of course it is. But it illustrates something important. You can't understand how genes for morality spread by looking purely at the group level.

Sure, cooperative groups do better than non-cooperative groups and, yes, that means more genes. But if genes that tell their bearers not to play by the rules do better *within* the group, then the rules won't last. Even the most successful of such super-groups will soon be overrun by Damiens and cease to be super-groups.

The rules have to be set up so that even on an intra-group basis, morality is the winning strategy. They have to ensure that individuals with a corrupted do-gooder gene do worse than those with the do-gooder gene; that Damiens fail to take over.

What's more, the benefit has to be in the short term. Genes can't say to themselves: 'If we stick with this morality lark then in a couple of million years there'll be nine billion of us and supermarkets and a welfare state. It'll be in our interests in the end.' We never get to the end if the genes don't spread in the interim.

Genes can't see into the future; their prevalence is entirely based on their performance in the past.

We can only affect the future

If you reflect on why you want to see certain people punished, or consult with philosophers, it's easy to get muddled: to imagine its purpose is rectifying wrongs, dispensing justice, satisfying honour, deterring others or comforting the victims. But if we keep an eye on the genes, we'll find that punishment's far more important than any of these.

Immanuel Kant was one of the champions of retribution. For him, the point of punishing was that the criminal got what he deserved, and got it good and hard. The sentence should reflect the wickedness of the act and nothing else: 'punishment can never be administered merely as a means for promoting another good'.

Jeremy Bentham disagreed. For him and other utilitarian types, the point of punishing someone is to prevent further harm in the future. You send a signal to other miscreants that crime doesn't pay.

For what it's worth, when several hundred Princeton students were quizzed, they expressed a strong preference for deterrence over payback. But when asked to sentence various criminals, their decisions suggested that they really leant towards Kant's view of the world rather than Bentham's.[40] While Bentham would punish most harshly the white-collar criminal who is unlikely to get caught (in order to make stealing a choice with a poor expected outcome), Kant and the students would come down harder on the murderer even if his capture is certain.

It's another example of what people think differing from what they think they think, and both of these differing from what's really going on. These philosophical theories take aim at individuals. They hurt the person who has hurt, or they incentivise others not to hurt. But the reason that punishment works, the real reason that people behave themselves, is because punishment hits the genes that tell them to misbehave.

A lag in jail might be getting sex, but he's not fathering any children. Prisons may be a recent invention, but they're not harsher on the malefactor's DNA than what came before it. Stoning, exile, hanging, maiming, confiscation of lands, ostracism. All hit where it hurts, preventing the guilty from having children or from gaining the resources to bring them up.

Other punishments even more obviously target the genes. In the Old Testament, God promised to visit 'the iniquity of the fathers upon the sons to the third and fourth generation of those that hate me'. In China four thousand years ago, villains were castrated, and for the most serious crimes (including the study of immoral books) not only was the offender killed but his or her family too. Stalin sent families to the gulags under the 'Repression of Family Members of Traitors of the Motherland'. Bedouin tribes still kill male relatives of offenders when they can't find the miscreant himself.

Most punishments are smaller in magnitude. Being snubbed at a dinner party or passed over for promotion can be punishments. We don't know what the prehistoric equivalents were:

being given a ropey piece of meat from a kill or put on guard duty, perhaps?

But we can be sure that, on average, the sentences were such that people who did what was expected of them did better than people who defied society. And we should also remember that the escalation to bigger punishments means that we accept the small ones. I can try and get the promotion by roughing up my boss, but then I might have an assault charge to face. I can avoid that by going on the run or shooting the officer who comes to arrest me, but ultimately the risk of escalation means that it's in my interest to accept the smaller punishment.

Bentham and Kant could have such divergent views on what punishment is for, while both agreeing that we should punish, because the real function of vengeance, the reason we've evolved to desire it and carry it out, isn't one we have access to.

It doesn't matter *why* people think they're punishing. If they thought that flogging criminals caused the fairies to cheer it wouldn't make a blind bit of difference to the punishment's effect on the punished's genes.

What matters is that they *do* punish. They damage malefactors who do things that would otherwise be beneficial to their genes: stealing, killing competitors, raping. They punish those who don't fit in with society's expectations, whatever they may be at the time. And, as we have just seen, their chastisements are of a type that harm the perpetrator's genes' chances of spreading.

The mountain hare grows a white coat in the winter, the hedgehog covers itself in spines, the poison dart frog has a body full of toxins. I'm sure that not one of these creatures has the foggiest why they are so. I'm also willing to bet that the fox, the weasel and the eagle have no idea that their predation makes it so. But nevertheless, the existence of predators ensures that any mutant offspring without these defences doesn't get to pass on its faulty genes.

Humans are self-domesticated. They don't behave ethically for the good of the group. They especially don't do it because philosophers have elegant theories. They do so because other humans ensure that if they don't, they won't get to pass on their dodgy genes. That these other humans don't understand why they punish or what effect their punishment has doesn't change a thing.

Vengeance is a virtue

Punishment incentivises behaving well, so what incentivises punishment? Dishing out retribution's an expensive business. Those jails cost money. If you tackle a bag snatcher, there's every chance you'll get a black eye for your trouble.

It's possible to squint a bit and see that society works better thanks to have-a-go heroes and stern teachers. But evolution doesn't act on society, it acts on genes.

Is mercy or justice rewarded?

And doesn't society reward lenience in its members anyhow? 'Turn the other cheek,' 'let he who is without sin cast the first stone' and so on.

We have seen that others' vengeance was the genetic imperative that created morals. Jesus and Gandhi tried to take an axe to the evolutionary incentives that made morality possible in the first place.

However, in their fight against hundreds of thousands of years of selection, these rabble rousers have lost: retaliation, reprisals and revenge are still an intrinsic part of what we think it means to be good. Researchers at Yale and Harvard demonstrated this with an elegant pair of games.[41]

In the first game, there were three players. Let's call them Alice, Bob and Carol. Alice starts off with thirty coins, Bob twenty and Carol nothing at all.

Alice chooses whether to share half of her thirty coins with Carol.

If Alice doesn't share, Bob is given a choice. He can forego five of his coins to make fifteen of Alice's coins disappear. What do we expect Bob to do? Keep the coins he has, or spend them, thus exacting retribution?

Bob hasn't been affected by Alice's mean-spirited hoarding. The game's played over a computer; Bob will likely never meet Alice or Carol in real life, and wouldn't be able to identify them if he did. Yet still, almost half of all participants who play the role of Bob choose to sacrifice some of their own bounty to rob Alice of her stash.[42]

If Jesus isn't having it his own way, nor are the liberals. Alice is stung not for harming anybody but for a failure to do good. This in itself is important: harm isn't the sole basis of morality; humans also impose an obligation on others to actively help.

So humans do frequently punish, even at an obvious cost to themselves. But why? What could they hope to gain?

In the second game, Bob is paired with a new partner, Dave. The second game is a trust game. Dave has thirty coins, and can trust some of these to Bob. Any money Dave gives to Bob is tripled. Bob then chooses how much of the tripled money to send back to Dave.

Before deciding whether to risk any of his capital, Dave can see whether or not, in the previous game, Bob sacrificed some of his coins to harm the misbehaving Alice. What this second game is testing is whether people trust people who punish more than they trust people who turn a blind eye to others' misdeeds.

And they do. They send a third more of their money to players they know have paid to punish the selfish than to those who chose not to. What's more, it's a good bet. People who punish *are* more decent: they send back more of their winnings to their trusting partner.

This suggests that punishing people is a signal of your own virtue. It's typically a trustworthy signal: people who punish also cooperate. It's a recognisable signal: when people pay to fine defectors, third parties know they can trust them.

So what happens when somebody plays as Bob who doesn't need to signal they are trustworthy because they've already established that fact? To find out, the researchers varied the terms of the experiment a bit.

Now participants played the first game twice, once in the role of Alice (deciding whether or not to share) and once as Bob (choosing whether to punish). Then they played the trust game with Dave.

Deciding whether to share is clearly the more relevant signal to the trust game: you give money to somebody else and the stake is higher (fifteen coins instead of five). Dave, deciding what to do in the trust game, might be expected to pay more attention to how somebody plays in that role than in the punishing role.

And indeed he does. In the trust game, sharers receive more than twice as much as those who don't share. Sharing is also a more reliable signal: players who split their pot in the first game returned twice as much when playing the trust game.

So what happens to retribution? If you have a strong signal, the weaker one becomes less important. Dave is going to pay more attention to what you do when you're playing Alice than when you're playing Bob. So why waste your resources on punishing? In the three-game version, the rate of punishing drops.[43]

It's easy for Gandhi, Jesus or Nelson Mandela to preach forgiveness. Everybody knows they're good men. It's the not-so-good from whom you should fear retribution.

If you're ever in front of the beak for sentencing, your lawyer will no doubt extol your virtues. But these experiments suggest a counter-intuitive play: sing the praises of the judge. The higher her moral standing, the less need she'll have to demonstrate it by giving you a long stretch.

Players aren't being cynical

In the terms of the games, none of the above was rational. We can see this by looking at the final game and working backwards.

If you're Bob in the trust game, and Dave has just given you some money, what should you do? You're the last person to make a decision. You're never going to meet any of the others again. So you ought to take what you receive and scarper.

Now imagine that you're Dave, trusting Bob with some money in that final round. You know that Bob has no incentive to do anything but take the money and run. So you shouldn't trust him with a dime.

Now put yourself back in the role of Bob playing one of the

sharing or punishing games before the final trust game. You know that in the last game you're incentivised to leave with whatever you're given. You know that Dave also knows this, and so Dave, if sensible, isn't going to give you anything.

Therefore, you shouldn't bother signalling in the earlier games. You shouldn't waste five coins punishing or fifteen coins sharing.

That's not what happens. Why not?

It plays out the way it does because humans didn't evolve to play closed games. In the past, our ancestors didn't deal with people they'd never meet again; they couldn't take what they wanted and scarper without consequences. One-shot interactions were a rarity.

Today, we trade with people we'll never see again. On tube journeys we avoid the eyes of con-specifics we wouldn't recognise if we saw them later that day. We hook up on Tinder or Grindr and have intercourse with bodies that are quickly forgotten.

This is as much an aberration as the tiger who jumps through hoops or the dolphin which catches a ball. We can do these things because we have a moral sense: but our moral sense didn't evolve for doing these things.

Participants were trusting, sharing and punishing to help their reputation. That their reputation wasn't worth what they paid to support it in these games didn't matter. Even Bob, who made a good return on the five coins he spent impoverishing the non-sharing Alice, wasn't cynically calculating that the new partner, Dave, would trust him more.

Indeed, to put this beyond doubt, two of the researchers who conducted the experiments re-ran them without the trust game at the end. Bob still punished when he had the chance, and he still punished less when he had the opportunity to share in another game.[44] He acted *as though* there was somebody to signal to ahead of a later interaction.

There was no one to signal to, no one to cooperate with or gain from. Reputation was truly worthless. Yet still they clicked into a moral gear that was formed when reputation lingered, when we didn't live in cities or communicate anonymously, and before researchers manipulated us in controlled experiments.[45]

A *cheap shortcut*

Being prepared to punish is like the masonic handshake; it's a way of signalling that you're part of the group. So if you're among people you may want things from in the future, it seems worthwhile dispensing some justice.

If somebody knocks your beer, you shouldn't cringe and say 'it's alright old chap, I've had enough anyway'. You should whack him over the head with a pool cue. Better still, you should appoint yourself as the guardian of the pub.[46] If anybody knocks anybody else's beer, you should whack them with the pool cue too.

But this, of course, is dangerous. In my experience, the sorts who jostle my arm in crowded bars are bigger than me.

And most signals have a cost attached to them. That's why they're reliable. When somebody gives up coins as Bob did in the game, or puts his jaw on the line in a bar-room brawl, we know that they are serious in their ethics. What would be ideal here is a signal of your virtue that had costs in the past, and therefore attracts all the reputational goodies we want, but which doesn't have those costs any longer.

Long ago, when humans banded together in groups of no

more than a few hundred, asserting that somebody was in the wrong wasn't just a way of letting off steam: you were stating your willingness to do something about it.

Serious crime is, and likely always has been, a young man's game.[47] So when you puffed up your cheeks, slammed your fist into your palm and declared something ought to be done, you were setting yourself against one of the stronger members of your social circle.

Because you were putting your body on the line, people took your fury seriously. And people still do. Condemning misbehaviour is a convincing signal of virtue: declaring your anger at those who engage in some misdeed improves hearers' perception of you more than if you simply state that you don't engage in the transgression yourself.[48]

However, the pain that your ancestors had to risk in order to signal their punishment-giving credentials can be avoided. You don't have to put your money where your mouth is. You can rant at the Sultan of Brunei's new anti-gay laws, at the cheating athlete, at overpaid CEOs or at the President of the USA.

Your bluff won't be called. You won't have to join a posse to oust the president from the White House. You're not going toe-to-toe with the steroid-enhanced boxer. You can vent your moral ire at people you'll never meet, and who won't retaliate. You can display anger on topics over which you have no influence.

In reputational terms it's not as effective as actually punishing a wrongdoer. It's a long way behind sharing half your wealth. But it is at least a bit effective. And it's completely free. It's a loophole in morality that's outlasted city living and a centralised police force. So use it.

It's particularly important to signal your moral credentials if there's any suspicion that you might not be moral. So if I see a tweet saying 'Outraged at Beyond Bad #PaleyIsEvil,' I'll know that you're a satisfied customer covering your tracks.[49]

Retribution is fun

Perhaps you don't want to hold back. It's entirely possible that, in telling you how to gain some of the reputational benefits of punishing without the messy and dangerous business of actually doing so, you feel I've missed the point.

If being seen to punish was in your forefathers' interests, maybe your brain motivates you to see justice done. Research suggests it does – for some of you.

Scientists at UCL gave men and women some prisoner's dilemma tasks.[50] If the players cooperate, both get a decent pay-off. If the other player defects, he wins more at your expense.

Losing out isn't nice, and both men and women rated defectors as less likable and even less attractive. But men expressed a greater desire for revenge.

The researchers didn't take participants' word for it. Perhaps men and women said what they thought was expected of them.

So they repeated the game while players had their heads in a brain scanner. And they punished the cheat. Not merely by docking them a few coins, but by zapping their hands with electric shocks. To get a control reading, they sometimes zapped cooperating players too.

The flow of blood in women's brains suggested that they experienced an empathic response when anybody's hands were shocked; men only experienced this when decent players were electrocuted.

The scientists also looked at the nucleus accumbens. This is generally active when something nice happens to you, such as winning money. Men apparently got a kick out of seeing the cheat punished; the researchers couldn't find any equivalent evidence that women did.[51]

There's a stereotype that men prefer action and war movies, films with plots that hinge on bad guys eventually getting their comeuppance. Women prefer drama and romance.

If it's only men who receive the payoff when they see Dr No boiling to death or Goldfinger sucked out of the aeroplane, we might expect them to get more out of it. The stereotype could be true. And so it is.[52] When men and women rate which genres they like, the average ordering follows the stereotype closely.

So if basking in the moral glow of an outrage-laden tweet isn't enough for you, and there aren't any appropriately sized crooks at hand for you to batter, you might make up for your lack by watching Sean Connery duff them up on your behalf.

Morality's all in the wrist

There used to be a certain amount of tosh talked about tool use and human uniqueness. The argument was that big brains were needed to manipulate our surroundings and this gave us an advantage over other animals.

With hegemony over our surroundings we could feast at will. We could tolerate long childhoods where our offspring learnt skills and their brains developed. Big brains could cope with language and abstract reasoning and moral thought. This cemented our advantage in what management gurus might call a 'virtuous flywheel'.[53]

In the opening scene of *2001: A Space Odyssey*, Kubrick suggested that this step in our evolutionary development was so magical that it required the intervention of some extra-terrestrial obelisk.

Now we know that crows can use tools: dropping stones into a water-filled tube to get at food floating on the surface.[54] The sparrows outside my window take all kinds of oddly shaped sticks and twigs and figure out how to weave them into a nest. Dolphins stir up the seabed with sponges to search for prey.[55] Degus – chinchilla-like rodents – can learn to use toy rakes to pull sunflower seeds into their enclosure.[56]

There's nothing intrinsically special about using tools or manipulating the environment. Instead, and as we have been considering, morality and social life is at the bottom of nearly everything that we think of as uniquely human: big brains, consciousness, reasoning, language. Only once they could cooperate were all of these social adaptations advantageous to our ancestors.

But what set us off on this wild ride? From where did the initial impetus come? Why did morality take off in *Homo* rather than wolves or big cats or some other group of apes? What made us ready to make use of it before we had all the other adaptations that came later?

In trying to answer this question, we can only speculate. We can't manipulate the deep past and re-run it in a test tube or in the lab. What we can observe of it is piecemeal: old skeletons and bits and bobs found nearby.

What we can do, too, is create stories that fit with the evidence we do have and our models of how evolution works. Some stories are, of course, more plausible than others; some fit better with the facts. The thrust of the tale in the following section was first authored by a scientist, Paul Bingham.[57] If it isn't quite right, it's at least cogent and it's certainly the most elegant narrative of our deep past I've come across.

This tale starts by noticing something other than our brains and our behaviour that's unusual about humans. We're physically different to any other species. *We can throw, and we can use other weapons at a distance.*

A chimp can hold a stick and wave it about threateningly. But his thumb's not long enough or strong enough to stabilise it against his palm when he swings. His wrist's too weak and his bones aren't in the right place to properly cock it before he bludgeons another chimp's skull.

Hand-to-hand, ape-on-ape, you'd lose against a gorilla, but however much he beats his chest and hoots, his physiology's all wrong for accurately throwing a spear any distance.

In one study, wild chimps were observed to throw objects forty-four times. They only scored five hits, all at two metres or less, and none of them caused any serious damage. In contrast, humans can sometimes kill a man at thirty metres with a rock.[58]

Our ancestors seem to have developed this ability early. *Homo erectus* had the physique for it two million years ago.[59] And we kept it up until recently. Arrows and the atlatl (think a cross between an arrow and a javelin) became widespread a mere forty thousand years ago. Australian Aborigines never developed the bow and arrow: when Europeans turned up, they were throwing clubs, sticks, stones and boomerangs to kill.

Our bipedal stance, our delicately crafted, hyperextendable wrists, our ability to turn elastic energy stored in our shoulders into a fast, accurate bowl, seem to have nothing to do with morality or language or consciousness. Most likely, the evolutionary benefit which favoured our malforming forebears (who rapidly lost the ability to climb) was the increased ability to hunt.[60]

Can it be coincidental that we have this physical oddness and the mental weirdness that allows morality? We are the only animal that can heft a club and kill at a distance and are also the only one that has developed morality.

Most thinkers who have a go at delving into our deep history try to find a way to connect the two. One hypothesis is that hunting allowed for teamwork. Bringing down big game was easier in groups. A good kill could feed it. Hence, morality.

But this can't be quite right. Families are big enough to man a hunt. Big cats do it: a lion, his harem and his offspring. And anyhow, the better human weapons have become, the less hunting they've done: they turn to farming and herding.

Darwin wondered whether war could have been the driver for morality. Perhaps the real arms race drove the moral arms race: you need soldiers to fight rather than hide at the back and make off with the spoils. Groups that couldn't cooperate well were wiped out by groups that could.

But again, this doesn't quite stack up, at least in the early stages. Winning wars and whatever comes with them, whether women, slaves, territory or stores, can only be valuable once humans have reached their niche at the apex, once they were masters over their environment and other animals. Until then, the bigger and more important fights are with the land, the elements, predators and members of your own group.[61]

If humans could only dominate the environment by virtue of their big brains, their advanced weaponry and their coordinated action, then you need morals to come *before* warfare rather than *after* it. Our ability to wage war is surely a consequence of morality: it can't have been the cause of it.

A more plausible story is that humans' ability to kill at a distance in some way made reprisals against wrongdoers more viable. Imagine that there are no clubs, axes, spears, arrows, knives or guns. Some miscreant with a heavy brow and a hairy back wrongs me in some way. Maybe he steals my antelope or grunts sweet nothings in my woman's ear. He's ripe for some punishment.

To do this, I can go up and bop him on the nose. But he's going to try and bop me back. If he's the same size as me, my chances are probably only 50:50 that I come off better. Unlike in films, there's no rule that says the good guy always wins. Might is going to beat right.

Perhaps I could go out and raise a posse. We all agree that the knave requires a hiding. Now, it looks like morality might be in with a chance. If the locals all agree on what is right and wrong, and that they should gang together to punish those in the wrong, then it seems as though those who we agree have done wrong will suffer. Genes for behaving morally might do better.

But it's not as easy as that. In hand-to-hand combat, you have to get close to the person you want to bop on the nose. Somebody's got to be in front when you're chasing him. And that somebody might come off worst before the others catch up.

I'm not sure that I'd back even half a dozen men of my own physique to take down a Mike Tyson or a Tyson Fury. Even if we did eventually overpower him, there's a good chance that a few of us would be handicapped in the struggle. Genes for being big, strong and called Tyson are looking a better bet than genes for being good neighbours.

But the ability to throw rocks at Tyson changes the dynamic completely. Imagine that I'm standing some distance from my nemesis. I throw a rock at him and he throws one back at me. Let's say that, on average, it takes about five minutes of lobbing stones to get one that takes the other out. Maybe a bit less if your aim is better or your muscles stronger. We're still in a roughly 50:50 game.

Now I come back with my posse of five. Because we can fight at a distance, we're all in the battle at once, together. And something nice happens to the mathematics.

If we're all aiming equally well, it won't take five minutes to bring the brute down, it'll only take one minute. And in that time, he'll have let off a fifth as many shots as if he was only exchanging rocks with me.

Even if he aims all of his shots at one of us, he's therefore only got a one-in-five chance of landing a disabling blow. So he'll get his comeuppance with certainty, and each member of my posse only has a one-in-twenty-five chance of being seriously injured.

Increase the posse to ten, and it gets better. The fight's over in thirty seconds and each member's chance of getting hurt has dropped to one-in-a-hundred. Double the number of punishers and you quarter the chances of any particular good guy getting hurt.

This rule of warfare is known as Lanchester's square law. It was discovered during the First World War, when the projectiles were a little more powerful than rocks. But the same maths holds, broadly, whether you're strafing bullets in an air battle, firing Tommy guns in Chicago or slinging stones at Tyson. When fighting at a distance, the larger team not only wins, but also suffers fewer casualties.

Because they can't throw things properly, no other animal can cooperatively fight from a distance. Therefore, they don't have this mathematical advantage when it comes to ganging up on parasites, cheats and malingerers.

On the other hand, for early humans the risk-reward equation changed dramatically. Suddenly, it made sense for groups – even non-genetically-related groups – to decide what the rules were and to see off people who broke them. At that point, cooperation became both possible, and more useful than it could ever have been before.

We don't know quite how the next step took place. What mutation first arose that allowed us to take advantage of Lanchester's law? What types of things were first punished, and how much of this was simply instinctive and how much reasoned? We'll likely never know.

But after mob justice was meted out, we were off. Genes that ensured that we maintained our reputation within the tribe, and on the side of the mob, were advantageous. Once people had an incentive to protect their reputation, we had a reason to trust them.

The rest, as they say, is history. And it truly was. For what is history other than a fascination with why people do as they do, for what motives and morals propel action? What drives the epochs forward so well as new ways of organising society and better methods of propelling objects in order to kill people? Morals, coordinated action, killing: this is what makes us human.

And as a nice side-effect, Bingham's theory also explains the second great mystery of human evolution. Why are grown men so fascinated by team games with balls? Rugby, football, baseball, cricket, basketball, American football: all involve groups of men firing projectiles.

Kubrick missed a trick. At the end of his beautiful opening sequence, he had one of the furry proto-humans heave a bone into the air. It's a terrible shot. My grandma could throw better from her moto-scooter. But it was possibly that physical capacity, that brutish hurling action, unique to our ancestors in all the animal kingdom, that set *Homo* off on their magnificent and terrible, exhilarating and terrifying trajectory to where we are today.

If you're going to be punished, you want it one-on-one

From time to time, some of you are going to slip up. You'll be caught in the act. You'll plead your cause, promise to do better next time, and affirm your ethics. But however great an actor you are, saying sorry doesn't always cut it.

You'll receive your medicine and be made to drink it. Just how foul this tonic is depends as much on the person giving it as how terrible your crime. As we've seen, some people get a kick out of applying justice, while a few are meek, mild and merciful. If your boss, spouse or former friend have a hyperactive nucleus accumbens this is horribly unfair.

You might imagine, then, that this is an advantage of juries. You won't get let off by the faint-hearted softy, but the vengeful hothead is also talked down, or at least outvoted. Behind the closed doors you imagine some sort of averaging is taking place.

But hidden in this chapter are clues that things might not be so simple. Punishment is a group undertaking.

Given how dramatically juries can change somebody's life, and how rarely people act as we expect, legal scholars and psychologists have (belatedly) started investigating what happens in the deliberation room. The results do make very uncomfortable reading.

In one study, researchers paid three thousand adults in Arizona to watch actors give the details of cases in which someone was hurt.[62] Participants decided how harshly to punish those responsible, assigning a dollar figure to the punitive damages. The researchers then put them into groups of six and the freshly formed juries had to agree a collective verdict.

Some of the cases were fairly benign. A secretary claims she is chronically ill from exposure to her computer monitor; an elderly woman injures herself while using an exercise video. Others cry out for justice. A motorcyclist is injured when his brakes fail; an employee is needlessly exposed to benzene while working.

Did the juries agree on a fine that was close to the median of their individual estimates? Hell, no.

For the truly guilty, the reprisals shot up: jury fines were up to five times larger than you'd expect from looking at the individual assessments. For every fifteen minutes the jury was out, the motorcyclist got another half-a-million dollars.[63]

Even for the smaller mess-ups, the juries' deliberations whacked up the payment. It seems that jurors egg each other on.[64]

People use punishment as a way of signalling. Placing a dozen men and women who hardly know each other in a room and asking them to talk about what some malefactor ought to receive could have been designed by psychologists to maximise the penalty. We all know that justice is blind, but the news is she's also psychopathic.

When two or more get together, what seems to one a crazily harsh sentence becomes feebly lenient after another has accepted it and raised it. If you get caught out at work, do your best to make amends. Express your sorrow; flaunt your guilt. More importantly, stop your colleagues talking about you. Stalk the water-coolers, barge into the toilets, join the smokers at the entrance. Go to meetings early and leave last.

But most of all, if you're going to sin, avoid the public eye.

If juries of six turn into slavering lynch mobs, then imagine what the deliberations of a hundred or a thousand might be. Or log onto Twitter and see.

Punishment isn't what it used to be

For one or two million years, humans have created an environment in which those who can maintain their reputation do better than those who don't. Our rock-throwing forebears have nearly killed off – literally – the ability to think differently.

Humans believe in human rights, duties, sharing, kindness, virtues, vices, good, bad and any amount of other junk not because these things are logical or true, but because picking up and believing the ideas of people in their group was a successful strategy for our ancestors' genes.

Punishment rather than love; judgement rather than mercy; stoning rather than forgiveness. These are what have brought morality into being; chopping out the malingerer, the miscreant and the malefactor.

No doubt, the people who got caught were for the most part simply defective in some way. Our prisons aren't full of clever cynics. Two-thirds of inmates have a personality disorder, a tenth have major depression.[65] In parts of the UK, a quarter of convicts are dependent on opioids.[66] These aren't people doing a cost-benefit analysis; they're people who've lost control of themselves.

What human society isn't protected against is a systematic attempt to look for its weak spots. Prehistoric scoundrels didn't have the benefit of controlled experiments to show them the loopholes in justice. They knew nothing of neurons, norms or natural selection.

City life, as we've seen, is full of one-shot interactions. Our brains haven't caught up: they still assume that every interaction is with somebody they'll meet again.

As I say, morality functions on the basis of reputation. But the point I want to develop here is that it doesn't function in the way that it did. People worry that privacy is invaded by Google or Facebook. They should. But the level of privacy we still have is unprecedented.

I grew up in a little village. The lady in the post office and the pub landlord seemed to know nearly everything about nearly everybody. Historic tribes were smaller still. Everybody knew who wasn't pulling their weight, who was sleeping with whom, who had insulted whom and fought whom.

Reputation still matters, but it's entirely possible to manage it so that different groups of people know different things about you. Within a hundred feet of where I write live a hundred people who don't know my name; during the day, I sit among people who don't know the colour of my wife's hair, let alone what I get up to in the evenings.

Gossip spreads the news, but people's bandwidth is taken up with stories that they can't influence and people they'll never meet. Celebrities, politicians, the characters in TV series. They're more beautiful, more dramatic and more scandalous; the actions of people we do know become dull in comparison and, by and large, we let them get on with it.

In the close-knit groups of our distant past, expressing guilt or outrage was a strong signal. Other group members would verify that it was backed up by the costly actions they implied. Now they're cheap tricks.

The law and the state further weaken ethics. When moral brains evolved, the same people who observed you, gossiped about you and knew you were the same ones who applied the ultimate sanctions of stoning or exile. They surely took a holistic view, and as mob justice is notoriously unpredictable, your more sensible ancestors will have kept well clear of the danger areas. Now the lines are written down, and you can tiptoe close to them: provided you don't break the law, there's little your neighbours can do to stop you. If the noise you make is a decibel under the legal limit, then you can keep the party going all night. They are also lop-sided. As we've seen, Bob will punish Alice for a failure to share: we're incentivised morally to do good as well as to avoid doing bad. But the law searches only for active harm according to the statutes: you can be jailed for hitting somebody, but nobody is sent to prison for failing to donate to charity or missing a chance to be kind.

For all of these reasons, modern society is ripe for a plucking. If Damien were born today, he might not do so badly. If he knew what he was doing, yet wasn't held back by the moral qualms most of us struggle with, he could get much of what he wanted without suffering the consequences. Indeed, the results of chapter two suggest Damien might be living among us already, enjoying the high life as a billionaire or a fêted artist.

FOUR:

How to keep up appearances

In the first chapter, we saw that many people imagine that morality is 'altruistic'. Morals, they imagine, are about helping others at the expense of the self: that's what they are for, and that's why we have them. We are now going to begin drawing a distinction between morality and altruism.

The bee dies to protect the hive. The starling wears her little wings out, and risks being eaten by the hawk, to try and ensure that her hatchlings are well fed. The kindly tree grows food for monkeys. Altruism's common, even among plants and animals.

But the reason that we see altruism, and find it remarkable, is because we are looking at the wrong level and on the wrong timescale. In each and every case, the personal sacrifice, when averaged over many individuals, confers a genetic advantage. The sterile bee might die, but the queen is more likely to survive and produce more bees with the warrior gene; some starlings are eaten, but more often their babies are well-fed and carry the hard-working, risk-taking, selfless genes to another generation.

Altruism's an optical illusion of the mind. Human brains focus on individuals; selection acts on genes.

It can be tempting to perceive morality as another mechanism which generates the illusion. As we've seen, humans have evolved to be moral, and maintain their reputation, to avoid punishment of a type no other animal can inflict. But the consequence could still be that morality makes humans altruistic. However, this is wrong.

Morality includes prohibitions on usury, fasting, finding and killing witches, beating up gays, female genital mutilation, blind loyalty, sacrificing children to gods, you name it. None of these are obviously altruistic; it's not clear how they improve the lot of any man, woman or humankind. Yet they would all be described as moral actions by people who do them. If we want to describe human morality and behaviour, then we have to include them all as examples.

You might balk at this. You might think in each case that moralists were simply mistaken. The witch hunters thought they were saving their neighbours from pestilence. The child sacrificers were preventing famine. The gay bashers and stoners of adulterers were protecting the family. They may have been wrong, but they were trying: they *thought* they were improving the lot of their fellow man.

But that is simply the rationalisation, and we'll have plenty more to say on this later. Why we frequently dress up our moral commitments as being altruistic, as preventing harm to, or helping, others is a puzzle we'll also look at again.

The fact is that group punishment ensures that individuals are incentivised to do what the group expects of them: to adopt the norms, proclaim the principles, bend the knee. It's not written anywhere that these expectations must always be things that help, or even aim to help, other people. It isn't altruism that has driven the evolution of morality.

Seeing minds prevents us from seeing the truth

In day-to-day life, we don't focus on genes as even indirect causes of behaviour. As we know, nobody punishes somebody else with the thought that the malefactor's lousy genes won't be so prevalent in the next generation. No mother cares for her child because she's decided this might be a good thing to do for the various genes which enable her to do so. Genes are the ultimate reasons we do and can do such things, but they aren't the immediate, proximate causes of our behaviour, or the way we instinctively explain it.

Instead, we see culpability and love. We see altruism because we are preoccupied with people's *minds*.

At this point, you might want your money back. Why am I telling you something so obvious? Surely only individuals think, make decisions, act, help and harm? Only they are kind, cowardly, saintly or evil.

But perceiving the obvious as obvious is one of the greatest barriers to scientific progress. It would help greatly if we could see our focus on people's minds as a little stranger than we do, and that is the subject of the rest of this chapter.

An alien[67] sending a postcard back after holidaying on Earth might explain things rather differently. Perhaps they'd be fascinated by the way that cells act together to make a body. They might latch straight onto genes as the things that interact with the environment to create collective behaviour. Possibly, they'd be most interested in population-level behaviour. Given that groups enforce norms, they might think of cultures as the basic unit of morality. It's surely unlikely that they'd think the decisions made in individual brains were the most interesting or influential.

This, you might counter, is because the alien is missing some information that you have. You are aware of making altruistic decisions, or of choosing not to. You perceive yourself as cruel or kind; good or bad; guilty or carefree. Because you know how you make moral decisions, and it's in yourself and through your thoughts rather than in your genes or through your group, you also think you know that individuals are the most useful and interesting level of analysis.

This logical leap is flawed. In fact, it's back-to-front. But explaining why it is so is to deal in what is quite possibly the hardest concept in all of science. Once you've grasped it, you will see the world in a totally different way: upside-down and inside-out compared to common sense. But it's from that perspective that many of the things that seem strange about morality will come into focus. That will be the topic of chapters five and six.

This chapter aims to show the following:

- We judge other people, and change how we behave towards them, based on what we think is their character and in their minds: what they think, feel, desire and intend.
- The minds and characters we attribute to other people can't be their real minds. What we glean is a product of our own brains at least as much as theirs.
- If we are to keep in others' good books, then we must ensure that other people infer good character in us.

If each of these statements seems trivially true to you both now and at the end of this chapter, that's splendid. Because in later chapters, we'll use them. We'll ask what we might predict of an animal which judges and is judged in this way.[68]

And these predictions won't be trivial, or obvious, or pleasant. But experiments show that they are right.

Morals need minds

Harvey is sitting next to Megan. He turns a little to his side and puts his hand on Megan's knee. He gives it a squeeze. What do you think of him? Did he do wrong? Ought he to be punished?

If Megan is Harvey's wife and she is weeping at her mother's funeral, you might think it a compassionate gesture and judge Harvey positively. Megan, you might think, is comforted by the squeeze. She feels cared for. Harvey wants her to feel loved.

If Megan is a nervous but beautiful young actress, desperate for her first big part, and Harvey is a powerful producer who has invited her to his bedroom, you might conclude differently. Harvey might not come off so well.

To distinguish between the two, and to make a judgement, you need to give character to the characters. What is Harvey thinking, and what does Harvey think Megan is feeling?

The content of your judgement might also depend on your beliefs about what is right and wrong. You might think that sleeping with a producer is fair game for an actress who wants to get ahead in Hollywood. That a pretty young thing who enters a man's bedroom knows what she's in for; has already made a free decision. Alternatively, you might think that touching someone outside of marriage is always sinful, or that to try it on in this way is an appalling abuse of power.

But wherever you stand on these things, you don't get far until you've given Harvey a mind: intentions, beliefs, emotions and thoughts.

If Harvey rests his hand on the arm of his chair, there's nothing to judge. A leaf fluttering against the windowpane has no moral content. Unless we can find a mind somehow: a negligent gardener who was paid to cut the branches back; a lad throwing a stick up to your daughter's bedroom window.[69]

To philosophers, ethics are abstract, knotted arguments about which types of acts are right and which are wrong. But, in practical terms, morality isn't about judging acts, it's about judging people and deciding how to treat them. And to do that, we grant them minds and work out what is in them.[70]

If you want to understand how morality works, the first step is to understand how people infer those minds, what they put in those minds, and how those minds change how they behave.

You are what you intend

Clearly a very useful reason for inferring a mind in somebody is to help you predict what they will do in the future.* If you decide the muscle-bound man is angry with you, you're more likely to expect him to thump you than if you infer that he's pleased with you. If you think your friend is cowardly, then you expect him to run away if the angry man comes for you.

And, of course, it can only be beneficial to predict others' actions if doing so changes your own behaviour. You might try and appease the enraged bodybuilder, get out of his way or find new, and less cowardly, friends.

It's because reading minds can improve our outcomes that we have the ability to do so. But if we infer somebody's character

* This is a plausible assumption, but it's worth saying that it's an as yet unproven assumption. [71]

to help us forecast what they will do, then it is to be expected that we will only use *some* of their actions to build that character.

Drop a rock and it will fall to the ground. Let it go from anywhere on the Earth and, within a smidgen, its acceleration as it plunges will be the same. It's easy to model and predict the behaviour of a falling rock.[72]

Humans aren't so straightforward. Put Harvey near to a leg and his hand won't always reach out to it.

From observing Harvey's behaviour, we can build up a sense of his character that enables us to predict under what circumstances his hand will shoot out. Perhaps it's just the legs of blondes. Maybe blondes with a certain figure and a stated desire to be actresses. And maybe it only happens when he's in a hotel room.

In our Harvey-hand-watching project, not all of his actions are predictive. He's a big man and let's say he's been drinking. He gets up from his chair. He wobbles, he stumbles and he starts to fall. His hand, which we're keeping a close eye on, extends and he grips the leg of the red-haired lady he was talking to. He blushes, apologises and makes his way unsteadily to the bathroom.

If the point of judging people is to predict their future actions, then what we care about when it comes to morals are *intentional* actions. We want to know how Harvey's brain directs Harvey's muscles. When Harvey's body moves in a way that he didn't order it to, or the consequences of those movements aren't what he anticipated, they're not telling us so much about the brain signals.

Broadly, this is how moral judgement works.[73] When volunteers assess vignettes, they rate women who poison a friend accidentally (thinking they were giving them sugar) better than those who tried to poison their friend but failed (because the sugar and toxic powder were mixed up).[74]

Scientists know which part of the brain converts assessments of intention into judgements of morality. They can switch it off with magnets and leave volunteers with childlike indifference to what Harvey meant to do when he grasped the red-head's leg.[75] For our purposes it mostly doesn't matter which part of the brain does what (it all has to happen somewhere), but it's interesting that this part of the brain seems to be something that only humans have.[76]

These studies seem to confirm what we suspect about the purpose of moral judgements. However, they rely on the author of the questionnaire knowing what the woman intended when she put the powder in her friend's drink.[77] In life, of course, we can never know for sure.

We have to work out what people intended to do for ourselves. Was Harvey quite as drunk as he seemed? Was he really falling, and was the woman's leg seriously the first thing he reached out for?

We can only get at this from his actions. And an astonishing chunk of (often uniquely) human brainpower is taken up inferring what other people meant to do and why from what they actually did.

Where was Harvey looking as he fell? What was the expression on his face? What was the time-lag between his stumbling and his hand finding the leg? What's his reputation?

We put all this together and – wham – we infer the contents of a mind and reach a judgement. It happens fast. It seems easy. But that doesn't mean it is, or that it's flawless. Flying's hard. Yet birds, bats and even bumblebees do it with remarkably little training. Inferring people's minds is much, much more complicated.

Smile when you're good and frown when you're bad

When we judge other people, we treat them differently based on what their intentions were, what they wanted and how they feel. But, as I say, these emotions and intentions that we use can't be their actual, felt emotions and real intentions: that's not possible. We don't carry around brain scanners with which to probe the inside of others' heads. We can't be sure from the outside whether Harvey feels guilt or affection or lust or indeed nothing at all. Morality's entirely based on the minds that we invent in others: granting minds is a gift we give.

Science is cataloguing the ways in which we infer intention and character from people's actions and signals. Some of these are complicated, but some should be obvious even to children.

And, of course, if we know how we read character and intentions in other people, then we are also learning how to modify our own behaviour to change the minds that other people grant to us.

When I was young, my mother thought I ought to help around the house. I disagreed. 'I'm doing my homework,' I'd shout back, grabbing a book in case she came to check. She'd call again. And again. Finally, I'd traipse downstairs and dry the dishes or empty the bin or whatever with a frown on my face.

One of my brothers was (and is) very different. This chipper little lad did his chores with a smile on his face, and asked Mum whether she needed help with anything else.

Mum would ground me, cancel my pocket money and give me a stern talking-to. I thought this very unfair. She could have her slave, but she needn't expect him to whistle while he worked. And with that I'd stomp back up to my room.

As well as being an unpleasant child, I was a fool. My mum was scrupulously even-handed: I ended up doing just as much work as my butt-licking brother, but never got any of the credit for it.

Scientists in New York thought my story might not be unique. They asked volunteers to watch films of actors.[78] Some helped others, while others harmed them.

For example, Brian agrees to give his colleague a hand with a tricky project. In some videos he grins and nods. Other times he grimaces, looks down and mutters 'okay'. Tina knocks coffee over her assistant's desk. Sometimes Tina looks pleased with herself, and in other clips she looks mortified at what she's done.

When the actors agree to help willingly, the volunteers rated their characters highly. However, the way they went about their chores and villainy also mattered. When they grudgingly give their time, most of the good work from helping is undone. When Tina grins like a psychopath after drenching her employee, she comes off badly; but if she shows a little embarrassment she's rated nearly as highly as the Brian who helped but was grumpy about it.

It makes sense to do your good works with a smile on your face, and to look ashamed if you've done wrong. But there are limits to how far acting might take you. If the point of reading other people's characters, of delving into their minds, is to predict what they will *do* in the future, then in the long run what they actually do should outweigh their expression while they're doing it.

If Brian grouses a lot, but always helps out, and Tina has a knack for 'accidentally' soaking people she doesn't like, you know who to ask for assistance and who to keep clear of.

It takes about three good deeds done with a frown before you're judged as well as somebody who's done one good deed with a smile. After that, it doesn't matter how you present yourself. The more helpful acts, the better the rating.

With misdeeds, the crossover's faster. You spill the coffee and loaf in a joint project and you might as well have laughed like a cartoon baddie after chucking the drink.[79]

Be good quickly, or don't bother

Ask a friend whether he'd sleep with his mother. If he thinks hard before answering, it doesn't really matter what he finally says.

Estimates of human brain computing power vary, but a reasonable guide is that neurons fire a hundred thousand billion signals a second.[80] Just how many calculations does a man need to do to know that he doesn't want to sleep with his mum?

So it is with ethical questions. If morality was about judging acts, as used to be thought, then it wouldn't matter how long people take to get to the 'right' answer. But if it's about judging people and intentions, then it does.

The virtuous seem to do what they believe is right in a blink. They're not doing a careful cost-benefit analysis in which the pros and cons are balanced. From this, we can infer that the moral aspects of the choice outweigh everything else, and we can predict that they will do so in the future: we know how they'll behave.

One such experimental race[81] asked people to judge a man who found a cash-filled wallet. Sometimes he returned the wallet and sometimes he swiped it. Sometimes he made his choice quickly, and other times he deliberated first.

When people delay over returning the money, they are judged just as poorly as those who thought long and hard before keeping it. They lose the money *and* their reputation. The man who pauses only long enough to check he's not been seen comes off worst, and the do-gooder who immediately turns the purse in gets the best rating.

The moral of the story is clear. And irritating. If your deliberations lead you to conclude that in such-and-such a circumstance you ought to behave as if you are good, then to gain the benefit you need to act quickly, as if you hadn't stopped to think at all. Don't dither.

Guilt is the next best thing to innocence

When film producers, actors or politicians are caught raping women, feeling up boys or sexting teens, the first thing that their PR agencies have them do is express profound sorrow. To say how bad they feel and that they're getting help, stopping drinking, examining their behaviour, have changed. They don the hair shirt.

If their audience is above six years old, it's worth a shot. German psychologists told children about two boys who were playing with toy cars.[82] The researchers announced that the boys had stolen the cars from a friend. To young children, taking another kid's toy is the height of evil, up there with scribbling on the wall and having sweets before dinner.

The researchers then showed pictures of the little pilferers. One of the boys was smiling because he was pleased to have the shiny car. The other looked sad. He was sorry because he'd pinched it from his friend.

'Which child is worse?' the researchers asked. To four-year-olds, there was no difference. How the boys felt after they'd done their carjacking was irrelevant. Among six-year-olds, a majority thought the happy kid was worse, but it was only at eight that ninety per cent of the children they spoke to had a clear view that being sorry makes you less reprehensible.

Do the fallen stars' *mea culpas* work out for them in the judgement of adults? Once again, our judgement will boil down to what we imagine is going on in their minds. If we judge them badly, the problem is perhaps that we don't believe that they're sincere. We suspect that their tweets and press releases aren't the product of a long night of soul searching but are drafted by advisers.

On the internet, you can find articles explaining what components an 'effective' apology should include. None of them are naïve enough to suggest their client actually has to *feel* the emotion. To convince adults, you need to do more than plaster the appropriate expression on your face and woodenly repeat the script you've been given. You'd think they'd know that in Hollywood.

Your innocence makes others guilty

If you can express remorse convincingly, it seems to be one of nature's greatest wheezes. Why do moralists set such store in a sincerely felt apology?

As we've seen, moralists *enjoy* punishing transgressors; thrashing the immoral and the amoral is one of the pleasures of being moral. Sad, but true. I've also argued that it's punishment that creates morality. Deciding who to punish is surely one of the reasons that we've evolved to judge people's characters in the first place.

But punishment can be costly. Guarding prisoners and feeding them is expensive. It reduces the size of your team. Even boiling them in oil isn't free.

Guilt is the compromise. Displaying it is at best a convincing promise about your behaviour in the future.

Experiments show that people who are reminded of past transgressions are afterwards more likely to give to charity and less likely to cheat on a maths test.[83] They're more willing to hold their hands in ice-cold water for extended periods. Yakuza gang members in Japan even chop off parts of their finger to atone for their misdeeds, and present the severed digits to their boss.

But the best evidence that guilt changes behaviour is that people will pay to make us feel it. While public relations firms try to convince us that their clients feel guilty, advertisers and their clients frequently want to induce it in us.

Charities want us to feel bad that we're stuffing our faces while others are starving. Phone companies want you to feel remorse for not calling your parents as often as you should. Anti-smoking ads pile the pressure on parents; mums, and working mums in particular, are known to be suckers for campaigns that suggest they aren't looking after their children properly unless they buy whatever it is that's being sold.[84]

But it's a tricky thing to get right. A carefully crafted ad ('You shape your children, so don't let your family down') leaves viewers feeling miserable about themselves until they do what the company wants them to do. Lay it on too thick though ('It's YOUR responsibility . . . DO IT RIGHT!'), and the target doesn't feel shame at all. They feel manipulated and angry.[85]

The mum stops worrying that she ought to buy new dental floss for her kid or cook healthier meals, and looks for the mind that's attempting to exploit her. Rather than feeling guilt herself, she infers malevolence in the company that is trying to make her feel bad. Purchasing intentions fall rather than rise.

From your earliest schooldays, you've been learning to give the impression you're remorseful and to induce it in others. Teachers are more lenient when they think you're truly sorry about the missing homework. Aunts are more generous at Christmas when reminded they forgot your birthday.

Now you're an adult, multi-billion-dollar corporations with the full force of academic research behind them are trying to turn the tables on you.

Being good makes people bad

Moral people don't do good for the sake of doing good (though they might imagine they do): they do good to keep their reputations within bounds.

When they are caught doing wrong, they try to make amends and restore others' good opinion of them. But what about when they are already in moral credit?

In one Canadian experiment,[86] volunteers split into two groups. The first received money to buy items from an environmentally friendly store: energy-saving lightbulbs, organic crisps, natural deodorant. The second spent their allowance in a shop where products were marketed on taste and quality rather than boosting your environmental credentials.

In Toronto, buying green is a virtue. The first group had done their good deed for the day.

After selecting their groceries, both groups took part in a 'visual perception task'. The task was easy to cheat by lying about what you saw. The volunteers then paid themselves from an envelope based on their performance, meaning they also had the opportunity to steal.

Those who'd done their bit for the world felt licensed to take a little back. They cheated more on the test, and on average took an extra fifty cents from the envelope.

Toronto students aren't unusual. It's a common finding that being a little good allows people to be a little bad[87]:

- People who reflected on their less pleasant qualities donated more to charity than those who first wrote about their more positive traits.[88]
- Obama supporters who received a chance to endorse the then candidate were more likely to choose a white officer as police deputy than Obama supporters who didn't first get to demonstrate their non-racist attitudes.[89]

It's important to us that we're perceived as moral people, that others believe that we behave in an acceptable way.

But few are aiming for sainthood. Bill Gates operated an aggressive monopoly, but donates to charity. Trump grabs women by the pussy but is affectionate towards his children. Gandhi fought apartheid and colonialism, but made young women sleep naked in his bed.[90] Most of us balance our moral accounts on a far smaller scale.

If you can be virtuous later, you'll enjoy your vices now

Who watches *Schindler's List* for fun? Who enjoyed *Four Little Girls*, a true story of racial terror and the civil rights movement? So why do we watch such things?

One reason might be that we think they improve us. People describe watching lowbrow films as a vice, and viewing difficult films as virtuous.[91]

This common belief allowed experimenters to test volunteers' moral accounting.[92] They gave students a survey. Participants could choose a movie as thanks for taking part. Some of the films were highbrow (depressing dramas and documentaries), others offered more immediate pleasure (comedies, daring heists).

Half of the volunteers believed this was a single choice. The other half thought they'd be back in a fortnight and get to choose a second film.

These were serious students. Whether they actually wanted to improve themselves, or just to signal to the experimenter what sort of person they were, most of them chose a highbrow film. But when they believed they'd have a further chance to demonstrate their virtue, the proportion owning up to liking a spot of throwaway action or sloppy romance doubled, from twenty per cent to forty per cent.[93]

A friend of mine has a huge stock of difficult films to watch; some of them even have sub-titles. In his bank account, a portion of his savings are mentally ring-fenced for charitable donations at some point in the future. He fully intends to help his wife with the cleaning next week. All this prospective do-gooding serves an important function: it lets him have fun today.

Looking angelic is almost as good as being angelic

Within a fraction of a second, with only a photo to go by, people form an impression of who is trustworthy and who isn't.[94] The malformed malefactor. The angelic innocent. And almost everybody agrees on which is which.

There's considerable debate on whether this is a profitable thing to do. Some argue it's plausible that hormone levels distort facial shapes, and hormone levels affect behaviour. It's equally conceivable that trustworthy faces are simply those that resemble a child's; there's a mix-up in our neuronal circuitry that throws off these pernicious prejudices.

Some studies find that quick judgements do correlate with behaviour. Others find no relation at all. Yet others claim that baby-faced boys take advantage of their looks and grow up wild.[95]

It's almost incidental for our purposes whether these snap judgements are adaptive or not. People make them. And because our lives are affected by others' assessments of us, our faces change what we can get away with and where we end up.[96]

If your eyes are too close together, if your eyebrows knit in the middle, if your cheekbones are crooked, tough luck. Life is hard. If you can't afford the surgery necessary to correct your defects, rob a bank: nobody will be surprised.

Morals are character-creating

In this chapter, we've found that people infer your character from what you say and do, how quickly you do them and even from what you look like. But what about your moral commitments – those oughts and oughtn'ts, duties and virtues that you proclaim? In this section, we'll show that these also affect what other people infer about you. If you want people to trust you, it's not enough merely to have moral attitudes, you have to profess the right ones.

I have a friend round. He's a decent, frightfully moral and extremely rational individual. He's a utilitarian. So it makes sense that after dinner he slips into my bedroom. He pockets my cufflinks and puts my laptop into his bag. The next day he sells them and sends the money to an orphanage in Venezuela.

The expected consequences are certainly an increase in happiness. I served him some jolly good wine, so he guesses that I'll be able to afford a new computer and something to wear to work. I'm pretty careful and indeed the book I am writing was backed up in a couple of places. I won't invite him to dinner again, but he doesn't mind that: I'm a terrible bore when I've drunk too much. Meanwhile, the poor orphans get some new shoes and a feast of a meal.

Rational or not, there's something a little unsettling about the utilitarian. You shouldn't trust them with your spouse: 'what the cuckold don't know can't hurt him, darling, and if he ain't hurt and we're happy that's morality innit?' They won't generally feel a duty to keep your secrets, and they'll never have your back if stabbing you in it improves the lot of others.

It seems that cooperating with them could be difficult, and psychologists have a way of testing this. In the trust game, as we saw earlier, volunteers are given a sum of money. You can keep it, or give some of it to a second player. The money that you give is doubled, and the second player can then return some or all of the money they've received.

Let's say you're given a dollar. You give the whole lot to the other player. In his hands, it's doubled to two dollars. If he sends back one dollar and fifty cents, you're both richer than when you started.

But if he's rationally selfish, he wouldn't send anything back at all. He'd be two dollars up, and you'd be a dollar down. If you think that's what he'll do, and you're rationally selfish too, you shouldn't share with him at all. You keep the dollar, and he leaves empty-handed.

The trust game's widely used.[97] It turns out that people aren't rationally selfish. We do send money to our partner, but the amount we send, and how much we get back, depends on a whole host of variables.

In this study,[98] researchers first told participants about various moral dilemmas. An example is the train track dilemma. A train is about to run into five people. You're standing on a bridge next to a fat man. If you push him onto the rails, he'll be squished, but the other five will live. Would you push him?

The experimenters asked participants what they would do, and then told them what someone else had decided. After learning of the other person's decision, the volunteers were asked to play the trust game with that person. Did they trust the rational, utilitarian moraliser or the squeamish sort who refused to give him a shove?

It was the latter: and in the dollar-lending test, volunteers passed significantly more money when they thought that the person they were playing with deviated from the moral mathematics.

The experimenters also wanted to understand why people reacted the way they did. What did they think, how did they feel, about people who made one choice over the other?

A lady wins some money. Should she give the money to her grandson to get his car fixed or donate it to a charity that provides polio vaccinations in the developing world?

When asked whether she was 'moral' or not, participants thought she was equally so whichever option she chose. (She could always have blown the cash on a new TV.)

But in which scenario did they think she'd make a better friend or spouse or the President of the US? Overwhelmingly, they thought the lady who favoured her own would do better as a friend or partner, but less well as a political leader.

Let's be frank, it's a matter of perspective. I want my prime minister to put her country first, my boss to put his team first and my friends to put their friends first.

My wife's rather a looker. She might well increase the happiness in the world if she puts herself about. I'd rather she didn't. She's smart. She might do more good in the world if she left me and our daughters to our own devices while she did some charity work. But I really, really don't want a utilitarian wife.

Utilitarianism's an attractive idea. It's pleasingly symmetrical; elegant in its disregard for groups and self. More than a few psychologists have concluded that it's the obvious 'correct' morality. Emotions and prejudices and loyalties are all errors that prevent people from being truly good; conquer them and you'll be a secular saint.

But boil away your emotions, burn your biases and favouritisms and what you end up with isn't morality at all. Even if you did end up with a utilitarian bent, utilitarianism isn't fit for purpose. By design, it makes cooperation more difficult.

Morality's about working out how other people will behave. It rests on us trusting that others *won't* behave rationally: we want them to be emotional, prejudiced and to favour us. So, if somebody reveals that they are a utilitarian, you can update your picture of their mind – and steer clear of them.

The most important thing about other people is that which doesn't exist

In this chapter, we've found that minds are how we predict people and judge people. Their moral commitments, their expressions, their actions, what they say and how fast they say it, and even the proportions of their face all enter our brain as data. The details of quite what happens in our brain are still mysterious to science, but we know at least some of what pops out.

Minds. Characters. Emotions. Intentions. All imaginary, all a product as much of our own brains as the brains of the people we imagine possess them – but all useful.

If you're good at reading minds, and working out how to use what you've read, then it's sensible not to ask your boss for a raise when she's cross with you. You'll be able to steer clear of malicious coffee spillers, and you'll know not to trust a utilitarian with your laptop.

These minds are essential to morality. A victim can only be a victim if he can suffer; you will only perceive somebody as a victim, and therefore possibly help them, if you give them a mind which actually suffers.

Similarly, we've seen that a wrongdoer is only culpable if he *intends* to do wrong. You will only perceive him as answerable if you both give him a mind which is capable of goals and attribute malicious intent to that mind. You will only gang up with others to punish him if those others also infer similar things. Indeed, you will only join forces if each member of your posse is able to infer about the other members that they too have vengeful minds. Getting minds right is important. It's essential to social life that you can understand people and that their actions don't come as a shock too often. If you couldn't infer minds, other people would be unintelligible objects doing random things at unexpected moments. Faced with such a confusing environment, your own actions would surely be inappropriate and, sooner or later, you'd suffer the social consequences, even if you couldn't work out why.

You can't, of course, see a mind, nobody's ever seen a mind, you can only create them from the outside. You understand

and predict other people by creating the invisible from the visible, the imaginary from the audible and the intangible from the corporeal.

This, we said at the start of this chapter, should seem more remarkable than it does. Minds are a very particular way of modelling people and their behaviour. In the next chapter, we're going to investigate something even stranger. We're going to find that the only reason we have a mind ourselves is because other people are granting us minds, predicting our behaviour from those minds, judging us on those minds and deciding how to treat us based on them.

FIVE

Without morals you wouldn't even have a mind

As we've seen, vigorous punishment ensures that those who engage the righteous anger of their fellow humans don't generally do very well. For hundreds of thousands of years, there's been intense evolutionary pressure to avoid castigation and engage kindness. Genes that have enabled their human bodies to do this have flourished; those that haven't have mostly gone the way of dodo DNA.

We have also seen that what matters is what other people think goes on in your head. Other people build models of you. They invent a mind for you. If you're lucky (or giving off the right signals), they'll assume that you're capable of feeling guilt, resentment and remorse.

They give you a character. From your actions, from what you say, from your pauses and expressions and from gossip they've heard, they'll decide whether you're trustworthy, kind, decent or a monster. Based on these imagined minds, they decide how to behave towards you: whether to trust you, share with you, stay away from you or group together with others to stone you.

So the formidable force that has acted on our genes over the millennia hasn't been to be good *per se*. It has been to *convince* people that we're good. In other words, we change others' behaviour towards us by changing the models that they have of our minds.

We do this, more or less cynically, all the time. A certain sort of man might buy flowers for his frail, elderly, boring – but very rich – great aunt. He hopes that she will think he's fond of her. He hopes that this will change her behaviour: that she'll adjust her will in his favour.

I, too, buy flowers. I give them to my wife. I hope they'll make her smile. But, over time, they perhaps change the model she has of me: she believes that I want to make her happy. Maybe that's why she married me.

My wife takes the gerberas and puts them in a vase. She smiles, and then she kisses me. I believe she's pleased. She'll probably get flowers again.

Social life is a grand and tawdry, ugly and beautiful jig of inferring other people's minds and having our own inferred. Of acting on what we infer, and others acting on what they infer. We read people's minds. They say things and do things which change the minds we invent for them. What we read changes how we behave towards them, which changes what they read in us, which changes what they say and do, and so on. From a baby's first cry for milk to an old lady's last deathbed sigh, we dance the dance all our lives.

But if we do it all the time, that doesn't mean it's easy or without risk. Take those flowers I gave my wife. She might have read in me that I gave them to her because I feel guilty about something. She might have become angry because 'only yesterday, we agreed to save money'.

What is really going on in my brain – the elusive, ephemeral, electrical processes – that led to my buying the gerberas and giving them to her isn't nearly as important as what she infers about me from my actions. It's the latter that changes what she reads in me, the latter that then changes her behaviour. It is really useful therefore, if when I contemplate getting those flowers, I consider how I might be perceived.

What I am doing when I imagine how I might be perceived is *modelling* myself from the outside in. I am in a sense reading my mind in the way that other people read my mind. Other people use my facial expressions, what I say and what I do, to determine what my emotions are, whether I am guilty or blameless, and I build up my own sense of what my mind contains based on what I perceive to be others' reactions to me.

In this chapter, we'll see that we do have just such a self-model.[99] It tells us not why we do what we do, say what we say, or feel what we feel: it tells us what other people might determine. And that, in turn, determines our sense of self. It's a fact that's as easy to explain and to scientifically demonstrate as it is difficult to accept.

This chapter simply aims to show that you have such a model of yourself based on other people's models of you. However, this self-model wouldn't have evolved, couldn't have benefited our genes, if we didn't use it when deciding what to do: we'll see how it manipulates you into manipulating others in chapter six.

We feel how we look

After a tiresome day's work, my wife sees me with the flowers looking pleased with myself. They make her happy, so she smiles. I see her smile, and so I know that she is happy. It seems that the order of events is (i) something happens, (ii) that changes how she feels, (iii) her feeling changes her expression, (iv) her expression changes what the rest of us are able to read in her mind.

But if my wife has a self-model, something that's trying to work out what other people are reading in her, we'd expect it to work slightly differently. It's her expression and posture and what she does that allows me to work out what's in her mind. So we'd expect these things to alter how that model perceives her emotions: it should work backwards from the outward signs, just as I have to do.

It might seem difficult to test this directly. It's only when the self-model within my wife's brain influences her behaviour in some way that I can begin to measure its effect. But, thankfully, one of the things that the model changes is what she says. There's lots of evidence that what people say is influenced by their outward expressions.

- After people adopt 'power poses' (arms akimbo, feet apart, that sort of thing) for a couple of minutes, they say they feel more powerful.[100]
- When your face is formed into a smile, you claim to find cartoons funnier. When you frown, you find them less so.[101]
- If you give people positive feedback when they're sitting up straight, they report being prouder of their achievement than when they're slouched.[102]
- When people do a very boring job, then tell somebody else that it's interesting (because they've been asked to do so), they later recall the task as being more enjoyable. Unless you pay them for their lie: in which case they remember the job being as boring as it was.[103]

For a long time, philosophers, writers and the rest of us believed that there was a fundamental asymmetry between the inferences we make about ourselves and those of others.

You smile, and therefore I know that you are happy. You sit up straight and therefore I know you are proud. You tell me something is interesting and I trust that you enjoyed it. You put your hands on your hips and thrust your chin in the air and I know you're on some sort of power kick.

But I imagine that I smile *because* I'm happy. I am proud and therefore I sit up straight; I tell you something was great because I thought it was. I've never had any great office of state thrust upon me, but if I did I'm sure that I'd start strutting about powerfully.

It seems that with ourselves we know our feelings first and our behaviour follows. But these experiments suggest the opposite.

Our gestures are surely messages to other people.[104] They signal what we are feeling. But if our self-model aims to work out what other people think we are feeling, then they are also signals to us. We infer how we feel about things from our behaviour, from what we say and do, in much the way we infer other people's feelings from *their* behaviour.

A confession makes you guilty

I was once questioned by the cops about an alleged assault on a housemate. Before I spoke to them, I called my uncle, a former policeman. He told me that, whether or not I'd done it, and whether or not they arrested me, I shouldn't say anything without a lawyer.

When somebody makes a voluntary confession, we believe them. We've all heard stories of men jailed for murders they've owned up to that later evidence proves they couldn't possibly have committed. These, we imagine, are morons. We've all heard political prisoners admit to absurd conspiracies and depraved acts that no human could plausibly have thought fruitful. These, we know, are the consequence of imaginative tortures. But if someone with more than half their wits, and without a cattle-prod or scalpel in sight, says they did something wrong, why wouldn't we accept their testimony?

People in the know, like my uncle, don't think it's so simple. With the right technique, you can create a situation where it's easier for someone to own up to wrongdoing than not, whether or not they did it.[105]

In one experiment, Princeton psychologists gave a tricky maths test to students.[106] They were to stop work after fifteen minutes. The researchers returned to the room after seventeen.

There wasn't any money given out for high scores, so there was no incentive to cheat. And nobody did: there was a hidden camera in the room which the scientists checked.

But the psychologists had a police interrogation handbook and were itching to try out some of the procedures. Their aim was to make the innocent students admit to something they hadn't done.

The first procedure aimed to coerce the students into a confession. The researchers told the students they had no choice but to come clean about having cheated. The experiment couldn't continue until they did.

The second technique they tried involved minimising the magnitude of the crime. The wannabe coppers told the students that it was common and entirely justifiable to use an extra couple of minutes to try and do a good job; the student was surely lost in the puzzles rather than watching the clock. It's not a big problem. Of course, you don't have to admit to cheating, but it would be very helpful to the experiment if you do.

The third strategy emphasised the consequences of being found out without a confession, and exaggerated the interrogator's certainty that the interrogated is guilty. The researchers said that if a student used the extra time without owning up, it would distort the experiment's results and trash the whole project. Cheating's a violation of the college's honour code. There could be severe consequences if the student doesn't sign a confession. Moreover, there's a video camera in the room and the experimenter will use the tape if the student doesn't sign.

In the first condition, nineteen out of twenty students signed a confession because they were told they had to. The second and third techniques had a three-quarters success rate.

This isn't such a surprise to psychologists as it might be to the rest of us. They have long known that the way other people present our choices to us has a larger impact on those choices than we expect it to. We imagine we wouldn't give near-lethal electric shocks just because we're told to, but in fact we're pretty obedient. We think we're independent-minded, but we pick up our morals from others; we mimic their behaviour, follow their fashions and tastes, and we even give the wrong answer to puzzles if everybody else does. Confessing to a crime we didn't do is just another example of us doing what scientists expect of us.

But how do we feel after we've made our false confession? Do we feel duped? Angry? Silly? Do we marvel at how unexpectedly compliant we are?

No. We feel guilty. Sometimes.

A day after they'd made their confessions, an apparently distinct research group asked them to take a personality questionnaire that included items on how ethical they thought they were, and on their self-esteem.

Members of the first group, who felt they'd been coerced into signing a confession, told the second psychologist that they were innocent, and continued the next day to believe they were ethical people with high self-esteem. But those who in the second and third group, who felt they'd had a choice whether to confess or not, came to believe they were guilty: they told the second psychologist they were, and the next day their self-esteem had dropped; they even rated themselves as bad people.[107]

We infer our own minds in the way that other people would infer them. If I knew your confession was forced, I'd discount it. But if I heard you'd caved at the slightest pressure, I'd believe your soul was rotten. And so, it seems, would you.

Fear makes people feel good

We don't need help when we're dozing happily on the riverbank. We don't seek assistance when we have our feet up by the fire.

I've argued that moralists are moral in order to change what other people infer about them, and they do this in order to change how other people act towards them. So when do we expect people to be most moral; when they're at peace or when things are hairy? And if we infer our emotions from external cues, how might we know that we're afraid?

Researchers in Canada designed an experiment that allows us to test both at the same time. They strapped heart rate monitors on participants' wrists.[108] The monitors made a sound like you'd hear from a stethoscope. Half of the volunteers heard a steady, normal sixty beats a minute. The others heard the more urgent thumpety-thump of nearly a hundred.

This manipulation sounds hokey. Why would listening to a recorded heart convince me that my own was beating faster, far less change my behaviour? It just doesn't seem plausible.[109]

But plausibility isn't one of the guiding principles of human design. Outside of research on morality, psychologists have been tricking volunteers with false heart rate recordings for half a century. Bump up the rate, and you increase men's ratings of erotic pictures.[110] Slow it down while ophidiophobiacs view pictures of snakes and you can reduce their fear of the reptiles to the point that a majority of them will afterwards handle one.[111]

Artists more or less elegantly, and more or less knowingly, manipulate our feelings through this effect. The pounding drum rhythms of a certain sort of music. The soundtrack to films such as *Jaws* and *The Shining*.[112]

So what did the Canadian researchers have their volunteers do while manipulating their perceived heart rate? In one experiment, the participants played a game with a partner. The partner could choose option A or option B. Option A paid eight dollars to the person strapped to the heart rate monitor and two dollars to the partner; in option B the payoffs were reversed. The partner didn't know this, but the main participant did, and was allowed to send a message to the partner about what the payoffs were. If the monitor-wearer lied, and told the partner they were better off choosing option A, then they would expect to win more money. In a separate study, the researchers offered other subjects the chance to volunteer for charity.

In both experiments, the higher heart rate prompted a greater proportion of participants to do what they thought was right. Lying rates fell from two-thirds to one-third. Volunteering rates more than doubled.

Our heart rate is a crude instrument for knowing ourselves. We feel it jump when we're frightened, but also when we're in love or working out. If we're running for the bus and nearly get knocked over, how do we know how much our palpitations are due to the running and how much because we're shocked at our near-death experience and how much because we're worried we're going to be late?

We can't know and we don't know.[113] If you scare a bunch of straight men in the presence of an attractive women, and don't frighten a second group when they're with her, members of the first group are more likely to ask her out. They're also less likely to say they're afraid than men who were scared without the woman: they've misattributed their high heart rate to the woman rather than the fright.

The stronger your self image, the easier it is to change

As a smokescreen, researchers gave irrelevant personality tests to some volunteers.[114] On the way out of the exam hall, half the participants were then asked to sign a letter to the president advocating more assistance for the homeless. Nearly everybody agreed to do so, and afterwards they were given a sticker to wear 'There are millions of homeless in America – think about it'.

A few days later, the experimenters were in touch again. There was a food drive for the homeless at the weekend. Would they help?

Of those who'd been allowed to leave the hall quickly, less than one-in-six agreed to do so. Among those who'd signed a letter and worn a badge, the number significantly shot up, to about forty per cent.

This experiment has three stages. It relies, first, on people's view of who they are – the sort who helps the homeless – changing as a result of agreeing to do something.[115] Secondly, it relies on this change in self-view persisting over days. Thirdly, people's behaviour has to change as a result of their new self-image.

If any of these stages breaks down, you won't get a change in behaviour. It's impressive, then, that the experiment has such a strong result: one in four people who wouldn't otherwise have volunteered their time do so because they put a sticker on their bag.

In fact, you can get similar results even more simply. It's not necessary for people to have learnt something about themselves; they just need to believe they have. Some researchers have given volunteers a quiz.[116] The quiz tells them nothing about how helpful the participants are, but the experimenters pretend it has.

They tell half the volunteers that the survey suggests they are extremely helpful, and the other half that they aren't. As the volunteers leave the test room, a woman clumsily drops a stack of pamphlets. Those who'd recently learned that they were helpful were more than twice as likely to pick them up for her.

These types of manipulations generally work with the average person. But not with everybody.

Some people seem to have a clear idea who they are. If you ask them whether they're careless or careful, timid or bold, warm or cold, they'll give answers. If you ask them the same question about four months later, they'll give broadly similar ones.[117]

Others seem more doubtful. They're not sure they're one thing or the other. Test them later, and they'll have changed their minds. People in this group are more likely to be neurotic, anxious and depressed.

We might guess that the strategies work best with the second group. The first sound like they've got their heads screwed on: their self-image won't be altered, nor their behaviour changed, by a simple manipulation a week earlier. They already know who they are. The second group sound like they blow in the wind.

We'd be wrong. It's the first group.[118] Either you find out who you are from your actions, from observing what you say and do, or you don't find out who you are at all.

People argue for what they've decided rather than decide based on the arguments

The best experimental psychologists are good at deceiving their subjects. If volunteers cotton on to what the study is really about, some of them say and do what they can to please the researchers, while others do what they can to mess the experiment up. Double-dealing is therefore in the psychologist's job description, as is caring in the nurse's and cruelty in the dentist's.

Psychologists aren't the first professionals to make a career out of duplicity. Illusionists were plying their trade when medics were still drilling holes in the skull to relieve mental illness.

To understand better what goes on in the head, Swedish psychologists borrowed a technique from their conjuring predecessors.[119] With strong glues, a pre-prepared clipboard and false pages they created a trick questionnaire. Volunteers marked their answers on page one, then turned over to fill in page two. When they turned the page, they unwittingly stuck part of the first page of questions to the back of the clipboard. When the volunteers flipped back to their original answers, these questions peeled off, revealing a new set that had been hidden underneath. The net effect of all this trickery was that some of their answers had been switched.

For example, you might be presented with the principle 'Even if an action might harm the innocent, it can still be morally permissible to perform it'. You reflect and decide that it's seven on a one-to-nine scale (1 'completely disagree'; 9 'completely agree'). You do the second page, go back to the first and find you've marked a seven next to the statement 'If an action might harm the innocent, then it is *not* morally permissible to perform it'.

Hardly anybody noticed the magic. Some, on reviewing their answers, thought they must have filled it in wrong. But the majority were fooled. They thought that the flipped answer represented their considered belief.

This is surprising.[120] The statements in the questionnaire were often controversial. Is it morally defensible to purchase sexual services? Is it commendable to harbour illegal immigrants?

In Sweden, both these topics have been publicly debated: ten years before the experiment, Sweden changed its prostitution laws; a few years after the experiment, a political party with white-nationalist roots gained one-in-six votes.

This was reflected in the strength of opinions that the volunteers gave. The average rating was 7.2 when participants agreed with the statement, and 2.8 when they didn't.

After pulling off their trick, the experimenters asked the participants to explain their answers. Why is buying sex acceptable; why shouldn't you harbour illegal immigrants?

At this stage, people's arguments and passion and moral certainty came into play. The more extreme their view on the questionnaire, the more forceful was their defence of it. But it was a defence of the flipped answer rather than the one they originally gave.[121]

At the start of this book, we saw that moral views can't be reached through considered moral reasoning. The types of facts that any such argument would rest on simply don't exist. Moral reasoning must be doing something else.

This experiment suggests that a part of what it's doing is

giving a social justification of our moral choices. Rather than forming views based on arguments, we create arguments to defend our views.

It's not only psychologists who deceive their subjects; we all readily deceive ourselves. And, for my money, the results are more dramatic than any cape-clad ham yanking a rabbit out of a hat or making an elephant disappear.

How you think and how you think you think are different

On the internet, you can get snuff movies. I've watched a few. My favourite is set to soft, Vangelis-like music. But it's the visual content that gets me every time.

Centre stage, nearly filling the screen, is a large, aggressive amoeba. It's hungry, as a tiny paramecium seems to realise only too late. The amoeba reaches out with its tentacles. The paramecium struggles and tries to escape, even as the arm surrounds it. As its end nears, the paramecium goes into a frenzy, wriggling and butting and squirming. If not for the music, you could be sure it's screaming. Finally, it succumbs. Its body is dissolved.

It's really hard not to feel sorry for the little critter. Yet the amoeba's a single cell, less than a millimetre across, and the slipper-shaped paramecium is an order of magnitude smaller. They don't have a neuron between them.

An accurate description of what is going on wouldn't use concepts like hunger or struggle or trying. It's all done with chemical gradients and reactions and responses. But I'm human, and the language I naturally reach for is that of a struggle between minds, between desire and suffering, pleasure and fear. It's nearly impossible not to.

In describing humans, there's exactly the same problem. Your behaviour is caused by thousands of neurons acting in concert. Specific genes churning out proteins. Hormones pumping through your body.

To explain your behaviour, we don't need to bother with all that detail, just as to explain how the Sun and Earth orbit, you don't need to calculate the gravitational pull between each and every atom in the bodies.

But we do need to distinguish between the causes of your behaviour, the inferences other people make about the causes of your behaviour, and the inferences that you – as a result – make yourself about the causes of your behaviour. These are three very different things. Indeed, the third is a part of the first.[122]

You can't feel a decision

Your brain is a set of complicated, interconnected switches. Neurons receive electrical signals from other neurons. Based on these signals, they send signals of their own. Some of these signals cause muscles to contract: your body moves, your mouth opens, your vocal cords vibrate.

Try and feel yourself making a decision. Try and work out which neuron is sending what signal to where. You can't do it. None of us can experience the switches that make our decisions.

Most of what we are aware of is a simplified model of ourselves. This model is much like the one we have of other people. We feel guilt and happiness; pain and fear. We have desires and beliefs.

And this model of ourselves, as I've already suggested, is created in much the same way that we create models of other people: from the outside in. It is influenced by our expressions and our posture, by what we say and by what we do.

We have this model not to work out why we do what we do, or why we feel what we feel (what would be the evolutionary point of that?), but to understand what other people might infer about us.

We work out why we did what we did after doing it

We could fill a book with evidence for the self-model and details of how it works. (Much of my first book – *Unthink* – was.) But by now, hopefully we've got a sense of how broad it is.

Whether you're working out how you feel, whether you're guilty, what you believe in, or even what reasons you have for believing in what you believe, you don't have direct access to the inner workings of your own brain. Instead, your self-model is influenced by what other people might perceive and what it knows they believe.

However, experiments show that it goes even further than this. Our self-model also works out *why* we do what we do.

One such study was conducted by José Delgado.[123] Delgado was a medical researcher, so he had a legitimate reason to slice off the tops of people's skulls. The brain doesn't have any nerve receptors, so his patients didn't feel anything when he pushed electrodes into their motor cortex. But by passing a current through the electrodes, he could make his patients move.

He made one of his human puppets turn their head. Then he asked them why they did that.

They didn't experience a loss of self-control. They didn't realise that it was electrons from Delgado's equipment that were sending signals through their neurons to their neck muscles.

Instead, they said they were looking for their slippers or they were restless or they'd heard a noise.

His patient invented plausible explanations for why they did what they did: explanations which nobody would have questioned if they didn't have electrodes sticking out of a hole in their head. In the experimental setting, it seems strange, even macabre. But that's what we all do all the time: invent reasons for why we do what we do in the way that other people might.

Hurting hurts

You touch a hot hob and pull away in milliseconds. A bee stings and before you know what's happened, you've shaken your limb. Step on a thorn and you're hopping to relieve the weight.

The actions that your body takes to prevent further tissue damage are automatic. For them to work, you don't need to be aware of anything. A fly doesn't contemplate the afterlife when it struggles in a spider's web, and nor does it hurt when it strains its wings in the attempt. A single-cell paramecium, swimming rapidly from an amoeba, has no feeling that life is unfair nor does it experience death-throes as it is gobbled up. The animal world is full of fast, reflexive actions.

The *feeling* of pain is something entirely different. It's there for a social purpose. It's telling you something about what other people will read in your mind: what they will expect of you and what they will do to you or for you. It's part of your self-model. If you're hobbling on the football pitch they won't think so badly of you for missing the shot; if you shout as the bee stings, you won't be blamed so much for knocking the picnic off the table.

If felt pain isn't merely physical, then it's not such a surprise that placebos work. If you think that the doctor thinks you'll feel better, you feel better. The opposite's also true. When researchers pretend to pass an electric current through volunteer's brains, the dupes report headaches afterwards.[124]

The interaction between what we think others think and how we feel is stronger still. Our experience isn't modulated merely by what people expect us to feel, but also by what they want us to feel.

Researchers at Harvard paired volunteers for some tests.[125] Participants believed that they might do one of several tasks: compare the relative pitches of various sounds, match colours, estimate numbers – or evaluate how painful some electric shocks were.

In truth, of course, they were all going to be electrocuted. However, half of the participants believed that their partner chose the task for them. The other half believed that they were getting shocked in spite of their partner's attempt to win a less unpleasant exercise for them.

Those who believed that their partner intended them to get hurt found the shocks more painful. Moreover, the researchers were able to test another quirk of pain perception. We habituate to it. The more times you experience pain, the less you experience pain.

You might think that this is a problem for bullies, torturers and sadistic nurses. The more effort you put in, the less reward you get for your trouble. Indeed, the great spy writer, Eric Ambler, discussed the concern in one of his novels.[126] His solution was to beat the victim about the knees, which he thought less prone to the effect.

But if your job, or your hobby, involves inflicting pain on others, you needn't worry. People who thought they were getting the volts in spite of their partner's efforts found the shocks successively less painful, as expected. Those who believed that their partner wanted them to hurt experienced no such diminution.

The feeling of pain serves a social purpose. It's telling us something about what other people are thinking as much as what we are thinking, and therefore it's changed by what we believe they are thinking.

Morality causes all the world's suffering

As the last section highlights, moral mind perception is head-hurtingly circular. We invent minds to model other people. Yet, because we have models of ourselves as others model us, we end up with something similar to the minds they're inventing.

But we hypothesised at the start of chapter four that an alien, trying to explain why humans behave as they do, might not resort to granting us minds at all. They might model us in a different, and perhaps more accurate, way. So let's return to that thorn you've stood on and try to understand why our less accurate mind-based model of others' behaviour might be more *useful*, and tease out some of the implications for the way we model ourselves.

You step on the thorn and begin hopping. What happened? Your sensory neurons are stimulated. They send electrons along nerve fibres to your central nervous system. This does a quick calculation and sends some electrons back down along your motor neurons, and these cause the muscle cells in your leg to contract, so lifting your foot off the ground.

Why do you work like that? In the past, there were probably some people who didn't behave like that. Some mutation stopped their sensory neurons sending signals, or their central nervous system didn't function in quite that way. They didn't lift their foot and more damage was done to it by an embedded thorn. They didn't pull their hand back from the fire. With a dodgy, infected foot and a crippled hand, they were less able to run from predators, fend for themselves or look after their children. Their genes didn't spread and so you don't have them.

What happened and why? You stepped on a thorn, it hurt and so you drew away.

All of these explanations are simplifications. Only the last is completely wrong, if by 'hurting' we mean what you experience. You've lifted your foot long before that.

But in order for me to predict your behaviour after you step on the thorn, the last explanation, while wrong, is the most useful. What I care about is whether you're going to keep walking with me, or sit down and hobble back. What goes on at a neuronal level is neither here nor there: until recently, there was nothing I could do about that. Knowing, or guessing, your evolutionary history is similarly unhelpful. But estimating how much pain you're in gives me my answer.

It's the most useful of the explanations even if you didn't *feel* any pain at all. If humans had never evolved consciousness, thorns and fires would still damage us and, more importantly, our genes' chances of spreading.

We'd still have evolved mechanisms which lessened the harm from them. As unconscious automata, we would writhe and struggle to be free of the trap, we'd nurse our blows, tend our wounds, run from the predator. We'd learn to avoid plants that made us sick. Women would try not to be raped. All of these behaviours improve the spread of the genes which cause them, and none of them require consciousness.

When the fruit fly isn't escaping from spiders' webs, it can be trained[127]. You fill its tube with perfume and give it an electric shock. You fill the tube with a different scent and don't shock it. You do this a few times and then put it in a contraption with two exits, each with a different smell. The majority of flies sensibly choose to leave by the second door. Fruit fly brains have about a hundred thousand neurons: one for every million you have[128]. There's nothing so very special about learning to avoid things that harm you.

Whether you're trying to predict the behaviour of a human, a dog or a fruit fly you can get a long way with the concept of pain. They're responding to pain, avoiding pain, being disabled by pain. Pain doesn't have to exist in the abstract. It's a useful shorthand, underwritten by evolutionary pressures you need know nothing about, in much the same way that the rule 'things fall to the ground' is generally true due to more complicated laws of gravity.

But if pain's part of our model of how animals work, if the experience isn't necessary for any of these things, why are we cursed with it?

In a crowded train, you stumble and feel a searing pain in your thigh. You cry out. Those of us without plugs in our ears look up. We quickly build a model of you. You're in pain. You're clutching at your leg. We make predictions about you. And we make predictions about the people around you.

Right now you're vulnerable. You want to make predictions about us. You want to know how we'll behave. You may well want to change how we behave.

Maybe I'll stop banging on about thorns in the foot and come to your aid. Perhaps the man behind you will take advantage of your plight and steal your bag. If there's a woman next to you with a grin on her face and a hairpin in her hand, perhaps we'll wrestle her to the ground.

The likelihood of any of these is affected by how much pain we think you're in. If I think you're shamming, I'm sitting still. The more likely we think that the woman with the hairpin deliberately inflicted pain on you, the more likely we are to punish her. The thief's weighing up just how distracted you are.

So if you're going to predict our behaviour, you need to estimate what we're inferring about you. This is a social question as much as a nervous system question. And you have a model of yourself from the outside in to do the calculations.

Pain, like happiness and guilt and pride, isn't a reflection purely of our physical state or the truth of the world: it is an inference of what others might infer. It's why seeing your nasty wound leads you to feel more pain than when it's covered, why placebos work, why seeing the malicious smile of your assailant burns. They're all signals we're using and therefore they are all signals you should be using.

Your felt experience of pain evolved to predict other people's behaviour. That fruit fly has no reason to create a flawed model of herself. No other fly is going to come to her rescue when she's trapped in a web. She can't talk the spider round. Other flies won't gang up to punish the eight-legged fiend. So she doesn't need to infer what others are inferring about her. Nobody cares, and neither should she.

Her genes will be a little less numerous in the next generation if she doesn't escape. But genes that meant she had more than a hundred thousand neurons in her brain and wasted some of those on building a self-model will have done worse in the long run. Her plight on the web is not cold, lonely, painful or angst-ridden.

Your ancestors' genes won out in a very different environment. They lived in groups. People behaved according to moral rules. They helped and punished and shared. Knowing what other people might do was important. So you create models of other people, and a part of that model is their model of you: your self-model.

If other people didn't infer pain in us, and behave differently as a result of that inference, we'd have no reason to infer it in ourselves. It's because other people generally try to avoid hurting us, come to our aid and punish people who cause us to suffer, that it's important that we know what they think we're feeling.

Moralists think they're a good thing for humankind. If there were more like them and fewer like us, they imagine that the world would be a better place. There'd be less pain and suffering. But next time you cut yourself, stub your toe or suffer a scald, remember that the only reason you feel the pain is because of them and their ilk.

You *are* your morals

Which bit of you is you? If you believe in everlasting souls that whizz off into the ether with your last breath, which of your characteristics does it need to contain to mean that *you* have eternal life?

When my daughter's teeth fall out, she readily cashes them in with the tooth fairy: she doesn't grieve for an essential part of herself. My hair is thinning on top; I'm a lesser me than I was a year ago, but I'm still me.

For most people, it seems obvious that they are somewhere in their minds. Smash their body up, put them in a wheelchair and they'd be none too pleased, but they'd still be them. Rich old men who don't have quite the funds for whole-body cryonics elect to have their brains frozen instead.

But which bit of your mind? If your after-life budget only extends to preserving a single slice of grey matter in the bottom of your children's freezer, which slice should you choose?

To get to the bottom of people's intuitions, researchers concocted a story.[129] They told participants about a futuristic Jim living in 2049. Unimaginatively perhaps, they explained that Jim had been in a car crash. Self-driving aircraft may not have taken off in their future, but medical science has advanced: doctors are able to give Jim a partial brain transplant to replace tissue damaged in the smash.

Volunteers received one of several slightly different stories. Some learnt that the brain damage affected Jim's ability to recognise objects. Some that the accident had messed up his memories, or made him apathetic. A final group learnt that it was Jim's conscience that had been damaged: his ability to judge right from wrong and empathise with others' suffering. Participants then rated the extent to which Jim was still Jim after the transplant.

The ability to recognise objects wasn't essential: participants thought he was as much Jim as if the accident had been purely physical in its effects. Loss of memory and drive were more important: raters were split over whether the post-op person was Jim or somebody else. But when the accident destroyed Jim's moral sense, participants were clear: Jim was also destroyed.

Researchers gain similar results when they ask about aging friends. When memories go, something of the person is lost. Declining attention span; loss of feeling in limbs; a change in tastes, whether it's a loss of interest in the football scores or a newfound passion for classical music: all of these create a person who is different. But far and away, it's changes in the morality of the friend – an emergent cruelty or racism, a newfound selflessness or humility which participants said meant that their friend was no longer the person they once knew.

Inferring others' morals is the first and most important thing we do to know them. It tells us how they'll use their other characteristics. It tells us what to expect of them, and how to treat them. It is who they are.

Equally, our morals are a huge part of who we are. We can't understand ourselves without understanding our own morality. People's drive for consistency, their reluctance to change stance or question the foundations of their views, their association with those who hold similar ethics, even their disgust at alternative ways of life – are part of a battle for survival.

Morals might be made up. Inferred from our behaviour. Manipulative. We'll see that moralists go to great lengths to prevent others, and therefore themselves, from finding out what they're really like. Yet that glimmer that they do glimpse is the part of themselves that they judge most them.

This suggests an uncomfortable question for you and me. Over the time that I've researched and written this book, my attitude to morality, what it's for and how it works, what I ought to do and how I judge people, has changed. Is my wife still married to the same person she walked down the aisle for? If reading this book changes your own perspective, if you follow my advice and abandon morality altogether, will it kill you? Will a new person close the cover and take over your life?[130]

SIX

How your mind manipulates you in order to manipulate others

I don't believe in telekinesis; thought alone does not change the world. What goes on in your brain can only benefit you, or your genes, if it changes what you say or do.

For us to have evolved a model of ourselves as others model us, for genes that gave us this ability to have spread, it must have conferred some advantage on those who had it. This model must change our behaviour. It seems likely that this advantage is a social advantage: the model changes what we do in such a way that other people act more favourably towards us.

When I pick up flowers, the self-model can tell me what my wife will think of me if I buy them. It can tell me I'm a nice guy, eager to please her. It can tell me that I'm an irresponsible spendthrift. But that doesn't do me any good unless it makes me more or less likely to buy them.

In previous chapters, we've seen that there's a huge pressure on our genes to ensure we avoid punishment from other humans, and are trusted. We've seen that people decide how to behave towards us based on what they read in our minds. We've seen that we have a model of ourselves that is built in the way that other people build their models of us.

This chapter completes the circuit. It shows how our model of ourselves, created from the outside in, changes our behaviour to maintain our reputation.

We've seen some hints of this already. When our reputation is low, when we've been caught doing wrong, we express guilt and amend our behaviour. In the last chapter, we saw that people express guilt not because they have cheated, but because other people believe they have.

In the following pages, we'll explore how the self-model protects us, how it helps us manage what other people read in our minds. The real causes of our behaviour might frequently be unseemly, but the self-model will only go so far as to change our behaviour when this unseemliness could be perceived from our actions. The evolutionary pressure that formed our minds is to *seem* good, not to *be* good.

The machinations of the self-model can seem breathtakingly cynical until you see how the trick is done. Because moralists read their own minds from the outside in, they have no idea that the real causes of their actions are different to those that they believe to be the causes.

These results will be picked up in later chapters, when we look at the behaviour of groups. Many of the most pernicious effects of prejudice are caused by people who imagine themselves free from bias. How can this be so? The answer lies in the way we read, and fail to read, minds in other people – and in ourselves.

In the final chapter, we'll argue that many of humanity's most pressing difficulties can't be resolved by morality; indeed, are worsened by it. One of the reasons for this is the quirky way we read minds.

Mindreading and self-mindreading are enormously powerful. But we didn't get these tools by magic; as we've found, we got them because our ancestors did better for having them (or, more precisely, our ancestors did better for the genes they carried by having them): these tools solved social problems that our ancestors faced. Their social problems aren't our social problems.

Immorality only matters when it can be inferred

John Darley and Paget Gross at Princeton performed one of my favourite experiments.[131] Their study elegantly demonstrates that the self-model leads to changes in our behaviour, and that it acts not to prevent us from being unethical but, instead, to prevent us from being *perceived* as unethical.

They invited seventy undergraduates to a 'teacher evaluation' study. They split the students into groups, and showed each of them a video.

All the groups saw a video of a nine-year-old girl called Hannah. The first group watched Hannah playing in a concrete yard in a run-down urban area. Her father was a meatpacker and her mother struggled as a seamstress.

The second group watched Hannah play in a tree-lined park. Her neighbourhood was one of large houses in landscaped grounds. Her parents had degrees; her dad was a lawyer and her mother a writer.

The experimenters then asked the undergraduates to estimate Hannah's ability on a range of academic topics.

There's a stereotype about parental background and scholarly performance which, on average, is accurate. If all you have to go on is the wealth of children's parents, and you predict that the one in the nice house will do better at school, then you'll be right more often than wrong.[132]

But applying such stereotypes is widely considered immoral.

Perhaps there's no surprise then that in the experiment both groups ranked Hannah about the same. To rank her as anything but middling would have shown that the undergraduates were using the stereotype; that their assessment was based on illicit views.

The experimenters also showed the clips to a third and fourth group. The third group only saw poor Hannah, and the fourth group only rich Hannah. But these groups also saw a second clip of her. In this extra video, they watched Hannah being tested at school; doing maths, reading and science. She wasn't great, and she wasn't rubbish either. Both group three and group four saw exactly the same second clip. Then groups three and four answered questions on Hannah's performance.

How do you think they answered? They saw the clips of Hannah's background, just the same as groups one and two, and groups one and two both said she was middling. They also saw a more relevant clip of her doing schoolwork, but both groups saw the same clip. So presumably groups three and four came to the same conclusions about her abilities?

No. The third group, who'd seen her in a poor background before watching her doing schoolwork, thought she was behind. The fourth group, who'd seen her lovely garden, thought she was ahead.

We know, because we can compare the results from groups three and four, that Hannah's background influenced their scoring.

For individuals in groups three and four, the second part of the video was *clearly* the most relevant. If you are asked to assess somebody's academic performance, then surely watching them perform academically must give more useful information than watching them walk around their neighbourhood.

If I'd seen you, and only you, watch one of those videos and give your assessment, I'd be confident that it was based on her performance. You could defend yourself. You saw how quick she was to answer the maths question, or you thought she stumbled when trying to read.[133] An outside observer, in a non-experimental setting, wouldn't be able to find any evidence that you were biased towards rich kids.

There's no reason to imagine the students were acting cynically. Why would they? Instead, it seems that the brain is forever proposing things that we might say or do. Some of these actions might be based on stereotypes, and some of these actions might be considered immoral.

The self-model tests these hypothetical actions. It doesn't know how the rest of the brain generates its proposals. It can't tell that prejudice was or wasn't a part of it. Instead it calculates how we might be perceived if we carry out the action. In groups three and four, the proposals passed: the self-model couldn't see any reason to do otherwise, any more than we could without the control groups. And in the absence of the experimental set-up, both observers and the students would come away believing they'd acted decently.

The immediate lesson is clear. If you have children and attend parents' meetings, wear your best togs and polish your shoes. Affect a plummy accent. It's *because* the teacher can convince himself that he's not influenced by this outward display, because he believes that his judgement is sensibly based solely on what happens in the classroom, that it will change his assessment of your child.

But there's a broader message. If people can act immorally, yet convince others and themselves that they aren't, they will. Their model of themselves isn't there to judge what actually went into a decision, only what can be inferred from that decision.

If fate's to blame, we're not

There's something monstrous about suicide bombers and kamikaze pilots. It's not just the demented belief of the brainwashed minions who strap on their explosives or climb into the cockpit. The most chilling aspect is the commander who sends them to their death.

In conflict, deaths are certain. Even when a superpower thumps a developing nation with all its airpower, the president knows there will be bodybags making the return journey. Nevertheless, it's rare to send any particular soldier on a mission knowing for sure that he won't come back. In the trenches of the First World War, a suitably drunken general could convince himself that a fighter might just make it when sent over the top. A chance is a chance.

Few of us make such weighty decisions. But we do play the odds. Uncertainty absolves us of guilt.

Psychologists frequently use variants of the dictator game to test people's ethical choices. They place their volunteers in pairs. One member of the pair is randomly assigned the dictator role. The dictator makes a choice. He or she can receive six dollars themselves and give one dollar to the other participant. Or they can split ten dollars evenly, with both members receiving five dollars. That's it.

It's a puzzle to classical economists that, even when the pairing is done anonymously (e.g. there are twelve people seated in the room at computer terminals, you aren't told who you're partnered with, and you don't get to see anyone else's responses), most people still choose to forego part of their pay-out to make someone else richer. In this experiment, three-quarters of participants did the 'decent' thing.

So the psychologists made the experiment a little funkier.[134] They told dictators that they'd be playing one of two games. In game A, the payoff was the same as in the above (i.e. six dollars/ one dollar; five dollars/five dollars), but in game B, the partner was better off if they chose the six dollars for themselves (i.e. if they selected six dollars for themselves, the partner would get five dollars; if they chose five dollars for themselves, the partner would get just one dollar). The dictators could find out whether they were playing game A or game B if they wanted, or make their choice without knowing.

There's no cost to finding out which game you're playing. If you want to be fair to your partner you need to know; if you just want to maximise your pay-off, you can find out and then choose the six dollars regardless. But only about half of the players chose to find out.

The trick to understanding the result is to consider what it was possible to infer about participants from their behaviour when they knew which game they were playing and when they didn't.

If they'd learnt which game they were playing, and found that it was game A, the dictators would have had to decide whether to maximise their own rewards at their partner's expense or play fair. They'd have been perceived badly if they'd taken all six dollars. By choosing to play without unveiling which game they were on, they left the other player's winnings to chance. It wasn't the dictator's fault if they only got a dollar. And so the number only getting a dollar rose dramatically.

Most of us are aware that some clothes, toys and gadgets are made using child labour or in sweatshops. Many would avoid the brands if they knew which they were. But they don't. Why? It's not hard: a minute on Google gives a partial list. It's not laziness: we all look up reviews before we choose a restaurant, select a bottle of wine or buy a new phone. They'd prefer not to know.[135]

If people don't know which of their T-shirts was sewn with little fingers, it wasn't their purchase which stole the worker's childhood. They can buy the item they'd like and sleep soundly in their possibly-not-sweatshop-produced pyjamas. It seems that being ignorant *is* an excuse.

Our own pain is worth less than others' pain

Once upon a time, aspiring traders answered the following. 'Would you prefer to be beaten up, beat somebody up, or run around the block naked?' In the days that you could ask this sort of question, when star dealers were known as 'big swinging dicks', perhaps they hired the candidate who replied that he would walk slowly down the street calling 'Come and get it laydeez'.

The question is in the tradition of magazine quizzes that attempt to judge our character, our ethics and our taboos by comparing what we would be willing to undergo with what we'd be willing to do to others. For a million, would you eat your faeces, sleep with Trump, cut off your pinky, slap a baby, poison a neighbour's dog, punch your father, pimp your sister? Donate a kidney, or push a button that killed someone you'll never meet?

We answer these posers by posing: giving the answer which we think will show us in the way we want to be seen. The job candidate who searches his soul in the interview room and admits he'll reluctantly take the beating just isn't going to cut it. The teen who thinks she's learnt something deep and meaningful about herself and her friends from their scores in the quiz is mistaken. Businesses as well as scientists want to know how people really answer the question when there's money on the table.

How to make these tests more real? Unfortunately, university ethics committees won't let you chop off participants' fingers. Psychology department budgets aren't large enough to fund a politician's harem. When psychologists want to hurt someone without fear of arrest or dismissal, they reach for the Digitimer DS5 bipolar constant current stimulator.

Dr Molly Crockett and her colleagues in Oxford and London had one of these.[136] It's a black box, about the size of a ream of A4 paper. On the right-hand side of the box is a yellow triangle with an exclamation mark, and next to the triangle is a bright orange switch. You attach a cable to the box, and fasten the other end of the lead to the back of volunteers' wrists.

In the Materials and Methods section of academic papers, there's a lot of detached discussion about the 'titration process' and fitting responses to a 'sigmoid function'. But the truth is, you flick the orange switch and electric current flows from the box into the subject, shocking them. You ask the now regretful volunteer to rate the pain on a 0 to 10 scale (0 indicating no pain, 10 intolerable), adjust the voltage up a bit, suppress a manic laugh and hit the orange button again.

You go all the way up to level 10, because you need to fully fit the sigmoid function, and you deliver each shock three times because that improves the accuracy of your fitting. (People's subjective rating of pain isn't directly proportional to the current that flows into them, and some people are more sensitive than others. These steps simply aim to find out for each participant where the dial needs to be set in order to deliver a specified amount of discomfort.) If you're a dentist because you like inflicting pain, you've missed your calling.

Once you've completed the titration process, you can break the good news to your subjects. In the main part of the experiment, all shocks will be a mere level eight.

In this study, the researchers paired off their volunteers. One of them was designated the decider, and the other sat out of sight awaiting their fate. The decider made a series of choices: they could earn money, but someone would get fried. Sometimes that person was the decider, and sometimes it was their passive victim.

For example, one trial might be worth fifteen pounds, but the decider herself would have to suffer eight shocks. Another might be worth just twelve pounds, and come with eleven shocks, but those shocks would be given to the person waiting behind the door. Yes or no?

If you're a dentist, a psychologist or a superstar trader, perhaps you'd let your partner receive shocks until their eyeballs popped out. Easy money.

That's not what the researchers found in their volunteers. People were willing to receive shocks for cash. They were also willing to get paid for others' pain. But the amount they demanded in return for letting the psychologists wiggle the orange switch was less when it was their own arm attached to the DS5 than when it was someone else's.

This experiment gives us a baseline. It suggests that the effects of the reputational harm of being seen to hurt somebody else is typically greater than the physical harm of being hurt yourself. This certainly isn't an explicit calculation that the participants made themselves: in this study, they could collect the money, walk out the door and never again meet the person they'd scorched.

Instead, it's a calculation that's embedded in most of our brains. We've evolved to make decisions that value our reputation highly because in tribal times having a poor reputation usually came with life-threatening costs.

Hedge fund managers believe they're a bit different to ordinary folk. It takes something special to profit from shorting a company which employs thousands. They're right to believe they are special. And if they want to recruit the next generation of bright young things to fleece the muppets in the market, then a Digitimer could be the best investment they make. At any rate, interviews would be livelier.

We dislike harming others, but not as much as we imagine

In chapter four, we looked briefly at the answers volunteers gave to various hypothetical scenarios. We found that when people answered in a coldly utilitarian way, other people trusted them less. In this section, we're going to look in slightly more detail at such conundrums, ask just what we can read into people's responses and explain how the self-model guides the answers we give.

There's a train running along a track. Ahead of the train, some maniac has trussed five people to the rails. You're standing next to the switch; if you pull the lever, the train will be diverted to the siding. However, the same or some other fiend has tied a person up in that path too. Would you pull the lever, saving five and squishing one?

Most say they would. All else being equal, five people's lives are worth more than one. So let's vary the situation a bit. You've taken up trainspotting. You're looking over the bridge at the Flying Scotsman, hooting and throwing up steam in the distance. Next to you is a fellow enthusiast. As well as locomotives, it seems he's into pork pies. Great rolls of flesh pour over the top of his neck and wobble under his shirt when he cranes to take photos. Turning, you see the five people gagged and bound on the line.[137]

You calculate that if you give the stranger on the bridge a heave you could get him over the railings and onto the tracks. His bloated body is already halfway there, he's leaning so far forward to get a good picture. Even the mighty Scotsman would be stopped in its path if it hit him. It would be messy, but you'd have saved the other five. How about it; do you give him a quick shove?

This time, most people say they wouldn't. It's still five lives against one, but something's changed. What? Scientists give these dilemmas to volunteers while their brains are scanned.

Some dilemmas just activate the parts of the brains usually involved in reasoning: the first train scenario; giving a vaccine that kills some recipients but saves a greater number; stealing a boat to save endangered mariners. With these, people typically follow the mathematics, minimising the deaths.

Something about other dilemmas activates the emotional areas of our brain: the second train experiment; harvesting a healthy man's organs to save the lives of several patients; strangling a crying baby so that enemy soldiers won't discover your hiding place. This emotional reaction interferes with the utilitarian reasoning. They force you to imagine actually hurting somebody rather than merely causing them to be hurt, and people are less willing to do the deed even when the consequences are mathematically better.

We've seen why this might be so; we found that people who claimed they'd make utilitarian decisions in the face of emotional dilemmas were trusted less. There's a steep reputational cost to giving the wrong answer and revealing yourself as a heartless follower of the moral mathematics. Those emotional reactions that the scientists could see in the scanner were warning participants away: ensuring that they gave the response that would lead people to trust them.

Nevertheless, it's a friendly and oft-reported experiment. The image of the fat guy and the bridge. The scan of the brain where you can see the bit that lights up when you imagine pushing somebody. The conclusion's quite comforting: our emotions jump in to stop us hurting people just at the point we might actually do it. It's the kind of illogicality many are pleased to have.

But do we? There's a reputational benefit to giving the right answer to a hypothetical question, and most people give it. Yet that's not the same as proving that people would make that decision when the situation isn't merely theoretical. Unless you're a surgeon operating on Siamese twins, the question of killing one to save another is never likely to reach your in-tray. The scenarios are so impossibly rarefied that it's uncertain that the answers have anything to do with real behaviour.

We do harm other people. Often. But usually we weigh up harming others not against the greater good, but against our own reward. A boss, with her thoughts firmly fixed on her profit targets and end-of-year bonus, decides whether to make her subordinates work late, sack them or make them redundant. You choose whether to help a starving Syrian or to spend the money on a night out. We split up with our heartbroken partner because we think we'll be better off without them.

Cambridge scientists identified these flaws, and thought they could do better. They devised a devilish little test which allowed them to compare how we think, or at least say, we'd behave in a moral dilemma with what we actually do.[138]

It's not just Oxford psychologists who have shock boxes; they have them in Cambridge too. And in this experiment, the partner receiving the pain wasn't hidden behind a door, he was visible on camera.

In the Cambridge scenario, each participant would be given twenty pounds to start with. They'd then have twenty chances to stop somebody else being shocked for a pound. Participants could take the whole pound, and the recipient would receive the maximum shock. Or they could give up the whole pound, and the recipient would get off altogether. Or they could spend part of the pound so that the shock was milder than the maximum. To make the sums meaningful, whatever they had left at the end of the study would be multiplied by a random number between one and ten: the maximum winnings could be two hundred pounds.

In the first part of the study, the psychologists described their set-up to eighty-eight volunteers. They asked them what *other* people would do in the situation. And whether the answer would be different if the question was merely hypothetical versus being done for real.

Three-quarters of the volunteers thought that when real pain and real money were involved, their fellow humans would be less willing to profit from others' pain. People buy into the idea that, when push comes to shove, their emotions will kick in and they'll be kind. Hurting somebody else isn't nice.

The scientists then recruited some fresh volunteers. Some answered what they'd do using a questionnaire, and others played for cash. When the game was hypothetical, only seven per cent of volunteers said they would keep any money at all. They'd give it all up rather than let someone get hurt.

The real version was very real. Before it started, participants were seated in the chair that would be used to give the shocks. They met the person who would receive them. During the test, the experimenters did what they could to rack up the tension. After participants made the decision, there was a short pause to let the anticipation rise, to let volunteers reflect on what they'd said. Then they had to watch the shock being applied, see the hand buck under the impulse.

All of the volunteers took at least some of the money. On average, they took over sixty per cent of the maximum on offer.

People do dislike harming others, and they do value others' pain more than their own, but money is money. Our estimate of our own and others' emotional reactions to inflicting violence is way off. What we say we'd do in some theoretical situation bears very little resemblance to what we'd do in real life. And it's unclear that what we say we'd do to some fat bloke on an imaginary bridge with a made-up train running towards some non-existent people has anything much to do with anything.

Talk is cheap

You don't have vocal cords so that you can sing in the shower. All that messy mass of specialised neurons in your skull, that humans and humans alone have, and which enables you to read, write, speak and decipher other people's words isn't there by chance. It's not even there solely so that you can read this book (though that might be the pinnacle of what it's ever been used for*).

Your power of speech evolved under pressure to do just one thing: change other people's behaviour. It can do that directly: 'we saw the enemy in the distance', 'the stream has dried up', 'pass the salt'.

It can also do it indirectly. Whether you tell me 'I hate faggots,' 'I feel happy,' 'I'm a utilitarian,' or 'if I were given the chance to shock people for money, I'd decline,' you're inviting me to change my model of you. To believe that your mind has particular contents and you will behave in a specific way in the future.

If the consequence of using your speech were that people behaved less well towards you, it would be better that you were unable to talk. Vocal cords would have been selected out. So it's not a surprise that volunteers who were asked what they would do hypothetically nearly all said that they would leave the money on the table and the hands unshocked.[139]

The experiment shows that people aren't concerned to make accurate predictions about what they'd do, but instead to make accurate predictions about what they can plausibly claim they'd do. There's no reason to think that the participants who said they wouldn't inflict pain for cash were being cynical. They model themselves as others model them: because others would, and indeed did, believe them when they said they wouldn't hurt others in return for money, they believed it of themselves too.

---

* I jest, a little. But there is an elegant beauty in where we're at. You are one of the first humans to use consciousness to reflect accurately on what consciousness is for. Almost all humans who have ever lived, have died or will die without doing so.

When we model ourselves we make the sorts of errors about ourselves that others make. There's no reason for the self-model to give people an accurate insight into what they would in fact do: that's not its role.

Some moralists claim that money is the root of all evil. They don't know the half of it. Perhaps our brains simply haven't caught up with the sheer beguiling power of filthy lucre; in evolutionary terms it's a new concept. At any rate, in spite of all the evidence, we routinely underestimate its attraction to others and ourselves.

So you can get away with claiming you care for it less than you do; of downplaying what you'd do to get it. When others make similar claims, you can believe that they're telling you what they believe. But what they believe isn't the truth.

Speciesism is specious

The concept of animal rights is as muddled as that of human rights. But it's muddled in a telling, and enormously useful, way.

The argument, in brief, is that you oughtn't torture foxes because you cause them to suffer. It's a moral statement, incapable of being true or false, and, as we've seen, subject to all the general problems of moral statements. But it has an extra one thrown in for free. When they say that a fox can be hurt, it seems they might mean one of three things.

First, they might mean that a fox has evolved a mechanism to pull away from harmful stimuli. This is obviously true, but has nothing to do with morality. It's like saying you oughtn't drop a rock because of gravity.

Secondly, they might mean that the fox itself can feel pain. This is what they probably do mean. Of course, it's notoriously difficult to prove from first principles that anything does or doesn't have consciousness. However, we do know – from chapter five – why *humans* feel pain: to help them understand what other people are reading in their minds.

The circumstances that caused us to develop this expensive piece of brain kit simply don't play a part in the lives of many, if any, other animals. Without that evolutionary pressure, the probability that foxes got it is low.

However, there's a third thing that they might mean. The type of humans that we can trust are the ones who avoid causing suffering. Humans infer pain in the fox. Therefore, we cannot trust the sort of people who inflict what they perceive as pain on the fox.

If this were the argument they were making, they'd be right. People who harm animals are more likely to have empathic problems, behave callously to other humans and show psychopathic traits.[140]

This type of reasoning about what you can expect from other people using some other behaviour as a proxy wouldn't be unique. A Muslim might say about a friend that he's a good man because he prays five times a day. This friend may not be helping anybody by making his prayers. But the sort of man who is willing to give up that amount of time probably takes the other pillars of his faith seriously. It's likely that he gives alms, for instance.

Giving up meat and avoiding furs are signals that animal rights activists can make which show they care about suffering, that their empathy system is in good working order and that they often act on it. They don't necessarily think of it that way, any more than the Muslim realises that he's displaying his goodness when he's prostrated towards Mecca.

This is useful to us because we also need cheap ways to signal that we're moral if we're to get away with doing mostly what we want to do. So how to take advantage of this modern morality?

My wife, as so often, points the way. She has a thing for snails. When she sees they've wandered, or slithered, onto the road, she picks them up and puts them on the verge. The snail won't thank her; the snail doesn't know whether it's eating grass or being fried alive in garlic oil, but the people around her think she's a nice person. She is a nice person.

The self-model is amoral

When we say somebody is good, what we mean, of course, is that we infer from their actions that they are good. But those people, however good they seem, have a model of how their actions will be perceived, and that model promotes their interests while protecting their reputation.

This self-model enables them to act illicitly in exactly the circumstances they won't get caught. They'll take money at the expense of others, but only when the link between their choice and others' suffering won't be spotted; when it can be put down to chance, circumstance or ignorance. They engineer such scenarios by deliberately avoiding knowledge which might compromise them.

When their reputation is in good nick, they risk it, and they're more likely to do good when they're under a cloud. The self-model is ruthlessly practical, even with itself. It understands that whether or not you did some misdeed is irrelevant. What matters is what other people think. So when others might infer you're guilty, it kicks into reputation management mode.

Moralists don't realise they're doing any of this. Because they infer their morality from their actions, from the confessions they make, the badges they wear, the test results they receive, they are as fooled as other people.

Our models of ourselves are sophisticated and amoral. They monitor our actions for us and ensure that we can get away with the most we can get away with without damaging our reputations too far.

But there are reasons to think that our brains might be beginning to misfire. They no longer achieve the aims they're supposed to.

The brain evolved to be very good at dealing with the social environment thousands of years ago, before cities and laws, money and the internet. It evolved when humans lived in small groups and knew almost everyone they'd ever meet. When gossip effectively spread news of transgressions to all of them.

But, as suggested in previous chapters, it's bad at dealing with one-shot interactions and the anonymity of cities. That's why participants didn't give the shocks they could have and take all the money. The self-model implicitly assumes that everybody else knows almost everything you can infer about yourself. That's why those tricked into making a confession acted guilty when they met other people later, and why their self-esteem suffered.

In that sense, it misfires in a 'good' way: it protects our reputation even when it doesn't need to. Yet it also misfires in a 'bad' way. In the next two chapters, we'll see it's terrible at handling the different groups that it encounters. It can't cope well with people who hold different moral beliefs, follow different cultures or simply look different. What it does worked well when all members of its own tribe were one group, but breaks down horribly in the twenty-first century.

There's another reason we might be dubious about our self-model's stratagems. It gives us a mind, but it didn't evolve for the benefit of that mind. It evolved to promote the spread of the genes that create the mind.

It's not coincidental that what is good for your genes is often the same as what gives you pleasure. It's not in your genes' interest that you are cold or hungry. To predict your behaviour, I model you as wanting to avoid these things and as being happier when you don't suffer them. You model yourself in the same way: you *feel* pleasure at a feast or in a warm bed. But if our genes' benefits and our own desires usually go together, they don't always. That's why we have condoms.

SEVEN:
Cooperation means competition

In chapter three, we saw that one of the biggest differences between early humans and other animals was the way they could form groups to punish. We gang up on malefactors.

Punishment incentivised people to do what the group expected. It didn't matter whether what the group wanted was sensible or stupid, altruistic or evil, what mattered to your genes was that you avoided your group turning on you. This drove us to infer minds in other people and in ourselves: predicting what other people would do, and how they will judge you, became important.

In time, this made living and working in groups possible, and it was groups that policed it. But what happens *between* groups?

In a hunting party of ten, I will pull my weight and I will share and I will conform. If I don't, there's a risk that the other nine will pick up rocks.

Now our group stumbles into a clearing. A smaller party of five are already there and they have made a kill. Provided that the ten of us pull together (and coalitional punishment makes it likely), we're in for a treat. It's not fourteen against one, it's ten against five: and the same law that makes morality possible means that the five will scarper as fast as they can.

This suggests that cooperation within groups makes conflict between groups likely. Provided that groups ensure that individuals act in the group's interest, then the larger, stronger groups have the means to take from smaller, weaker groups.

This doesn't mean that there has to be any natural selection at the group level. Groups grow and split, and decline. We switch allegiances. There's nothing permanent about a group in the way there is a gene.

Instead, inter-group competition is just an instance of normal animal inter-individual competition. Within human groups, mutual punishment curtails it. Between groups, there's nothing to hold it back.

This chapter and the next are about groups. How they form, how they hold together, how they interact and how morality fits in with it.

We'll find some pessimistic predictions borne out. Split individuals into the smallest, flimsiest groups you can imagine and competition clicks into gear. People don't always realise that this is what is happening: research shows they simply don't infer minds in out-group members in the way they do members of their own group.

So far in this book, almost all we have discussed has assumed relations between two members of the same group. But in chapter eight, we will find that moral statements are group things. Moral claims, of the sort we found in chapter one can be neither true nor false; they create groups and strengthen them. They signal which group you belong to, and cut you off from others. Far from being altruistic in origin, they prevent you from understanding what is in the mind of out-group members, and thus set you against them.

We'll find that morality entails competition: tribes, armies, teams and companies all coordinate their behaviour to outdo others. Morality doesn't allow for the absence of bad guys; it needs a 'them' and 'us' to function.

You're human, so you're part of a group

If humans form competitive groups, it's natural to ask what it takes to form one. Do you need a hundred years of historical antagonism, or will a generation or a few years be sufficient? Do groups need to look dramatically different, or is it enough to have a different accent or wear a different football shirt?

Fifty years ago, Henri Tajfel, a Polish Jew who lost family and friends to the Nazis, thought it might take even less. He was struck by how common intergroup prejudice was at the time, whether it was racism in America, religious sectarianism in Northern Ireland or nationalism in Belgium. He also observed that it took common forms.

A friend in Slovenia described to him the stereotype of immigrant Bosnians. Tajfel presented the description to his students at Oxford and asked who thought that about which group. The students readily recognised it: it was what Englishman thought of Indians and Pakistanis.

If stereotypes form so readily and along such a similar course, maybe the details of the groups aren't so important. Maybe innate groupishness is more important than the cultures which express it.

Tajfel set himself a challenge. To create groups with as little background as possible. He recruited fourteen and fifteen-year-olds from local schools, eight at a time. In the first part of his experiment he had them express a preference for paintings.[141]

He told half that their choices meant they were Klee fans and the other half that they leant towards Kandinsky. He gave the news in private so that the kids didn't know who else had chosen the same way.

In the second part of the experiment, each child was asked

to allocate points to the others. The points would be turned into cash, and by the standards of the day there was a decent chunk of pocket money in play.

A spotty lad who'd just learnt that he liked Wassily Kandinsky might be asked whether he wanted to give seventeen points to member three of the Kandinsky group and seventeen points to member two of the Klee group (maximising fairness). Or he could choose to give twenty-three points to a member of the Kandinsky group and twenty-nine points to a Klee preferer (maximising the points awarded in total and to the Kandinsky group, but meaning that he gave more to an out-group member than an in-group member). Or he could give eleven points to a fellow Kandinsky lover and five to someone who didn't recognise the Russian's superiority (punishing the ignoramus, but at a cost to someone in his own group).

For all the lad knew, 'member two of the Klee group' might be his best mate and 'member three of the Kandinsky group' could be the bully who nicked his lunch money. Or vice-versa. Nobody told the teens to think of the task as a competition. You might have expected Tajfel's manipulation to be weaker than school *esprit de corps*: the shared assemblies, uniforms and classes.

Yet the kids weren't swayed by any of these factors. Maximising the difference between what members of their own group received and what the other group gained was more important. The more choices that Tajfel gave them, the stronger their discrimination grew. They wanted more for their own group, but at least as strong was the desire to keep cash out of the hands of the enemy.

Tajfel's grouping was the flimsiest, most arbitrary possible.[142] But that's why his studies are so important.

What Tajfel's experiments (and many since) show us is that humans form groups like water forms droplets.

But groups, once formed, are complicated things. To understand what's going on properly, we'll have to understand a little of the signalling, invective, history and propaganda that characterise them.

You've been groupish all your life

How do we get to be so groupish? Were the teenagers inevitably so, or simply a product of a school sports system that sorted them into teams and taught them it is better to win 1-0 than lose 5-4? Should football be banned?

Without doing any experiments, it's possible to advance any number of hypotheses. Maybe children are born group-blind and they learn prejudice from corrupted adults. Perhaps it's an inevitable part of development like teething or menarche. We could posit that children lose their groupishness as they mature and adopt egalitarian beliefs.

If you've still not cast off your morals, you might have an instinctive stance on this already. A Nazi sympathiser might think that as people learn more about the world, they will grow to recognise that other groups are scum. Again, a liberal egalitarian teacher might hope that groupishness is learnt: with a little careful nurturing his own charges can be steered from the abominations of xenophobia, racism, anti-Semitism, homophobia and lots of other isms and phobias.

Unfortunately for both groups' prejudices, it's a question that can be studied. Scientists in California and Harvard generated a series of faces. Some of them were unambiguously White, and some Asian. Others were more difficult to categorise. Half of them were happy and half of them were angry.[143]

The researchers asked White American children between the ages of five and twelve to sort the images: clicking one key for Asian faces and the other for White. They gave the same test to adults.

Five-year-olds are pretty basic creatures. If you tell them there are fairies at the bottom of the garden, they'll believe you. They've only just learnt that mum might be sad when she's smiling.[144] They're also blissfully unaware of adult sensitivities around race.

But young and unsophisticated as they are, the five-year-olds' performance on the test was indistinguishable from that of the older children and the adults. Sorting objects into groups is something that five-year-olds are good at.

They categorised the unambiguously White and Asian faces just fine. Yet where there was uncertainty about the race, angry faces were forty per cent more likely to go into the Asian bucket than happy faces.

It cuts both ways, and it can't be explained by infants quickly picking up on adults' attitudes or behaviour. In Taiwan, there are hardly any Whites. Children's main exposure to the race is through toys and Western media. When the researchers repeated their experiment there, both Taiwanese children and adults were more likely to categorise the angry faces as White rather than Asian.

These aren't lone experiments. In fact, you can replicate Tajfel's experiments with five-year-olds.[145] You put them in a 'red' group or a 'blue' group according to the disc they choose, and give them an appropriately coloured T-shirt to wear. You then ask them to distribute coins between two other children, one of whom is wearing a red T-shirt and the other a blue one. Children in the red group give more coins to others in the red group. If you ask them to rate the other children on likability, they give higher marks to those wearing the same colour T-shirt. And they get the dynamics: if you ask who is more likely to share with them, the blue kids know it's other blue kids.

As soon as infants are able to identify themselves as members of a group, groupishness kicks in. Even as they play with their dolls, they associate sharing with members of their own group, and conflict with others, and it remains roughly constant throughout life.

Humans can't have evolved to be racist

Racism's an explosive subject. It's almost taboo. In this book, I've evinced an admiration for Hannibal Lecter, I've told you how to escape the consequences of your misdeeds, and I've argued (and will argue again) that the best morals are those you don't have.

At a guess, I'll have made a few of you smirk, the deepest of you a little sad[146] and only really outraged the most delicate. But have I finally said something unsayable? Isn't the natural corollary of the last section, that even five-year-olds are implicitly racist, that a totally multi-ethnic society is impossible a contradiction in terms? That humans have evolved to be racist?

Answering this question here is important for practical reasons. Racism is a social problem. Inter-race discrimination and violence in America, the rise of anti-immigration parties in Europe, genocide in Myanmar. If you want to make society better, then understanding why racism is so prevalent, and whether morality can do anything to fix it, is important.

But it's also important for theoretical reasons. In this and the next chapter, we will draw conclusions about how groupishness works from experiments on racism. If humans evolved to be groupish *and* to be racist, then we're mixing up different things.

On its face, it seems plausible that racism and groupishness aren't the same. People choose whether to be mods or rockers, liberals or conservatives. Members of most groups actively signal their allegiance. Old school ties; surnames; football strips; masonic tiepins; attendance at church, synagogue or mosque; bumper stickers; tattoos; politicians' placards in their garden. But you don't choose your race, and unless you're Michael Jackson, you can't really hide it.

However, in this section we're going to argue briefly that humans can't possibly have evolved to be racist as an end in itself, and that the right way to think of racism is as a special case of groupishness.

We only have identifiable races because for a long period of time most members of a race didn't mix with members of other races (or at least interbreed). They were geographically separated.

Some hunter-gatherer in central Africa fifty thousand years ago doesn't know that there are Mongolian herders who look and speak differently to her neighbours. She'll go through her life without ever meeting one of them. So there can't be any plausible benefit to a gene that had a main effect of making her behave differently to a Mongolian if she ever met one.

Yet if we take her five-year-old descendant today, and ask her to sort faces, we'll find something unpleasant. It isn't likely that 'racism genes' have sprouted in the last few years of big cities and high migration. Instead, the face-sorting must be a sign of something else the old hunter-gatherer had; something that can have benefitted them in the tribal environment in which they lived[147]. We've seen why the hunter-gatherer might have evolved to be groupish, and why she might have expected aggression from members of other tribes; it is likely this mechanism that is misfiring when her descendant associates people who look different to her with anger.

This is far from being the only psychological effect that scientists have uncovered where a mechanism that evolved for one reason changes our behaviour in circumstances that can't have been relevant to the mechanism's evolution. One such effect can be seen in twin studies. Twins are catnip to developmental scientists. They are to them what races are to social scientists.

Identical twins, in particular, are quite exciting. Because they share the same genes, there's no genetic competition between them. A daughter of your twin is just as good as a daughter of your own at passing on your DNA.

So, having argued that our genetic interests underlie morality, we might expect less conflict and more cooperation between identical twins than nonidentical twins. This is just what researchers find[148]: in various tasks, identical twins help each other more and share more.

But nobody believes that there's a gene, or set of genes, for being extra nice to your twin.[149] The probability that you have an identical twin is about one in two-hundred-and-fifty. Because they're so rare, a gene that exists solely to make you nice to your twin would rarely find it had anything to do. And natural selection only acts on those genes that have an *effect*: that make us more fertile, run faster or act in different ways. A gene that sits idly by and doesn't often affect its holders' lives won't spread.[150]

More likely, the fact that identical twins cooperate well is due to some other machinery. We do live among siblings (half our genes are the same), half-siblings, aunts and uncles (a quarter the same) and cousins (an eighth).[151]

Genes that cause us to assess how closely related we are to

someone else, and make us behave more cooperatively towards those who share more of our genes, have spread. The twin studies simply catch the extreme end of it.

So it must be with racism. Because our ancestors so rarely encountered anybody of a different race, it's equally implausible that a racism gene can have benefitted them. It can't have evolved under its own steam; it must be hitching a ride on something much more prevalent: intra-group conflict. If we understand groupishness, we also understand racism.

The tighter your belt, the greater your loyalty

In a land of milk and honey, there is no need to fight. If there are a hundred, and food for a hundred-and-one, everybody gets fat and happy. If there are a hundred, and food for ninety-nine, somebody's going to die: and it's unlikely to be starvation that kills them.

In the animal kingdom, this point is well observed. When resources are plentiful, animals mark their territory and keep out of each other's way. When times are hard, teeth, claws and horns are used.[152] The harsher the environment in which they live, the more likely that females will kill the offspring of competitors.[153] Even cuddly meerkats aren't beyond ripping up another's cubs to ensure their own children get what food there is.

In humans, morality tempers competition between individuals. But if morality (and the group-inflicted punishment that creates it) does nothing to prevent inter-group conflict, we might expect to see something similar. We might anticipate that groupishness increases as resources become constrained.

Anecdotally, that's what we get. Every British schoolkid learns that Hitler rose from the economic deprivations of the Weimar republic. More recent data from forty-seven countries shows that the poorer you are and the poorer you perceive yourself to be, the less you like immigrants coming to your country.[152]

These findings do not necessarily demonstrate increasing groupishness. It's quite possible that the type of person who dislikes immigration is also the sort who finds it hard to thrive economically. Or it could be due less to groupishness than a level-headed calculation of jobs minus applicants. But it's harder to dismiss a neat study from scientists in Atlanta.

Since 1964, the American National Election Survey has been asking US voters about their attitudes to different races. The researchers compared these answers to state unemployment rates. Sure enough, when the economy cooled, Whites attitude to Blacks cooled too.[155] They also found that a rise in unemployment led to fewer Black congressman and fewer Black musicians scoring top-ten hits. Unpleasant, but nothing compared to studies of earlier data which show that when the economy stuttered in the American South, the number of lynchings increased.[156]

These aggregate stats don't tell us what is going on in individuals' heads. Do people recognise the connection between their empty bellies and their attitudes, or is there something more subtle going on?

Amy Krosch and David Amodio could (sort of) see inside individuals' heads using EEG and fMRI[157], which measure electrical activity and track where blood is being sent within the brain. They told some participants that there was a pot of up to a hundred dollars that they could share between others, and they told others that the pot was capped at ten dollars.

The researchers told both groups that a computer would

decide 'randomly' how much of the pot was available. To make this convincing, the researchers created an animated pie-chart which apparently showed the computer making its decision. However, the participants who thought the maximum pot could be a hundred dollars each watched as the pie-chart shrank to a sliver: the actual bounty they would play with was just ten dollars. Those who thought the maximum pot was ten dollars were lucky: the computer always gave them the whole ten dollars.

This is a well-known psychological trick. Frame ten dollars as the maximum payout and it seems a lot. Frame it as a mere tenth of what's out there, and it seems rather less.

The participants then set about allocating the money. They saw a sequence of faces and, based on how 'deserving' they thought the people were, they could give up to ten dollars to each of them. It probably won't surprise you that half of the faces were Black and half were White. Meanwhile, the scientists kept watch with their electrodes and magnets.

This is a fairly minor manipulation. Getting only ten out of a hundred dollars is not equivalent to drought, famine, losing your job or even missing a crucial pay-rise in a downturn. Yet it was still enough for the researchers to find what they expected.

When participants believed that resources were constrained, their brains emitted fewer of the signals that usually indicate they *are recognising a shape as a human face*. The patterns the scientists picked up in participants' brains were more similar to those you'd find if you tested somebody looking at an animal face or a scrambled picture.

But only when the face was Black. When the resource-constrained participants looked at White faces, their brains emitted all of the usual human-identifying signals (just as participants who were playing for a full pot did when they looked at Black faces). This wasn't a general effect to all other people, any of whom might be competitors, it was a specific response to out-group members.

Moreover, when their brains didn't do the usual calculations that turn a picture into a human face, it changed what the participants did. They gave less to the Black people. When the going gets tough, humans get groupish.

You can't feel what you can't see

In earlier chapters, we argued that reading minds is the key to understanding all morality. It's about inferring others' pain and others' intentions, and trying to manage what other people infer about us. This last experiment suggests that groupishness involves a failure to infer minds in people who don't belong to our group. That would explain why we don't apply the same moral rules, why we don't share or trust.

In *Danny the Champion of the World* (one of my daughters' favourites, so I know it almost by heart), Roald Dahl explains how smiles work.

I was glad my father was an eye-smiler. It meant he never gave me a fake smile because it's impossible to make your eyes twinkle if you aren't feeling twinkly yourself. A mouth-smile is different. You can fake a mouth-smile any time you want, simply by moving your lips. I've also learned that a real mouth-smile always has an eye-smile to go with it. So watch out, I say, when someone smiles at you but his eyes stay the same. It's sure to be a phony.

Psychologists give the smiles different names (eye smiles are called Duchenne smiles, non-Duchenne smiles are phony); otherwise they concur with Dahl.[158] But if Danny knew what to look for in a smile, how good are the rest of us at spotting who is really happy and who is just faking?

One group of scientists gave volunteers some pictures to look at.[159] Half of the photos were of people who were feeling twinkly; others were merely mouth-smiling phonies. Half of the photos were of Blacks, but none of the volunteers were.

The participants rated the twinkly smilers as happier than the phony smilers. But they were better at telling the difference in Whites than in Blacks: they could judge their emotions more accurately.

The hardcore racists (and healthy sceptics) among you might shrug. Perhaps Blacks smile in a different way to Whites, or maybe it's harder to make out creases in darker skin in photographs.

But the researchers also used a gadget that kept track of where volunteers were looking when they viewed the faces. When we look at a face, our own eyes jiggle about. Our focus swings from the eyes to the nose to the mouth and back up to the eyes again. Eyes might not be windows on the soul, but as Danny knew, they're certainly the best place to look for emotions.

The typical participant spent more of their time looking at the eyes in photos of White people than in photos of Black people. They knew their task was always to judge happiness, but that didn't stop them looking in the wrong places when the face was Black.

Still, the sceptic might be unmoved. Perhaps the noses and mouths in the Black photos were more prominent, that attracted attention, and the misjudgement was merely a consequence of physiognomy.

Another experiment puts paid to that theory. In this study, the researchers set volunteers a personality quiz.[160] Apparently on the basis of the test (but in reality at random), they told half of the volunteers they had a 'blue' personality type, and the others that they were 'purple'.

Participants then saw photos of others whom they were told had the same personality type that they did, and photos of those who didn't. They looked longer at the eyes of people they believed belonged to the same group. It's groupishness that prevents us from looking for, and therefore inferring, the minds of people in other groups, whether that group is a race or formed in some other way.

How groupishness can be used to sow division

If you work for a large corporation, you've probably done a fair number of personality tests in training sessions. You've learnt that you're a Shaper, a Plant or an Implementer. You've possibly been given a colour energy. You've shared your results and had a 'safe space' debate about what they mean.

When I first encountered these quizzes, I thought they were just dodgy thinking from a pre-scientific, Jungian age.[160] Then I thought maybe the psychology behind them was less interesting than the commercial angle: what can you flog to gullible HR departments?

Now, I wonder whether I've underestimated them. I think there might be a crack group of fanatical anti-capitalists at work. They know how easy it is to create groups, to turn off empathy and trigger conflict. Their plan is to fragment companies from the inside, test-by-test.

In one part of HR, you have Diversity teams trying to break

down groupishness that is imported from outside the company. In another part, you have crafty devils creating it where none existed before.

The other side hate what you love

Gaza's a tiny strip of land with just under two million inhabitants. From time to time, some Palestinians within the territory fire rockets into Israel. Israel bombs targets in Gaza. Teenagers riot on the border and get shot.

The EU, the UN and the US have all had a go at brokering peace at some point or other. I'm writing this section two years before this book gets published and I'm going to not-so-boldly guess that I won't have to edit a word in the first paragraph. Unless things get worse. It's as intractable a case of intra-group struggle as we are going to get. Good for scientists studying conflict; bad for everybody else.

What's going on? Why are the two sides doing what they're doing? Historians, politicians, economists, religious experts and military strategists could (and have) had a go at explaining. Psychologists took a daring approach: they asked.[162]

Their questions were deceptively simple. They asked Israelis whether other Israelis' support for bombing Gaza was due to their hatred of Palestinians or their love of Israelis. They asked the same group whether Palestinians typically supported the rocket attacks because they loved other Palestinians or because they hated Israelis. They put similar questions to Palestinians.

The Israeli answers were clear. They believed Israelis bombed because they loved other Israelis rather than hated Palestinians. They believed Palestinians bombed because they hated Israelis rather than because they loved each other.

Palestinians respondents thought differently. They believed Palestinians supported the rocket strikes because they loved Palestinians, and they believed that Israelis fired missiles because they hated Palestinians.

The Israelis must be wrong about themselves or about the Palestinians, and vice-versa.[163] In fact, we know that both groups are wrong about themselves *and* the others. Groupishness has its own unconscious dynamic; its own hard to access effects on our behaviour. Hatred and love are things we infer about our and other people's minds.

In the earlier chapters of this book, we saw that the way we inferred minds in others and ourselves is quirky, but generally it is aimed at making useful predictions. We infer minds in others to manipulate their actions. We infer our own minds as a self-protective mechanism against the inferences others are making. Accuracy is useful.

But we've also seen that this mechanism doesn't work in the same way when it comes to groups, and in this conflict the whole mechanism seems to have been blown up. Israelis aren't inferring in themselves what others are inferring in them, and nor are the Palestinians. Their mind-reading isn't helping them to understand what other people are thinking: it's obscuring it.

That's what groupishness does to us; it disrupts our ability to reason about the minds of non-members. As a territory, Gaza might rely on Israel for water supplies, electricity and phone signals. But individuals within the territory depend on other group members. Day-to-day, that's who they eat with, sleep with, pray with, trade with and dance with. Understanding other group members and being seen to be a member of the group is important: knowing exactly what emotion flashes through an enemy soldier's brain when he launches a missile is less so because there's little any individual can do to change the soldier's choice.

In the park, I see a man slap a woman. She cries; he hates her; I shout. Or: she looks surprised; he shows her the mosquito in his palm; she smiles; he loves her; I go on my way.

In the park, making the right inference is helpful. In Gaza, the enemy attacks and you attack. You infer that the enemy's bombing because he is hateful not because he's hateful but because that's an appropriate emotion for us to infer in people we punish. Your group doesn't fight him because he's hateful; he's hateful because you fight him.

Is this a freak result of a hot, multi-generational conflict? Something that sets in only when groupishness gets so far out of hand that there's blood and smoke and death? No.

The same researchers took their questionnaire to Republicans and Democrats in the US. What do Democrats think motivates other Democrats: hatred for Republicans or love for other Democrats? And so on. The results were remarkably similar to those found in the burning rubble of Gaza.

EIGHT

Morals make enemies

As we saw in the last chapter, a consequence of groupishness is that morals are switched off, or at least turned down low, as regards members of other groups. We're less willing to trust and to share. We don't bother inferring the rich, complex, subtle minds that cause moral actions. We don't even bother working out what minds out-group members are inferring in us: they are out to get us, so what's the point?

This makes signalling which group you belong to extraordinarily important. So how do people show which group they belong to? And how do people police these groupings, ensuring that they only trust people who are genuinely part of their group rather than those who are merely pretending? And how does morality fit in?

In the last chapter, we also saw that we form groups easily and arbitrarily. In this chapter, we'll see that the ways humans show which group they are in are similarly varied.

But we'll also find there's a particularly strong signal of group membership which forms an especially strong type of group. Right at the start of this book, we argued that moral statements of the type 'eating animals is wrong' and 'gays ought to be punished' were incapable of being true or false. Yet people spend an inordinate amount of time arguing about them.

Our moral beliefs and commitments aren't rational: it turns out they're signals. They tell us who is on our side and who is against us. We infer different types of minds in people who agree and disagree with us. Not because they are wrong and we are right, but because they are them and we are us.

Groups shout about it

When Caesar crossed the Channel in 55BC, the Brits were blue-painted barbarians charging about in chariots.[164] They wore strange facial hair and spoke a foul language. The Romans sported a natty uniform that not only protected them from the blows of my forebears, but also marked them out as a group of their own: soldiers of the republic.

You can create groups by telling one set of boys that they are Kandinsky fans and another that they prefer Klee. The changes wrought by groupishness are, and can only be, those in the brains of people. Groups are imagined things. Yet members of almost all groups go to great length to signal their membership and their place within it.

The short back and sides of the junior lawyer; the beard of the hipster. The over-enunciated vowels of the Manc and the dropped 'g's of the Scouser. Sports strips and military uniforms. Languages. Prison gang tattoos. The Phi Betta Kappa key. Bumper stickers and crucifix pendants. Tribal headdresses and the uwa-obi of the samurai. The bagpipes and the jig.

If we automatically, and from a young age, treat people who look different as members of other groups there's a reason. For far longer than interrace contact has been common, members of other groups have looked (and sounded and acted) differently.

You are what you eat

Two hundred years before Christ's birth, Hannah and her seven sons refused to eat pork.[165] This angered the king, whose wish it was that they ate. The first son's tongue was cut out, he was scalped, his hands and feet were chopped off. Then he was fried in a pan. His family held fast. Eventually all eight were killed in a similar way. Before the seventh son took his turn, his mother told him not to fear the torture but to accept death.

Hannah and her children were Jews; Hannah is remembered as a heroine and martyr. Jews don't eat pork. Hindus don't eat beef. Catholics avoid meat on Fridays, and fast during Lent. Some Buddhist groups are vegetarian. Muslims won't consume blood.

But if we think that food consumption is a group-membership signal that only religious groups use, we are mistaken.[166] If you eat quinoa and rave about craft beer, you're sending signals I can read.

You might well imagine that you like the taste, and that your enjoyment is nothing to do with what other people think or what other people of your ilk consume. But the evidence is against you. You infer that you like the beer (which is the same as liking it) because you drink it; you most probably drink it in the first place because that's what others like you do.

The best guide to how much fruit and vegetables students consume isn't how many times they've been told greens are healthy, but what their friends do.[167] Indian immigrants to Rome who identify more closely with their ethnicity are more likely to eat Indian food than branch out into pizza and pasta.[168]

But the strongest evidence comes from marketing executives:

fifty-three per cent of them run group targeting programmes.[169] These arouse group feelings (in, say, English football fans), tell you what members of your group do (drink Carlsberg), and punt their product to you.

You say your choices and tastes are individual; the money says they're groupish.

Steal a culture; kill a group

My first book was published in English, Thai, Turkish, Korean, Russian and Chinese. If I sound proud, it's because I am. I'd like both that and this book be read and discussed by as many people in as many different countries and cultures as possible.

I'm sure Shakespeare would have been well chuffed to know that his plays are performed in places he'd never heard of. Mozart would have been glad that you can stream his music around the world two hundred years after his death.

But not everybody is keen on creative work crossing boundaries. Some Polynesians have complained that their tribal tattoos are becoming mere street fashion. Some Native Americans have been upset that warbonnets appear in haute couture shows and their likenesses in sports mascots. Some Chinese Americans and British Indians have accused restaurants and food chains of 'inauthenticity' and 'cultural appropriation'.[170] White rappers take expletive-laden stick.

It's notable that the creators of these artforms aren't, and can't be, asked. Azealia Banks didn't invent hip-hop any more than Iggy Azalea.[171] Those who complain of 'appropriation' care about something other than the quality of the art, which can only be improved the more people who contribute their talents.

Culture isn't some grand expression of refined taste: it's a way of signalling group membership. If those signals cease to be signals, then it's harder to be a group.

Moral beliefs are group membership cards

We mentioned earlier in the book the peculiar temptation to conflate morality and altruism. To imagine that morals directly improve the lot of humans. But morality and altruism can't be the same.

If banning abortion is altruistic, then making it freely available isn't and vice-versa. Yet both are sincere moral views. Free love or stoning adulterers? Gay marriage or stoning homosexuals? Sex realignment at the state's expense or stoning trans people? Encouraging banks to lend to boost the economy or jailing usurers? Making prostitution safe and respectable or purging the profession? A soldier's duty is to follow orders or question the command to massacre?

You might in each and every case hold that one of the judgements is altruistic (and, surely, it's the one that you happen to agree with). But we're still left with the fact that at least half of them aren't.

The mental machinery that enables us to moralise is evolved; it's innate. *But it didn't evolve to make you altruistic.* The beliefs that slot so neatly into your brain might seem altruistic to you, but non-altruistic beliefs slot equally easily into other people's brains. And they believe in them, argue about them and fight for them every bit as passionately as you do for your beliefs.

In this book, we've found that morality is usually more about judging people's minds than directly judging their deeds. But people's moral beliefs form an essential part of those minds.

If you tell me that Hitler ought to have gassed *all* of the Jews, then I've judged you. It doesn't matter that you can't travel back seventy-five years, that you've not so much as spat at an Israelite, or that you're nice to your elderly mum and sacrifice much of your income to supporting your disabled sister. You're judged. What is going on?

In chimpanzee troops, the biggest, muscliest ape gets his way, whether or not what he wants is in the best interests of the troop or any other member.[172] It's in the interests of lesser chimps to side with the brawniest.

Humans are different. As we've seen, we group together to punish, and weaponry means that we do so more efficiently and with less reliance on the physical prowess of individuals. The muscliest men don't occupy the apex of society; *groups* decide what happens. Therefore, the pressure was on our ancestors to do what their groups expected of them, and to demonstrate that they were a member of the group.

In the remainder of this chapter, we'll find that one of the functions of our distinctive moral beliefs is to signal which group we're in. They are less about making people's lives better, and more about choosing sides.[173] This brings together many of the themes of the book.

- We choose how to behave towards others after reading their minds. The moral beliefs that they express change what we infer in them, and whether we empathise with them.
- We read our own minds from our actions and what we say. Expressing moral beliefs, and acting on them, changes who you think you are.
- Morality evolved under the threat of punishment from other members of our group. So it shouldn't surprise us that moral beliefs are groupish.

- We rationalise our beliefs rather than choosing them based on reason. Nobody imagines that they hold their moral beliefs as a signal of which group they belong to. Instead, they form arguments that their beliefs are objective, external and true: that they are the *right* beliefs to hold.

Morality divides

In a quirky little experiment, researchers in Chicago demonstrated that moral commitments are a fine way of separating otherwise similar people into 'them' and 'us'.[174] At the start of term, the scientists quizzed their students on their moral beliefs and how strongly they held them. One of the questions was on abortion. Weeks later, they asked the undergraduates back for a discussion on the subject.

The experimenters led each student into a room separately, where the student expected to meet another participant in the study. In the room was a chair, on the chair was a book bag, and on the book bag was a large 'Pro-Child, Pro-Choice' pin. At the far end of the room were more chairs. The experimenter said he was surprised the other participant wasn't there yet, and told the student to pull up a seat while he looked for them.

Abortion's one of the louder topics in US politics. Roughly half of Americans believe abortion is morally wrong, a fifth think that it's morally acceptable, and the rest apparently don't consider it a moral issue at all.[175] The stakes they are playing for are seemingly enormous. The pro-choicer thinks that women should be allowed to terminate their pregnancies.

We might be a little more wary of the pro-lifers. In the US, there are about six hundred thousand abortions a year. Some pro-lifers, at least, consider each of these a killing, and a killing of equal ethical weight to the murder of an adult human. That they're not all rampaging through the streets and blowing up abortion clinics is, on its face, more surprising than that a few of them do.

When the experimenter returned, none of the pro-lifers had unsheathed a knife or cocked a gun. They weren't waiting to dispense justice to a slayer of innocents, but nor were they relishing the opportunity to bring a sinner back to the fold.

As I say, the moralist's convictions aren't there to guide consistent action. They are there to signal who is in which group; who they belong with and who they don't. Pro-lifers sat further from the chair with the book bag than did pro-choicers, and the stronger their conviction, the further away they rested.

This might seem an odd measure of groupishness. But it's a measure that's been used before. European Americans sit further from African Americans the more prejudiced they are.[176] They sit furthest away when they believe that their prejudices are widely shared within their group: i.e., when they think that distrusting African Americans is a signal of group membership. Morality doesn't just metaphorically divide us; it physically separates us.

The greatest evil comes from good people

Manichean dualists saw the world broken into good and evil, everything one or the other: a swirling black-and-white pattern dividing the cosmos in two. On this view, there is a war between good and bad, the right and the wrong. And you can't have a good army without a bad. What's the point of Superman without

Lex Luthor; Mother Theresa without inequality; a Schindler without a Hitler?

Good needs bad like an alcoholic needs a drink or a martyr needs a painful death. The opposite seems to be true too. How could you know evil if you didn't know what good was? How could you offend decency if there wasn't such a thing? Innocent victims need to be innocent in the first place.

But this ancient dichotomous worldview is inconsistent with what we now know about morality. People act evil not because they are evil but because they are good. We'll explain that the two are intertwined not because they are opposites but because they are the same thing.

Take your pick of the most evil acts in history. Or, if you're already past believing in good and evil as real things, choose what you think your friends find offensive, or what you think they believe they ought to find offensive, or what they'd claim to find offensive if they were asked.

Maybe you picked female subjugation. Slavery. Massacres. Military invasion. Genocide. Or some specific instance. The bombing of Dresden or Hiroshima. The Spanish Inquisition. The Belgian Empire in the Congo.

No lone nutter could have carried out any of these. They were and are only possible because humans form groups. Because they are loyal, follow orders, fit in, do the right thing.

For a group to function effectively, the individuals within it must share, and act according to, an ethical framework. We know that they do this readily: hundreds of generations of punishment have weeded from the gene pool most of those who don't.

But this still underestimates the importance of morality to groupishness. It doesn't merely enable coordinated action and police it.

We'll see that moral statements are group signals of an extraordinarily strong variety. Whereas groupishness itself interferes with our ability to read the minds of people in other groups, morality *gives* minds to members of other groups: bad minds.

Moral statements aren't merely philosophical abstractions, or conundrums to toss around in the pub. They are paradoxically the cause of all that moralists find most evil.

Morals come from your group

If morals are to work as signals of group membership, we must get them from our groups, which suggests we are flexible. Yet once we've got them, we must hold to them hard.

Squint a bit, and this seems plausible. Mainstream views on having children out of wedlock, homosexual marriage and women in the workplace have all shifted in the last hundred years, at least in the bit of the world I live in. It isn't clear that there's some new scientific finding or discovered truth behind this change.[177] This supports our expectation that morals are malleable.

Yet once moralists have an idea in their head, it seems it is pretty hard to change. Can I think of an argument or a fact or a finding that would convince my friend that her three bastard children ought to be shunned (as they would have been in the not-too-distant past)? If you gave me a megaphone and the attention of the crowds at London Pride, is there anything I could tell them that would make them go home, hanging their heads in shame? In either case, it's more likely I'd get a black eye or a beating.

How do morals change? It's quite hard to study moral changes in the wild because by the time that you've spoken to somebody about their attitudes to homosexual marriage, they've already formulated them. You can't see the change that you want to watch.

Scientists in the US got around this by giving students moral dilemmas that they were unlikely to have thought about before.[178] Because the students hadn't seen them, the researchers couldn't watch a change, but they could compare their decision making in two scenarios: when answering alone and when they thought their group had a view on the matter.

Paramilitary terrorists capture you and your party (which includes eight children) in the jungle. At night, one of the guards wakes you. He tells you that the leader plans to slaughter you all in the morning. However, being the nice terrorist that he is, he will help you all escape. Provided, as an act of good faith, you kill one of the hostages for him. Would you take him up on his offer?

When American students answer this question in isolation, the vast majority say no. But in this experiment, the students weren't answering alone. There were three others in the room being asked the same question. Each of these, in turn, said they would roll up their sleeves, wield the machete, kill the single hostage and save the kids.

This changes the answer that the volunteers give. Trade-offs they'd shy away from when asked alone become more acceptable when their peers would do it, and vice-versa.

When given the question cold, moralists have only their self-model to guide them. It gives them emotional prompts which, in effect, tell them how their peers would judge one answer over another. In general, it's pretty good. That's why answers converge.

But it's only an approximation. When you have actual evidence of what other people would do, that's better than what your model can give you. So the answers change to fit in with the group.

In earlier chapters, we've argued that these vignettes tell us nearly nothing about how people would actually behave. In this context, that's not important.

You might have views on bull fights, fires in the Amazon and what to do in Saudi Arabia. But for the vast majority of you, your attitudes matter not a jot, if what we're talking about is practical action. They *do* matter if the purpose of talking about these things is to show whose side you are on: which group you belong to.

What's important is that your views shift to those of the group rather than you choosing your group based on your views. It's well known, for instance, that supporters of political candidates adopt the leaders' stance.[179] If you give them some policy, and tell them that their man promotes it, they agree with it. If you tell them the woman standing against him is championing the policy, they say it's wrong.

If you want people to take a moral position, you don't convince them with arguments. Like the marketers of lager, you need to convince them that their group has already decided for them.

Morals are hard to change

Moralists get their principles from their peers as flamingos gain their colouring from their food: without realising they are doing so, and with no way of stopping it from happening. If morals are group signals, it had to be so.

But we also said that, to serve as effective group signals, they had to have a second property. If we gain them easily, and pick them up from other group members, once we have them they have to stick. In a sense, they have to be like prison-gang tattoos. Before convicts have one, their skin is a blank page; in principle, they can apply the markings of any group. But, of course, they will only have the tattoos of the gang they belong to – and once they have them, they have them for life.

This can be tested in two ways. In one experiment, researchers asked Australians whether they thought that the government ought to apologise to Aborigines for the policy of assimilation.[180] They asked them whether they thought it was a moral issue, and how strongly they felt about it.

The scientists convinced some of the participants that most people agreed with them, and others that most people disagreed. Then they offered them the chance to have a short essay published in the local newspaper.

People who held strongly moralised views were much more likely to put their name to the piece, as we might expect. But what of the effect of others' opinion? Remember that morals come from others. If we asked a Texan who'd never given much thought to Australian Aborigines, we'd expect his answer to fall into line with what other Texans believed. But those Queenslanders who already had strong views were different: their willingness to go into print was completely unaffected by what they thought other Queenslanders thought. Queenslanders who held differing views were simply members of a different group, even if they happened to live locally. In the terms of our prison-gang metaphor, they already had their tattoo.

This demonstrates how strongly we identify with our beliefs, and how much more important they are than other signals of group membership. I'm pretty sure that a (sober) Manchester City fan, finding himself in a pub full of rowdy United fans, will swallow his pride and tuck his scarf in his pocket. Yet moral signals are so significant to their holders that they are equally willing to fly the colours among friend and foe. It's the stuff that martyrs are made of.

The moral beliefs that people signal are often controversial. People have bumper stickers, email sign-offs, Facebook frames and badges that declare their stance on abortion, gender equality, foreign wars and homosexuality. They are telling other group members that they are part of the club, even at the expense of signalling to people who hold different views that they are at odds.

The second type of test is even more direct. Researchers quizzed students on their attitudes to recycling.[179] They then convinced some students that their arguments for or against recycling were predominantly practical, and others that their answers were based on ethical principles. (This was in Ohio, where recycling apparently isn't quite as moralised as it is in some parts of the world.)

Finally, they tried to talk all of the students out of the attitudes towards recycling they came in with. But once the researchers had convinced the students that their beliefs were *moral* beliefs, they became much harder to change. You can alter your opinions on policy, but ethics are eternal truths.

These results are new to science, but not so much to politicians. If you can convince your party that your policies are moral issues, whether they be wealth redistribution, keeping immigrants out or even leaving the EU, they're more likely to follow you.[182]

The costlier the commitment, the stronger the group

As a first-year undergraduate, I took part in a strange and terrible rite. One dark and cold evening, I drank four-and-a-half pints of beer, spirits and dehydrated potato*. I lay on my back in the park while cream and Smarties were consumed from my chest. Afterwards, I was a member of the Tadpoles, a university swimming and water polo society. I was entitled to wear a purple tie with pale blue and pink stripes, and I did so with pride.

My initiation was lightweight. The Sateré-Mawé tribe in the Amazon sew dozens of stinging ants into gloves which boys must wear while dancing. The Mandans (of what is now North America) hung their initiates from hooks inserted under the skin of their chests. In Papua New Guinea, the Chambri slice a crocodile skin pattern into young men's bodies.

In some Aboriginal groups, men chopped off boys' foreskins and the children swallowed their own flesh. Once this was healed, the men held the boys to the ground, inserted a thin stick into their urethra and sliced the penis apart from underneath, tip to scrotum. The initiates thereafter squatted to pee, like women, but were men.

In earlier chapters of this book, we saw that we infer what we are from what we do. When the fee is extravagant, we infer that we must value our membership.

We might expect that, after the 9/11 terrorist attacks, Muslims in New York identified more closely with their religion. Not because they supported the bombings, but because they took abuse from non-Muslims. Declaring yourself a follower of Islam came with a cost.

A conveniently timed Columbia University study (running from 1998–2004)[183] found just this. In New York after the attacks,

---

* In a previous year, somebody was ill after the initiation. The mashed potato was a safety measure: it ensured that everybody vomited.

Muslims attached greater importance to their religious background and less to the 'ethnic, linguistic and sectarian differences' which divided them.

If you want to build a strong group, it helps if it's hard to join.[184] Cults don't brainwash their acolytes into believing and doing crazy things; it's the sequence of progressively more outlandish and difficult declarations that is the brainwashing.

This, then, is one of the ways in which moral beliefs create groups. The pro-lifer who declares that all abortion is killing suffers a social cost from pro-choicers, and her sense of group membership, and her belief in the cause, is no doubt stronger for it.

A moralist might say that gays ought to be allowed to marry. Or that transsexuality is evil. That racism is wrong or that Muslims ought to be deported.

As we have seen repeatedly, none of these statements is capable of being true or false. People talk about them to a degree, and with a passion, out of all proportion. They have the impression that they're true and reasoned in a way they couldn't possibly be.

Now we understand better the function they play. And why beliefs in any given statement appear in clumps, correlated with time, place and social status. Why people talk about them and yet rarely convince.

Moral statements are declarations of group membership. *They have a price: they cut you off from non-group members.* And in doing so, they strengthen your attachment to the group.

Even a bad group is good at being good

Members of a group aren't obliged to believe that their side is best at everything. They don't even have to think themselves the greatest at the thing they purport to do.

Derby County football fans know their team would lose to Barcelona. Luxembourg's army might take marching outside the Grand-Duke's palace very seriously, but they get that they're not invading Russia any time soon. Most University of Oxford graduates are smart enough to realise they're not quite as smart as University of Cambridge graduates.

However, there are limits to self-disparagement. Groups refuse to concede that their moral beliefs or their moral behaviour are inferior. This applies trivially to groups that are bound by their morality (anti-vivisectionists won't accept that medical researchers have the ethical edge). But it also applies in groups that outwardly seem to be nothing to do with morality.

Researchers told university students that a large survey of employers ranked graduates from a nearby institution as better skilled.[185] They told other students that the survey found that they were more employable than their neighbours.

The students then answered questions about their own university and the other. When they'd heard that their university was poorly thought of in the marketplace, they emphasised the superior social life on campus. When the students thought their degree was going to help them get a job, they conceded that the other place was fun.

But whatever they were told of their job prospects, they were certain that members of their own university were more honest and trustworthy. What's more, the study found that students' self-reported identification with their university, and pride in it, was more strongly related to how ethical they perceive it to be than how effective they thought the tuition or how much they enjoyed the parties.

If you praise people or groups on one metric, it's easier for them to concede your superiority on some other. I'm sure the

Spaniards would be impressed by Derby men's drinking prowess. The Luxembourgers might not be able to fight, but the creases in their khakis are the envy of the militarised world. Cambridge has nearly twice as many Nobel Prizes as Oxford, but what Oxonians lack in intellect, they make up in bluff: twenty-eight British prime ministers attended Oxford to Cambridge's fourteen.

But morality's non-negotiable. There's no trade-off in which a group accepts that it's superior at making money, scoring goals or advancing knowledge yet inferior in morality. Their ethical beliefs and behaviour are an essential aspect of what they are.

This is reminiscent of something we've seen earlier. Our own morals are a crucial part of our identity. It's losing those in an accident or through age (or on reading a book such as this one) that mean you'd no longer be you. They're your soul and your *self*.

Naively, we might ask which it is. Are moral beliefs collective things which define groups? Or are they individualistic things which define a person?

They are both. We construct our identity in the way that others perceive us. But other people are trying to work out how we will behave and how they should behave towards us. The answer to both of these questions depends in large part on whether we belong to the same group. If morals define the group then they also define the person.

When people champion individual liberty or the freedom to think differently, they are of course signalling their group membership just as strongly as those who argue for nationalism or subsuming the self in the greater good.

Moral beliefs are group things. Our self-inferences, our own minds, are also about group membership and our place within the group.

Citizens of the world are bad citizens everywhere

If groupishness and morality go together, we might also wonder about the converse. If you can overcome groupishness, do you also lose morality?

In 2017, a paper in one of the most prestigious social psychology journals[186] opened with a quote from *The Wall Street Journal*. 'Public universities in the U.S. recorded 5.1 reports of alleged cheating for every 100 international students, versus 1 report per 100 domestic students.'

We're surely looking for a twist. Social psychologists are notoriously liberal.[187] The authors of the paper are based in five universities across three countries. Their surnames – Lu, Gino, Maddux, Quoidbach, Chakroff and Galinsky – don't all sound stereotypic homegrown American.

We know that the punchline won't be a finding that US citizens are genuinely more ethical than foreigners. Is the clue in 'alleged'? Perhaps Americans are more likely to accuse foreigners of cheating. And, anyhow, what are psychologists doing reading the *Wall Street Journal*?

In the paper, the authors reported eight studies with over two thousand participants. They diligently tracked schoolchildren before they moved abroad and after they'd been there a year. They interviewed French-speakers who'd travelled a lot and those who hadn't. They quizzed domestic MBA students and foreign-born MBA students.

The researchers asked them how acceptable it was to fare-dodge, but also gave them chances to cheat on tests, to over-pay themselves and to lie in negotiations. The results from the studies were consistent: spending time abroad loosens your morals, and the broader your experience, the looser they are.

The scientists found some evidence that those who'd lived abroad embraced moral relativism: they stopped believing that one culture's rules were intrinsically superior. But this isn't the whole story. Cheating, lying and stealing are sins in almost all cultures. Nobody returns from a gap year in Canada having found that everybody cheats and it's a good way to be.

The benefit of foreign experience is that it broadens your outlook; gives you different perspectives. But that's exactly its problem from a moralist's perspective. It weakens the hold of any group on you. We've seen that morals exist to strengthen groups; if your tie to your group is weakened, then it's not a surprise that your ethics are too.

This relationship's long been suspected, and provides fodder to politicians playing to the home crowd. Theresa May, then the British Prime Minister, claimed, 'If you believe you are a citizen of the world, you are a citizen of nowhere'. Alexander Gauland, a German politician, made a similar case, writing against a 'globalised class' who moved from city to city with no attachment to their homelands. Gauland was predictably compared to Hitler, who decried an 'international, rootless clique' who felt at ease everywhere.[188] I suppose I ought to make a confession here. I have worked on three continents. I hold two passports. I have lived abroad for the last six years. But my ethical standing isn't in any doubt, is it?

The less we care, the more fuss we have to make

As I write this, my father is alive. When you read this, he will be dead. A few months ago, Dad was diagnosed with lung cancer.

Since then, the renegade cells have launched an invasion through his lymphatic system and they now occupy half a dozen organs.

Yesterday, he called to tell me about his funeral arrangements. Dad's booked the cars, decided who will lead the service and chosen the food we will eat afterwards. He's also bought his coffin.

The cancer wards are full of thin men, wasted by their disease and the treatment. My dad is against type. Ten years ago, he had the lean frame of the heavy smoker. Since giving up, he's ballooned all the way to what he calls porn-star large (XXXL).

So he wanted me to know that his coffin was the thinnest and lightest the shop had: he doesn't want me to strain my back. I reassured him that I've been working out regularly in preparation for the day. He laughed and then lost his breath and coughed.

To some of you, who haven't yet seen a loved one dying, or who don't know my father and me, our call might seem heartless. How can we take the mick out of his weight at a time like this? But (often bad) jokes and the most serious of things belong together.

In the 1970s, the British produced comedies poking fun at themselves and the Second World War. *Dad's Army*; *Allo, Allo*; John Cleese 'not mentioning the war' and goose-stepping around his hotel. It's not just a British thing. *No Man's Land* was released six years after the Bosnian War. A Serb and a Bosnian trapped in a trench with an amusing booby-trapped corpse.

Seventy-five years on from Germany's surrender, things are different. A light-entertainment star was photographed in a Nazi uniform on the way to an *Allo, Allo* themed party[189]. The Campaign Against Anti-Semitism said it was 'an insult to the to the British soldiers and civilians who died . . . and the six million Jews and many others who were murdered'. The presenter apologised. Prince Harry also took a lot of stick, and later said sorry, for bearing a swastika in fancy dress.[190]

What is going on? Why did the people who knew the dead well, and loved them, feel it was appropriate to make jokes about the war? And why, when there's hardly anybody alive who remembers any of them, is it outrageous?

At the time those comedies were shown, most Brits would have known somebody injured or killed in the fighting. They remembered hiding in air shelters, rationing, carrying gas masks. Black-out blinds in schools, conscription of sons, husbands, brothers and fathers.

My dad doesn't need me sobbing on the phone every time he calls. He knows that I wish he wasn't dying. I know, and he knows that I know, he's frightened. He figures (and I hope I'm as brave), that if he has only a few months to live, he might as well enjoy them, or what's the point in having them? So he continues gardening, planting vegetables he'll never eat. He walks his dog. He calls his sons and tries to raise a smile. What else should he do, and how else should I respond?

Our feelings are not in doubt, so we don't need to signal them. If we can laugh, we'll laugh: nobody will infer any less grief in us. It's the fact that the war is now so distant, so much less visceral, that people must go to lengths to show they care. But who to, and why, and how?

I'm doubtful that it's possible to insult the dead. It's surely one of the perks of not being here any longer. If the deceased continue to exist in some sense, if minds don't expire with the body, it's hard to imagine them taking a break from feasting in heaven to harrumph at the disgraceful dress sense of the cheeky chappy from *The Great British Bake-Off*.

We aren't expected to show emotions for all victims of war. I don't pretend to feel anything much at all for my poorly armed forebears slaughtered by Roman troops. If I go to a party dressed as Caesar, guests might laugh at my presumption (or my puny arms sticking out of the emperor's tunic), but nobody's going to accuse me of dishonouring the fallen.*

In our avoidance of swastikas and Nazi jokes, we're signalling our standpoint on an issue of *current* controversy (mostly anti-Semitism in Britain[191]).

This means of signalling group membership is common. You might not believe that Jesus is God. But he certainly sounds fun. He turned water into wine at the end of a party, when we might imagine the guests were already drunk. He got into fights. He told jokes and ribbed his disciples.

Catholics today turn bread into what they believe is Jesus' actual body. They place it in a gold frame. They kneel before it. They bow their heads and whisper. Children are told to be quiet.

The Free Tibet campaigner might light a candle and reflect on difficulties in a region they've never visited. The environmental activist talks reverently of the intelligence of dolphins. English left-wingers keep alive the memory of those who died in the Peterloo massacre.

Groups must agree on what is important. Individuals must *feel* for things that are important: minds, morals and groups are three parts of the same thing.

When emotions are raw, there's no need to tiptoe around the cause. It's once the emotions have faded, once we can't be sure

---

* This isn't inevitable. If pacifism ever becomes a dominant view to be signalled, or if I were a member of such a group, it's plausible that anybody appearing to glorify a war leader would receive similar treatment.

who feels what, once an event comes to stand for something as well as being something, that we have to be careful to give the impression we have the right emotions. We can't easily summon the tears, but neither are we allowed to laugh.

Immorality seems harmful

Moral beliefs are, we have seen, signals of which group you belong to. The costs of these signals demonstrate to others, and to yourself, that you're sincere. But to the moralist, they're not arbitrary in the way that a tie is, or a tattoo or a uniform. We saw earlier that they justify their moral beliefs after gaining them, rather than gaining them as a result of their deliberation. But what sort of justifications are acceptable?

To those who think homosexual acts are wrong, they damage family life and corrupt children. Vegetarians believe that rearing livestock entails animal suffering. Islam encourages violence. Porn stars are exploited. If you think that books like this one ought to be banned, perhaps I'm damaging readers or the people they meet or society; just possibly, I'm harming you.[192]

Moralists frequently justify their moral beliefs in terms of harm. Whether they're for or against porn or free speech, they argue that those they disagree with cause others to suffer. It's a wonderfully ironic way of defending their views. We've seen that moral behaviour is driven by the invention and inference of minds in others. But groupishness, which is the real under-pinning of moral beliefs, impedes the reading of these minds: it makes us more willing to harm.

This has led to an academic game of cat-and-mouse. Scientists have tried to find 'objectively' harmless vignettes, which they think some people might still find immoral. Somebody burning a flag.

A man having sex with a dead chicken. Siblings having sex with contraception. Many people do find these things immoral.

But they also find them harmful. This can be tested implicitly. For example, if you give somebody a vignette and then ask them to rate how painful an injury is, there's a strong correlation between how sore they rate the injury and whether they thought the actions in the story were wrong.[193] More directly, they might explain that the incestuous couple will have harmed their relationship, undergo 'a crisis' later or end up being tormented by their secret.

However, there's no such thing as an objectively harmless act. Harm is something that humans invent. It's a property of inferred minds. It's fundamentally subjective.

Take sex outside marriage, for instance. If incest can be harmless, and sex with a dead chicken is harmless (as the researchers wrote, 'carefully constructed so that no plausible harm could be found'), then surely a little pre-nuptial intercourse is too. If immoral at all, harm can't come into it: this *must* be something that adherents either can't explain or must put down to a nebulous notion of 'purity'. But Catholic writers talk of lust turning 'love into a drive to possess and control,' impoverishment of our natures and the 'personally and destructive impact' of sex misused.[194] They think it harmful.

Scientists' search for an 'objectively harmless' yet immoral act (and their belief that they can recognise them) is a measure of just how hard it is to empathise with other people's moral commitments.[195]

It's not at all clear to science *why* moralists feel they should be able to justify their moral beliefs. But whatever the answer to the mystery, they do. They seem to need to infer about themselves that their moral beliefs are rational, and that they hold them, declaim them and act upon them because they're good people, because they want to reduce the amount of harm done in the world.

For some moralists, the chain of reasoning stops after one or a couple of steps. Some philosophers have to spend a whole lifetime and write several books before they are satisfied that they have justified their beliefs. Remember Bertrand Russell's observation that they all (since Plato, at least) start their work knowing what conclusions they are going to reach.

Moralists might be hypocrites, but they aren't generally cynics. They don't realise that this is what they are doing.

Morality's about the stories we tell

In some ways, this whole book has been about the way that people create stories. That's what morality is. We model minds in other people to predict what they will do and to judge them. These minds aren't real minds: we have no way of telling what brain connections fire to create their behaviour; they're a way of assessing the contents of a black box (their heads) in order to guide our own behaviour.

We have seen that because other people are modelling a mind in us, we model one in ourselves. From our actions, and what we say and do, we give ourselves characters and emotions. We use this self-model to guide our behaviour: to manipulate what other people will think about us and how they will judge us. This model isn't right. It's not telling us which brain connections were made to make our decisions. It has to be wrong in much the same way that other people are wrong about us: if it wasn't, it wouldn't be much good at predicting what other people will predict about us.[196]

179

In neither case are people being dishonest. We now know about genes and natural selection and neurons, and we can run controlled tests on individuals. We can see the gap between the causes of their behaviour and what they imagine are the causes of the behaviour. But trapped inside themselves, individuals can't see any of this: they only have the models that served their ancestors well.

We know that it is coalitional punishment that guided the evolution of morality. That these pressures ensured that those who did as their group expected outperformed. But there's no reason for the moralist to understand that: they are being good because they are good people; they don't *feel* the forces acting on their genes.

Outside the groups that coalitional punishment entail, the same pressures don't apply. The constraints on naked competition are lessened.

But again, the moralist doesn't see any of this. She doesn't give more to her own group members than others because she's currying favour with those who (at least in the tribal evolutionary past of her ancestors) have the greater power over her interests: she sees a different type of mind. She sees fewer emotions and of a different sort. She infers hateful intentions. She's not even aware of the bias.

From the outside, you might imagine she'd see that the groups she belongs to and the signals that she uses to declare her membership are arbitrary. What's so great about being a Tutsi or a Hutu that makes you willing to kill and die for it? If she'd been born in the US, she'd have been lumped into the same grouping either way: 'African American', 'Christian' or 'woman' as the situation demanded.

The devout Hindu would, had the circumstances of his birth

been different, or a long-forgotten war ended otherwise, been a Muslim. The nation state's nothing but a recent invention of warlords. These things aren't who she is. Of course, she doesn't see it like that. She does the things her group does and comes to believe that's who she is.

The ruinously expensive wedding, the pain of basic military training, the gruelling interviews: the costs that these impose all help to make marriages, armies and companies forms of groups. The magic is the same colour as that which creates every aspect of your self-perceived character: you model yourself from what you do. And who you are changes what minds you infer in others; how you judge them.

Moral commitments are the ultimate group makers. If people exaggerate the traditions of their group, with morality they imagine it eternal, unchanging, true. If people are a little embarrassed by the evidence that they are in other ways groupish, in morality they are forthright. Those who disagree with them are harmful.

If sin exists in the modern world, it is a consequence of morality, not of its absence.

NINE:
The unfixable paradox of morality

Being ethical is stupid.

However, your capacity for picking up your group's morals, believing them, arguing about them, enforcing them and (sometimes) acting upon them is clever. It enabled the cooperation which has made humans masters of the Earth.

It also sparked an evolutionary arms race in which there was an incentive to predict other humans better, and to manipulate what they inferred about you. As our ancestors became better at reading minds, detecting lies, spotting bad intentions and coordinating to punish malefactors, they also became better at working out which of their actions would damage their reputation. More so than any other animal, human evolution has been powered not by the demands of the environment but by the demands of other humans.

That's why you're conscious. It's why you feel. It's why your brain is huge.

I, for one, am glad that my ancestors were subject to these pressures. That they won out. That they were seen as decent men and women. That they carried genes that ensured that they did what was necessary to maintain their reputation. It's because of their success in this evolutionary arms race that I'm here and that I have the capabilities I have.

But as I said earlier, I don't live the life that my ancestors led. The world has moved on. The things I have to do to get what

I need and what I want are different to the things that they had to do. I know things they didn't.

In this book, we've seen a number of reasons to cast off ethics, to cease being good and believing in good. But knowing these won't necessarily change what you say, believe or do.

So what *are* you going to do? Are you going to be amoral, or irreligious and moral and intellectually dishonest? Or join a faith you know to be absurd?

We haven't evolved the skills to face the conundrum that science has posed of us.[197] It's like asking a goldfish whether it would prefer a steak or the teriyaki chicken. It doesn't have the teeth to eat either, can't use a knife and fork and doesn't have the brain to understand what you're asking of it.

Groupishness and morality are anachronistic failings, but just wishing them gone won't make them go away.

Anyone who wants to save the planet and solve other global non-tribal problems is faced with a dilemma. In order to achieve their aims, moralists have got to understand what changes people's behaviour. They've got to act in a way that causes other people to act in a way that brings about what they want. The paradox is that that might mean abandoning the morality that made them want to change these things in the first place.

The apocalypse is finally coming

It's a rare society that doesn't imagine it's living in the end times. The Ancient Persians thought there would be a great and final battle between good and evil, the dead would rise and a final judgement would be pronounced. Jews, Christians and Muslims riff on the same theme.

Buddhists foretell the appearance of seven suns. The second sun will dry up brooks and ponds, the third the Ganges and the fifth all the oceans. The sixth and seventh will bake the Earth like clay, consume the mountains, and the land will blaze with fire.

Some Hindus think that we're in the last stage of a cycle; when it's finished, Shiva will dissolve the universe and create a new one. My parents had the Cold War, the threat of atomic annihilation and a nuclear winter.

Today, we have global warming. Since James Watt patented his steam engine, carbon dioxide levels in the air have jumped by more than fifty per cent and are rising another per cent every couple of years or so.[198] Carbon dioxide (unlike nitrogen or oxygen) vibrates at the same frequency as the infrared rays emitted by the sun. This means that more of the sun's energy is trapped in the earth's atmosphere rather than being bounced back into space. The little blue-and-green dot on which we all live is getting hotter.

In the short term, sea levels will rise, freak weather will become normal, corals will bleach, animals will go extinct. Drought will ravage farmlands. Starving people will migrate. We've seen that when times are hard, humans become more groupish, so we can probably add our own predictions of ethnic conflict and wars over resources.

Climate scientists tell us all this will happen if humans don't halve global emissions by 2030. In 2030, even my eldest daughter will still be at school. Given that worldwide emissions are increasing (never mind halving), what might happen if they are higher in 2040 or 2050 or 2060, when my youngest will be as old as I am now? Scientists are better at forecasting the short than the long term.

However, you might not believe in global warming. Or you might believe it is happening, but also believe that it has nothing to do with human activity. Because the topic is perceived as a moral issue, you will probably have already made your mind up, and it's unlikely that I could change it.

But to benefit from this chapter, you don't have to believe. You can consider saving the planet from climate change a hypothetical exercise. Whether or not they're mistaken, we can still ask whether the way morals work enables greens to change people's behaviour or if it gets in their way.

Saving the world can only be moral

From a purely selfish perspective, it makes more sense to fly out and see the coral reefs while they're still there than to stop flying and perhaps preserve them for somebody else to see. In my lifetime, I will not suffer any of the potentially terrible consequences. If England's a bit hotter in thirty years' time, that would be a good thing: it will warm my old bones*. If there are wars, I won't be called upon to fight.

If you think that we're living in the end times anyway, then conserving resources for the future's simply silly; we should be burning them with abandon and maximising our pleasure in the last days. As a moral standpoint it has impressive credentials. 'Eat, drink and be merry, for tomorrow we die' wasn't coined by a hedonistic amoralist; it's biblical.

---

* One academic study[199] claims that the climate of London could be similar to that of Barcelona. Wouldn't it be wonderful?

185

Only morality can be blamed for not saving the world

Morality explains why some people would like to save the planet and only morality can explain why they are failing.

We've known about climate change for a generation. The IPCC was founded in '88. The Kyoto Protocol was signed in '97. Thirty years ago, children watched Captain Planet battle the eco-villains. I recall books on slash-and-burn farming in my primary school library.

In the last three years, carbon dioxide emissions from burning fossil fuels have grown three per cent.[200] Methane and nitrous oxide concentrations are steadily climbing.[201] Greenhouse gas levels in the atmosphere aren't coming down, the rate of addition to them isn't even coming down, we're accelerating. Ignore the political declarations, look at the data, and it's clear that climate warriors' tactics have been utterly feeble.

There are two ways in which they may have failed. They may have failed to spread the message, to make enough people care and believe they ought to do something about it.

They may also be failing in a more intriguing way. People who believe that climate change matters, people who believe they are willing to reform their behaviour, people who believe that they *are* making sacrifices for the future, sincere, ethical, good people may not be reducing their emissions meaningfully.

They've failed in both ways. And we can explain why. Moralists might care about climate change because they have morals. But morality is completely unsuited to solving it.

Planets don't have minds

The most direct route to moral behaviour is through mind inference. Associating your actions with somebody else's pain.

On paper, this seems to be home territory for global warming. It's famine. It's drowned islands. It's extinction and wars and poverty. It's hungry people, displaced people and impoverished people.

But to change behaviour through this route, what's needed isn't an abstract or even a rhetorical recognition that climate change harms. We need to *feel* for the sufferer, to infer an individual mind about which we care. There are several reasons to expect this to be hard.[202]

- Serious climate change, on the scale we're told to worry about, hasn't happened yet.[203] It might make more sense to change our behaviour *before* it does rather than after, but empathy doesn't work like that. It's tricky to feel for someone living in the future, someone who might not have been born.[204]
- The numbers are too big. If morals did what moralists imagine they do, you'd expect them to be more willing to help when more people can be helped. But that's exactly the opposite of what happens. Whether you test it with appeals for the starving in Africa or hospitalised children, people are most willing to donate when you tell them of a single, named person who'll benefit.[205] We can empathise with a person; we can't empathise with a million people.
- The harm is indirect, and it's caused mostly to foreigners. Moral people are far more willing to harm others by failing to act than by deliberately acting, especially when the people

who get harmed aren't local.[206] The big polluting nations, the ones with citizens whose behaviour most needs to change, aren't the ones that will be damaged most in the early stages of any climate catastrophe.

Global warming could almost be designed to harm the minds we least care about in the way we least mind harming them.

You can get some traction by anthropomorphising the environment. Researchers put a donation box in a Korean coffee shop.[207] Sometimes there was a poster nearby with a tree and the message 'Save trees'. Sometimes the tree had eyes and a mouth, and the message was 'Save me'. With the latter, donation rates increased by a half, and the amount each customer chucked in the pot also increased.

But even then, it was small change. A much more dramatic demonstration of the power of mind inference followed the release of Sir David Attenborough's *Blue Planet II*.

Attenborough's stock-in-trade is telling stories about animals, anthropomorphising them; making us feel for them and empathise with them. In this film, the story he told was of animals suffering because of our actions. In the final episode, there was a heartrending scene in which an albatross fed plastic straws to her chicks.

It was hard not to think that the tube could have been one that you'd used yourself and thrown away carelessly. The queen banned them on her estates. Rock festivals went plastic free. US states prohibited them. A survey by a supermarket found that nearly ninety per cent of those who'd watched the series claimed to have changed their behaviour (at least 'somewhat').[208]

But giving up straws won't do much to save the planet. The greenhouse gases associated with their manufacture are negligible.

They're not even a significant proportion of the plastic waste entering the oceans.[209] One study estimated that coastal countries generate 275 million metric tonnes of such rubbish each year, of which somewhere between 5 and 13 million tonnes end up in the sea.[210] If you use a straw in Ohio, and put it in the bin, it won't ever go near an albatross.

Sir David Mackay, formerly the UK's Chief Scientific Advisor on the topic, wrote in the context of moving away from fossil fuels, 'Don't be distracted by the myth that "every little helps". *If everyone does a little, we'll achieve only a little*. We must do a lot. What's required are *big* changes in demand and in supply.[211]'

For most of us, giving up plastic straws is easy. Even if we all do so, it's not going to move the needle. However, what Attenborough illustrated was that you can quickly change people's behaviour, at least a little bit, if you can draw an immediate link between their actions and a mind that hurts.

On the much bigger and harder topic – reducing greenhouse gas emissions – nobody's yet made that empathic link tight. When people turn the key in their ignition, order a new computer, receive an Amazon delivery or pick up fruit that's been flown from another continent, they're not making an emotional connection with a suffering mind.

There's only one planet, but many groups

The other main route to moral behaviour is group signalling. Saving the planet has all the features – the controversy, the element of belief, the visible sacrifices – that we've seen you need to make group morality function.

If the moral belief that humans ought to act to prevent global warming is primarily a groupish one, we'd expect to find evidence that the belief correlates with membership of other, existing groups. Such evidence isn't hard to uncover.

In the US, ninety per cent of Democrats think the government is doing too little to combat climate change.[212] Among those who lean Republican, that drops to thirty-nine per cent, and among conservative Republicans it's less than a quarter.

We might want to put some of that down to the sitting Republican president at the time of the poll: to accept that too little is being done is to blame their leader. But the same survey asked to what extent humans contribute to climate change. Only fourteen per cent of conservative Republicans thought it was 'a great deal'; a whopping eighty-four per cent of liberal Democrats agreed with them.

Climate change activists might naively think that they can turn the tide (or at least stop it from rising) by tutoring the masses on the scientific evidence. But this misses the point. It is like pro-lifers imagining that they could convert pro-choicers if only they could explain why foetuses are living humans.

Morality starts with an answer. An emotional reaction, an inferred mind or the shared beliefs of a group. Rationalisations, as we've seen, come after.[213]

Group morality will never convince everybody. You might convert a nation or a social class or a race, a religion or a region. But it will only motivate followers so long as there is another group to define itself against.

And as long as you are defining yourself against them, they will define themselves against you. Donald Trump quit the Paris agreement and launched his own line of plastic straws.[214] He told Greta Thunberg to work on her anger management problems, watch a good movie and 'Chill Greta, Chill!'

The group approach to morality is fundamentally and

necessarily antagonistic. On an international level, China and India argue that historic polluters, the most developed nations, should meet their commitments before they make any. Their people agree. In China, only eighteen per cent of respondents claimed that climate change was a 'very serious' problem (a number which has been falling). A majority in both China and India think that rich countries should do the most.[215] (Americans, unsurprisingly, disagree.)

A moralist might concede that they have a point. But as half of all carbon dioxide emissions are from the Asia Pacific region[216], and they're rising quickly, climate change activists can't achieve much unless they find a way to make China and India feel part of the 'in' group.

On this, they're bound to fail. Greta Thunberg's speeches receive a poor response in mainland China.[217] 'Many netizens see [Greta] as representing the general liberal western agenda . . . There is this larger perspective that the west is ganging up against China.'

The problem with groupish morality is that it *is* groupish. You might like Greta. You might think she's saying things you believe. But if the Chinese aren't part of the group, and the President of the US isn't part of the group, then all the protests and rallies and marches and summits can do little beyond make attendees feel they are moral people.

It's not what you think, it's what you think others think

If action is what is wanted, psychologists can point to ways to prompt it, though they aren't necessarily what moralists would like.

A significant chunk of the energy you use is to heat, cool, light and power your home[218]. In one of the world's largest human experiments, a company called Opower conducted a series of two hundred randomized trials across twenty-seven US states with sixteen million households.[219]

Some of these customers received regular letters telling them how much energy they'd used and how they compared to their neighbours. They were also given a rating. If they were 'good' they received a smiley face; if they were 'great' they received two smiley faces. Others didn't receive the letters; they were treated like normal customers.

The carefully crafted missives worked. Households that received them cut back on their consumption. The amount of the saving, however, varied between states. In some it was a meagre 0.81 per cent. In others it reached the heady heights of 2.55 per cent. What could be going on?

Researchers also surveyed people. They asked them whether they cared about energy conservation, and they asked them whether they thought their neighbours cared about energy conservation. There was some correlation between the two, as we'd expect: our moral attitudes tend to match those of people around us.

However, states in which respondents claimed to care about energy consumption did no better than states where inter-viewees shrugged their shoulders. Instead, the states with the biggest change in behaviour from the letters were those in which people thought their *neighbours* cared about energy conservation.

We have seen throughout this book that moral actions are signals. They might not feel like it, but they're about showing other people what we're like and that we're a member of their group. So the best way to change people's behaviour isn't to convert them, it's to convince them that other people are already converted.

This is practical advice. It's a natural consequence of what morality evolved for, and how it works. But it's very hard for moralists to take advantage of.

Groupish morality evolved to form groups. Members believe that they are superior, and more ethical, than outsiders. They want to signal this. They want to berate others, tell them they're inferior and acting badly. It helps them to bond, yet this gets in the way of converting other groups to your cause. You get better practical results if you can convince people that everybody else – that *other people like them* – already believe.[220] That even now they're acting green. That if you waste carbon you won't be judged by climate warriors with dreadlocks and extinction-rebellion tattoos but by your next-door neighbours and colleagues and friends.

There's never been a pan-human endeavour. Yet many of humanity's greatest problems require just that.

Global warming. Regulating research into deadly viruses. Even poverty's not a local issue any longer. The import and export policies of Europe or North America can enrich or crush farmers and factory workers around the world.

What others can't infer, neither can you

A statistician will be rightly impressed by the study in the last section.[221] There's no ambiguity. The sheer size of the sample means that we can see, with great clarity, very small changes.

But there's the rub. In the states with the greatest social pressure, and with clear comparative numbers to motivate participants, the energy savings don't even hit three per cent. In terms of what we need to do to save the inhabitants of the planet, that's the square root of bugger all.

Understandably, Opower (or Oracle, who now own them), will scale up the energy savings from each household into an aggregate number, and because there are so many households, it will be a gobsmackingly big number.[222] If I was them, I'd do the same.

If everybody in the world reduces their household energy consumption by three per cent and sticks with it, the aggregate number will be even bigger. But it will still be a gobsmackingly small portion of our total energy consumption, and the world will still fry.

So what's going wrong? It seems that even those who have, or whose neighbours have, planet-saving tendencies aren't doing what they need to do.

In earlier parts of this book, we saw that moralists aren't 'good' for good's sake. They act in ways that gain the approval of, and avoid punishment from, others. They signal who they are and to which group they belong.

They're not knowingly cynical in this. They each have a model of themselves as others model them. They use this model to test out what they might say and do. If others couldn't infer bad intent, then they don't either.

We've seen the sorts of tactics people deploy. They avoid seeking information which might put their choice in a bad light. They are willing to do wrong when their choice could be attributed to some other, innocent purpose. They fashion plausible, and socially acceptable, excuses for their actions. And when they think they've done enough good to be in credit, they ease back.

Climate change lets people use all of these tactics to the full.

*If people can avoid information that puts their
choices in a bad light, they will avoid the
information and keep making bad choices*

It's hard to work out what matters and what doesn't. In the last year, I've seen posters on unplugging phone chargers. Printing less. Using hand-driers rather than paper towels. They're all highly visible actions, they're all easy to do and if we all do them we'll delay the planet hitting some tipping point by a few hours.

The people who draft these posters, print them and distribute them surely have ethical intentions. But most of you, in the back of your minds at least, will guess that the things that matter are somewhat bigger.

They all have a cost, either monetary, in foregone pleasures or in sheer nuisance. Stop flying on holiday. Give up driving. Install a condensing boiler. Pay extra for renewable electricity or put a solar panel on your roof. Go vegetarian. Purchase carbon offsets. Stop buying so much *stuff*: microwaves, TVs, computers, phones, clothes, wine and imported food.

However, unless you spend quite a bit of time researching, it's hard to work out which of the above matters most. How does a new boiler compare with a bottle of French wine a week? Is your vegan colleague who drives to work better or worse than the cyclist who eats muscle-building chicken sandwiches?

Moralists deliberately avoid information which might allow their actions to be judged badly. With climate change, that's easy.

*If people can show they are good in one way, they
will be bad in others.*

When people perceive they are in moral credit, they take it easy.[223] Put up a solar panel, and who's going to chastise you for drinking beer from an aluminium carton trucked all the way from Belgium? Recycle your rubbish weekly and you've earned your new phone. Buy a Tesla, and who could blame you for flying on a mini break?

Because stopping climate change involves so very many actions, people can pick and choose what they do, and yet still point to actions which demonstrate that they care. Provided that they do enough to be perceived as ethical by their group, people won't do more. Indeed, in an earlier version of the Opower experiment (before they added the smiley faces as encouragement), the letters had an unintended side-effect. When they told customers that they were doing better than their neighbours, those customers started using more energy.

If people's intentions seem good, then it doesn't matter what they do.

To judge people, you have to infer their intentions. When people judge themselves, they do the same. Outside of cartoons, nobody releases greenhouse gas for the thrill of it.

A friend of mine claims to care about the environment very much. He says it's the biggest issue facing the world. He was an early adopter of low-energy lightbulbs, he reads everything on a Kindle and he recycles. Yet he recently bought a great-big SUV. Why? Because if he's in a crash he wants to be sure his young son is protected as much as possible. Can we infer bad intentions in him; is he blameworthy? Or is this a selfless man making financial sacrifices for somebody he loves?

Of course, the atmosphere doesn't care about intentions. The gas gets there, it traps heat and it warms the planet whatever the reasons we do what we do.

But most people's brains, moral brains, *do* care about intention. They're designed to predict behaviour, to work out who's in the group and who isn't, who they can trust, who might harm them when it's in their interests. The mind inference that motors morality is ill-equipped to change behaviour that doesn't demonstrate to onlookers an evil motive.

If you want morals to change people's behaviour, then people have to fear that their reputation will suffer if they don't do what you want them to do.

This all makes it very difficult for climate change moralists to pick out who to blame. Who to punish. There's too much going on to work out who's really, deliberately bad, and too many mitigating factors.

What about the old lady with rheumatism who has her heating on all day? The overworked father who uses disposable nappies? The mother who buys fruit for her children every week, whether it's in season locally or a thousand miles away? Everywhere you look, people are frittering away the future. But they all seem to have blameless minds.

Perhaps this appeals to you. Maybe the environment can be the source of a kinder, gentler morality. Everybody does their best, and we leave judgement for thieves, cheats and fur-wearers.

But morality doesn't work like that. The Opower experiment reminds us that our moral acts are aimed at appeasing other people in our social groups. If moralists aren't blaming and punishing each other for their carbon footprint, then greens' models of themselves won't be either.

Flying might be the exception that proves the rule

If you're a green, then flying ought to be a bugbear. A return economy class ticket from London to Los Angeles releases somewhere between two and three thousand kilogrammes of carbon dioxide into the atmosphere. That's about half the carbon dioxide released by the average person in a year. Even that underestimates the warming effect of flying.[224] Those white contrails that aircraft leave behind them also trap heat.

The good news for environmental activists is that you can make flying a genuinely moral issue in the way that you can't most uses of carbon. Many of the problems of the last section simply don't apply.

- The relevant information is, or can be made, very visible. A flight is a single big-ticket item, rather than the accumulation of lots of small sins. Is it beyond what lobbyists could achieve to have tickets and boarding passes stamped with the number of kilos of carbon dioxide that will be released by the traveller?
- We all need to heat and light our homes. Life is difficult without computers or mobile phones. Unless you live in a big city, you use a car at least some of the time and you can't shop in a supermarket without accumulating a hoard of single-use packaging. But nobody *has* to go skiing, take family holidays abroad or hold stag weekends in foreign capitals. They're discretionary.
- It's hard to hide the motives for flying behind alternative, ethical desires. When people fly on holiday, they are sending a clear signal (to themselves as well as others) that their pleasure is more important to them than their impact on the environment. This matters: climate change moralists can *judge* fliers.

In 2019, the EU published a detailed survey on citizens' attitudes to climate change.[225] Ninety-three per cent thought it a 'serious problem'; seventy-nine per cent a 'very serious problem'; sixty per cent that it's 'one of the most serious problems facing the world'; twenty-three per cent that it's 'the single most serious problem facing the world'. In terms of stated opinion, the EU appears to be home territory for climate activists. It's part of the in-group.

But in 2018, the number of EU air passengers grew by six per cent compared to 2017. Flying increased in every single EU country. All twenty-eight.[226]

Greens can attach a stigma to flying. They can make it clear that it's inconsistent to say that climate change is one of the great problems of the world and then to hop on a plane for a jaunt. But if they do so, they're taking a huge risk.

At the moment, most people can say, hand-on-heart, that they're sincere environmentalists without doing very much. Even the Formula One racer Lewis Hamilton, whose job is to sell high-powered cars, can lecture us on social media about saving the planet.[227]

When the EU asked what practical steps its citizens were taking, respondents said that they were 'trying to reduce waste' (seventy-five per cent) and 'cutting down on consumption of disposable items' (sixty-two per cent). These are as easy to do as they are difficult to measure whether you're doing any better or worse than the average.

Yet from these people's responses, politicians are able to draw grand conclusions. From the survey: 'More than nine in ten (ninety-two per cent) agree that greenhouse gas emissions should be reduced to a minimum while offsetting the remaining emissions, in order to make the EU economy climate neutral by 2050'.

Do we really believe that? Did the survey spell out what is

involved and how it might translate into higher fuel costs, higher taxes and fewer flights? If you ask people whether they'd like lower taxes, I'm sure a majority would say yes, and they'd also agree that they'd like better schools, better hospitals, free public transport and more bobbies on the beat.

Some greens might not care whether people's answers reflect what they'd really like. If politicians use these figures to push through environmentally friendly policies, much might change. You can't electrify aeroplanes, but governments can switch a lot of power generation to renewables.

What might happen if you make flying a moral issue that is used to judge people? You'd change some people's behaviour for the better: 'flight shaming' might well generate the social pressure that gets people out of the skies.[228]

Others will be forced to infer from their behaviour that the environment doesn't matter so much to them. They'll go on that dream trip to Hawaii, have a lot of fun, and accept that they're not a part of the green group. Perhaps they'll stop bothering so much with recycling; they'll let their children play with plastic toys.

In the short term, that won't matter too much. Most people's behaviour isn't so green anyway, even when they believe they care. A tradeoff between making some people act in ways that actually help the environment, and allowing other people to conclude that what they're doing isn't helpful anyway sounds like a good one.

But once the fliers are forced to accept that they have other priorities, those poll numbers might start to fall. And that could have an effect.

Currently, subsidising green energy is a cheap signal for a politician to make. It's other people's money he's spending. He can point to the polls and say that they want it spending. Government finances are sufficiently opaque that taxpayers, in turn, don't know quite how much it's costing them. (Contrast that with hiking the tax on fuel. That might also improve people's behaviour.[229] The poll also suggests it's a safe move. But it's visible. As the French president, Macron, found out, Europeans are happy to ask for green policies until they can see the cost.)

Politicians, wealthy donors, celebrities who front campaigns: these are all frequent fliers who'd be forced to change their behaviour or accept that they too aren't the climate crusaders they'd imagined.

Flying can be made an emotive moral issue. I suspect it will be. We will use people's holiday choices to infer whether they really care about climate change, and so will they. It might even slow the growth of the airline industry. But the risk for climate change moralists is that, by attaching a costly signal to being green, they create an out-group as well as an in-group, and some members of that out-group might be people, such as those celebrity endorsers, they depend on at the moment.

Morality and saving the planet don't mix. Mostly, the nature of the problem and the nature of the solution prevent our moral brains from engaging properly with it. In the one area that activists could overcome that, they might be better off not doing so.

It's good to be amoral

Morals don't work. We don't need new codes, new virtues, new rights or a new way of thinking about ethics. We need to abolish the whole caboodle.

It's the intellectually sound thing to do. But it's also the practical thing to do. Our moral machinery evolved in, and enabled us to live in, a form of society that no longer exists.

We don't run around in small tribes. Instead, we live in cities.

The largest have populations comparable to the whole of Europe only a thousand years ago.[230] Walmart employs as many people as lived on the planet a hundred thousand years before you were born.[231]

We no longer converse only with people we know and that our friends know. Massive corporations with scientific advisers bombard us with their messages. Zuckerberg's and Pichai's and Bezos' computers decide what we read.

Our brain's implicit assumption that everyone we meet knows our business is a hindrance rather than a help. Our brain's implicit assumption that those talking to us are incentivised to behave well fails when algorithms monitor advertising returns and the stock market counts only profits.

Groupishness has become a problem rather than a benefit. We don't battle the local environment to survive, or trek out on a hunt. Instead, our collective actions will, most likely, destroy the globe.

It's morality that got us here. We needed its care in our infancy. That groupishness nurtured us when it was us versus the animals and tribes kept out of each other's way. The hard smack of intra-group punishment kept us in line. Those assumptions we make, while imperfect, were better than anything any other animal came up with. And they gave humans a unique environment in which ever greater brains were both possible and beneficial. Morality has been good to us.

But we're grown-ups now. It's time we left home.

ACKNOWLEDGEMENTS

I'd like to thank the researchers who carried out the experiments in this book (and the many others which I didn't write about but which enabled me to reach my conclusions), and all of you who pay for them to do their jobs.

Paul Bingham and Joanne Souza very kindly answered questions on their work and looked at mine. As well as being very helpful, I greatly enjoyed our calls and email exchanges.

My publisher, Mark Booth, has done a tremendous job: the book you have read is much better thanks to his suggestions. My agent, James Wills, has continued to be supportive.

My wife, Fiona, enabled me to write this book. On Mark's suggestion, she even read it aloud to me. If there are good people, she is surely one of them.

My daughters have also been helpful. Within a few minutes of tickling them, searching for a lost crown or pretending to be a frog, any irritation at a paragraph that won't hang together is gone and I can approach it with a fresh head. Georgina is old enough to be excited that I'm writing another book. But I'm hopeful she doesn't read it until she has left home.

NOTES

1   [173]

2   Why you believe so can itself be studied.

3   Hume's famous 'you can't derive an is from an ought' and Moore's naturalistic fallacy are arguments (or can be adapted into arguments) that science cannot reveal moral facts. But if objective moral facts don't exist, which they don't, then scientists can investigate everything knowable about moral behaviour.

4   It's still not assumption-free. We have to believe that our observations are somehow representative of the real world, that there's no elixir of life about to be discovered and that we haven't messed with an important variable (e.g. we killed the men on a Tuesday, and men are only mortal on weekdays). There's also the risk of 'black swans'. (All the swans in your random sample are white, but this isn't enough to be sure that there aren't any non-white swans.) A careful scientist would probably adapt the initial argument to: 'Most men are mortal. Socrates is a man. Therefore, Socrates is probably mortal.'

5   J. L. Mackie first made these arguments. [131]

6   Later, we'll argue that this is a sloppy use of the term 'desire'. But we're on philosophical ground here and they're quite happy with this sloppiness: don't even seem to realise it.

7   Ronald Dworkin called these special moral particles 'morons'. [56]

8   That people have different moral systems doesn't in itself tell us that there's no 'right' moral code. In the past, there were those who thought the sun and stars orbited the Earth and others who thought we were carried along on a giant turtle. There's still a truth to be got at.

But if you think that humans without fancy equipment can discern moral truths then it *does* pose a problem. How can you be sure that the magic particles you're receiving are the right ones and theirs are the wrong ones? If you can't explain how you get your moral facts, how can you demonstrate that they're the best?

Taken together, the oddness of moral facts, the impossibility of ever knowing them and their diversity suggest the tentative acceptance of a premise of our own: that moral facts don't exist. There aren't any magical particles that tell us we shouldn't kill.

9 Some philosophers do accept that we're in error talking of moral facts. J. L. Mackie, an Oxford don. Even without science showing how morality actually works, it was already possible to see clearly that his colleagues (and the rest of us) were mistaken.

Since then, the number of ethicists and meta-ethicists in university positions hasn't shrunk. So what are they doing with their days?

Philosophers are rather fond of thought experiments. If you and five others are hidden from soldiers in a cellar with a screaming baby ought you to strangle the baby and that sort of thing. We'll see again and again in this book that our answers to such questions are dramatically different to how we actually behave. The whole point of experiments is that you can't tell what the world will do from an armchair.

But thought experiments *are* good at showing how we think we think about morality, which is a different thing. And they're also good at showing how you can do a lot of very clever thinking about nothing at all.

Faced with the problems of the last few sections, some moral philosophers are currently engaged in a desperate attempt to save their discipline. How might one try and do this: to turn morality back into something where reason can reign and science can be kept at bay?

We can get a sense of their best efforts in a galaxy far, far away. After tens of thousands of years in space, the crew of the *Queen Elizabeth XII* have landed on the planet of the Polynosians, so named because they have four nostrils.

The Polynosians all live in a little city in a valley. Having checked the atmosphere and so on, the captain leaves the spaceship and hikes up one of the mountains to take a look at the people through a telescope.

She notes many things I'm sure: lack of military installations or spacecraft, sources of food. I expect there are training manuals setting out what to look for and in what order. But the most bizarre thing that she spots in this cramped town are the poles.

The streets are full of them. Blue poles, red poles and yellow poles. Twelve feet high and set about two feet apart. Like creatures in a pinball machine, the Polynosians scramble between these masts.

The funny-looking people seem quite adept at getting through their obstacle course, weaving and pushing, stepping aside to let others pass. But after a while, the captain notices that none of them touch the red poles. They make huge detours to avoid crimson thickets.

Not quite true. She spots one poor child, tears running down his face as two others try to push him into one. He's screaming and fighting with all his might, trying to hold onto a yellow rod. An older Polynosian shouts something and the boy's adversaries run off giggling.

One of the crew approaches with a local woman. In true *Star Trek* style, the Polynosians speak English. 'Hiya,' the woman says. All of the captain's training goes out the window. She doesn't inquire about the hierarchy or say she's come in peace. 'What's up with the red poles?' she asks.

'They're kinda contaminated,' the Polynosian replies, her Texan drawl made worse by the extra nose.

Over the following days our intrepid explorers learn all they can about the poles. Once a Polynosian touches one of the red poles, he's contagious. He's forbidden from having sex or washing or eating ice cream. It's ineradicable except at an annual ceremony of blue light, where he must stand naked at dawn on the top of the mountain.

At night, the ship's scouts, dressed in chemical protection

gear, take samples from the rods and test them in the laboratory. They take radiation readings and use mass spectrometry, look at the surface with electron microscopes and feed scrapings to the cat. They find nothing. In fact, all the poles seem to be coated with the same clear varnish.

They are right to be puzzled. This being a thought experiment, we can fill in some of the blanks. Shortly after the *Queen Elizabeth XII* left Earth, the *Trump Explorer* was launched to settle the planet. The *Trump Explorer* had the biggest and best engines ever, and arrived several thousand years before the *QEXII*.

Unfortunately, the *Explorer* was hit by a cosmic ray shower. The mutations in the embryo cargo caused the unsightly nasal cavities, and the captain in his suspended animation went a little mad. As he founded his colony, he put up the poles, destroyed the ship and all the robots that had built the city, and propagated the myth.

Once the space travellers accept that there is no contamination (and this will take a while; demonstrating a negative is notoriously difficult), there is still plenty to study. With thousands of years of evolution, it's entirely plausible that Polynosians' eyes are more sensitive to red light. Perhaps they gain a hard-wired fear of red things; do they avoid crimson clothing?

We can study Polynosian psychology. Why do they accept the contamination story so readily? (In fact, it's not so very different from how real humans work. Many people would prefer not to live in a house where a murder took place or where Hitler grew up. What exactly do they think is left behind?) How is the story passed on through the generations? Does what a Polynosian says about the contamination correspond with how he acts: if he touches a red pole unseen does he still abstain?

To scientists, it is obvious that there is no contaminant: the Polynosians are mistaken. But what about to philosophers? Philosophers who don't want to re-train or do experiments could take a variety of tacks.

1. Facts explain things. The easiest way to describe and predict the behaviour of the Polynosians is by way of the presence of

a contaminant. Any other means – by reference to their psychology, their evolved nature or their history – is inherently more complicated than simply saying that they avoid contaminated red posts. Therefore, the contamination has explanatory power. It plays the role of a fact. It is a fact.

2. Perhaps when Polynosians say they are contaminated that's not what they mean at all. Maybe they're just saying that when they touch a red pole they *feel* contaminated. And they lose all desire to wash or have sex or eat ice cream. That they use the word in the same way they would a real external fact doesn't signify. Indeed, we can observe Polynosians accidentally bumping into red poles and going 'Yuk!'; nobody takes that for a statement that could be true or false, yet it serves the same purpose as saying 'I am contaminated'.

3. Perhaps the contaminant really exists: as a projection of Polynosian's sentiments. Beauty doesn't exist without an appropriate observer, and yet we don't doubt that there are beautiful things. Knowing that the topic is subjective doesn't stop it from being true.

4. Possibly when a Polynosian says 'you are contaminated' what they are really doing is expressing an acceptance of the norms of Polynosian society rather than making a supposedly factual statement.

These lines are all analogous to currently debated philosophical theories about morality. Seriously. Hundreds of books and papers discuss each of them, and careers have been built defending them.

The linguistical nuances that hypothetical humans could possibly be using to make sense of reasoning that they don't in fact do is neither here nor there. Moral ideas are stored in real human brains, they are transmitted from human to human, they influence human behaviour. Studying these things might not be 'congenial to philosophers' or 'amenable to philosophical methods' (Mackie's phrases), but they are what matter.

10 Good introductions to the various efforts of meta-ethicists to

remain in work are [144] (an introduction) and [176] (readings and provocative commentary). If you want to follow one theory in depth, I'd go for Simon Blackburn's quasi-realism. Probably you have to start with [17] as later works assume that you're familiar with the debate. The arguments and counter-arguments and counter-counter-arguments are really neat. It's unfortunate that these fine minds weren't turned to something more productive.

11 In the *Republic* [160], the divine doesn't appear much; it seems you should be able to get to an ethical position through reasoned thinking. However, in the *Laws* [161] it does. Ordinary people are to be induced to believe in the gods. The rulers are also supposed to believe in them, but because they have gained confidence through intellectual effort. If one of the rulers finds a logical flaw in the proofs, that is fine so long as he keeps it to himself. It seems that Plato is aware that there might be gaps in his proof. He is not confident that the right response to a doubting ruler is to discuss his doubts and show him his error. Religion has a practical purpose beyond its intellectual soundness.

12 It's also not clear that greater knowledge of the diversity of religious belief is responsible. Knowledge of the diversity of moral belief hasn't (yet) killed morality. For Christianity to have grown it must have displaced other religious beliefs, and you can't do that without being aware of them.

13 [105]. Joyce describes moral fictionalism in greater detail in [104], and considers the evolution of morality in [106].

14 [166]

15 [149]. There are three obvious and extremely important flaws in the experiments.

Nearly all of the effect in Study A (pulling in front of other vehicles) comes from the extremely luxurious cars. Indeed it's unclear whether there's a substantial effect at all if you exclude the class '5' vehicles. It's clearly easier to pull in front of other cars, and to do so safely, if you have a powerful engine and can accelerate quickly.

In Study B (the pedestrian crossing) it's unclear what the

researchers did to ensure that the confederates who approached the crossing were hypothesis blind. Or, even if they did this, whether it could be the confederates' attitude to wealth, rather than the drivers' attitude to stopping at a crossing, that drove the effect. From experience, drivers' willingness to stop at a crossing is a function of how determined you look when stepping into the road. Do I play chicken with people I'm jealous of (and whose brakes I'm confident of) more often than little old ladies in clapped-out bangers? I think it entirely possible.

There's also some self-selection in the class '5' cars. Let's assume that rich and poor people are equally likely to be the sort of person who pulls in front of other cars. But let's also assume that the sort of person who pulls in front of other cars is also the sort of person who buys a flash car *if they have the means to do so*. If these were true, the 'lower-class' cars would be a mix of careful poor drivers, careful rich drivers and careless poor drivers; the 'upper-class' cars would be the careless rich drivers. We would see the effect witnessed in the paper. This second hypothesis seems entirely plausible. I know a lot of very wealthy people, and the set of them that drive nice cars definitely have different personalities to those who are more discrete.

However, the results of these studies are consistent with other (generally less punchy, and more lab-bound) experiments; they are a worthwhile idea in spite of their flaws.

For a review of the literature, see [118]. However, be careful. In part of their review, they are careful to define 'upper class' so that it is not just about wealth. Perceived status plays a part in their definition, and as many wealthy people work under even wealthier people, self-perceived status, even in a financial sense, isn't a straightforward function of income or cash in the bank. However, many of the studies that they cite use education or occupation or wealth or income as a proxy for 'class'. As a Brit, I find their definition of 'class' frightfully odd to begin with . . .

16 Study 1 in [158].

17 [116]

18 [159]

19 Study 2 in [158].

20 E.g. [115].

21 [59]

22 [85]

23 [29]

24 [49]

25 [133]

26 [117]. The results in this paper seem consistent with others. However, there are some clear question marks over the details of their study. Two of the four statements that individuals were asked to endorse or not in the 'biological basis' sub-scale were: 'Even after centuries, families will have the same social class as now' and 'A person's social class does not change from their social class at birth'. It's not clear to me that endorsing either of these statements implies a belief in a biological basis for class. If you think that class is partly determined by wealth, inheritance laws and the bank of mum and dad, this could account for a belief in both of the statements without implying any biological basis. So also could socially transmitted values that determine class, whether that's a posh way of talking or an interest in education.

27 [70]

28 [148]

29 [111]. See also [9] which found women preferred altruistic men for long-term relationships and dates, but couldn't discern any preference for altruistic men when women were looking for a one-night stand. (For those of you who read the paper, the phrase 'non-significant preference' means that we can't find evidence for any preference at all: not that there is evidence for a small preference.)

30 [94]

31 [47]

32 Philosophers reserve the term 'amoralist' for something else. But I think it suits those who are actively amoral better, so I'm nabbing it.

33 [119]

34 Even an apparently self-sufficient hermit in the forest is, knowingly or not, utterly reliant on the goodwill of other humans. He relies on property rights that protect him from developers, on governments not imposing a land tax he can't pay. He needs arsonists to stay away and war not to stomp through his paradise.

35 Some morals seem to be widespread culturally. See e.g. [39]. I'm uncertain whether these principles are in some way genetically determined or whether cultures without them wither quickly. I have my suspicions, but as the empirical evidence is inconclusive and it doesn't affect the narrative of this book, I shall keep them to myself.

36 [41, 42]

37 There are fish which bravely feed at the gills of sharks. They fill their belly and the shark is freed of parasites. It's a win-win, but it's only possible because the shark and the feeder fish don't compete; there's no conflict of interest. Similarly with pollinators and flowers. It's easier to cooperate with members of other species than with members of your own species.

38 [66, 163] More recent data in the UK shows that greater levels of education lead to later first births and doesn't directly chart the total number of children born. However, the later the first birth the fewer children women are able to have. https://blogs. worldbank.org/health/femaleeducation-and-childbearing-closer-look-data   https://wol.iza.org/uploads/articles/228/pdfs/female-education-and-its-impact-on-fertility.pdf

39 If we assume that there is a positive correlation between the education people receive and how smart they are. This seems plausible, if only because smarter people find educational toil less difficult.

40 [25] Just deserts and deterrence make different claims about who should get punished the most. Deterrence is most effective when the crime is well publicised (lots of other potential criminal will hear of the sentence) and most important when the probability of detection is low (if the fine for stealing ten pounds is fifteen pounds and you've only got a one-in-ten chance of being caught then there's no disincentive). Just deserts will calibrate the

sentence based more on mitigating circumstances (which reduces the wickedness of the action) and the seriousness of the offence.

41 [100]. Given that another experiment mentioned in this chapter suggests that men and women react differently to punishment, it would be interesting to know whether the same results hold in this experiment: are men more likely than women to punish? Other obvious questions: do men and women vary in their responses to punishers, and do we expect men to punish more than women?

42 Even six-year-old children are willing to incur a cost to punish other children who don't share candies fairly. [140]

43 This is another example of moral licensing, which we saw earlier. When you have two opportunities to signal your goodness, you aren't as likely to take the second compared to when this is your only shot. We need to demonstrate we're good, but not too good.

44 [101]

45 There's quite a lot going on in these studies. Indeed, when the researchers quizzed participants afterwards about the dynamics, less than half could fathom all the forces they were subject to.

Most people just aren't up to doing game theory in their head. But that's OK for them. Their big brains are there for calculating social consequences, and these rely on other people also not doing the game theory. (Or at least not doing the game theory associated with the one-shot games they are party to.)

46 There are more reputational goodies for avenging harm to others than harm to you: [90].

47 [42]. A remarkable book on who kills whom and why.

48 [45]

49 But be careful. Hypocrites are viewed negatively. (E.g. [102]) People who condemn a behaviour which they themselves engage in are treated more harshly than those who engage in the behaviour but don't condemn it. This isn't news. For example, politicians can get away with the most egregious sexual misbehaviour. But 'family values' politicians can't survive even the mildest hanky panky. Lying about it ('no, I didn't sleep with a prostitute') isn't treated as strongly.

50 [178]

51 It would be nice if, from this, we could pull out a broader message on how women and men behave differently in practice. In lots of individual experiments, men and women do play differently in various economic games (trust games, prisoners dilemma, dictator games and the like). However, drawing out a general and useful principle is difficult: at first sight, many of the results appear to contradict one another. An interesting review is [37].

52 [208]. If you're looking for a gender-neutral film, comedy is a good bet. Men like the genre about as much as action films, and women like it as much as romance films. However, the researchers didn't split the genre further: the black, twisted comedies that I like are quite different from the slapstick my wife prefers.

53 Jim Collins is the person behind virtuous flywheels. https://www.ft.com/content/60a08aa2-4006-11e9-b896-fe36ec32aece

54 [98]

55 [136]

56 [154]

57 [15, 16, 153]. Bingham's theory is so attractive because it explains what caused the environment in which humans developed big brains, language skills, social skills, group behaviour and consciousness without assuming that they were there in the first place: it doesn't require genes to see into the future. It explains how the incentives for *individuals* to punish were changed rather than relying on group selection. If it isn't quite right in some way, it deserves to be!

58 See [46] and references therein.

59 [164]

60 Or, possibly, to chase predators from a kill that the humans scavenged.

61 This might seem to cut across what we said in an earlier section. Surely, it's the pressure from defectors within a group that prevents wars being the main driver of early morality? But I think that this argument is additive, or at least highlights the very different dynamics of later warfare. Gaining territory from others is only useful once you have the capacity to make use of it. Generally,

you're better off sticking to your territory and leaving others to theirs. However, some other resources can be carried off.

62   [171]

63   This is only one of a large number of experiments showing that we are more willing to punish when others do, and the size of the punishment grows the greater the number. See e.g. [146, 183].

64   Intriguingly, when asked to score the punishment on a 0 to 8 scale, the results were very different. In the egregious cases, the group decided to punish the guilty a little more severely than the average juror had; when the misdeed was smaller, the jury was slightly kinder than its median member. It could be the scoring system that created this: putting things on a defined scale can have frustratingly odd effects on people's answers. There's certainly benefit to be had from framing things appropriately and choosing people's benchmarks, but you'll have to research them yourselves: there isn't space in this little book.

65   [62]. There's even a study showing that recidivist violent criminals and compulsive fire-starters don't handle glucose properly [199].

66   [132]

67   See how difficult this is? I immediately jump to an individual.

68   Note the asymmetry here. Once we accept minds as a way of judging people, we can derive some odd (but true) predictions. But from first principles, from the group incentives of the last chapter, we couldn't have predicted that humans would have used minds to judge. The bit of the thesis that seems obvious is the bit that, *prima facie*, should be a surprise.

69   Not all minds can do all things. You can hurt a baby, but you don't blame her for throwing up on your shoulder. Little ones have feelings, but they don't have agency: you judge me for how I behave towards them, but you don't judge them [73]. See also [76]: having more agency may mean you have less feeling and vice-versa. [205] offers a more detailed, alternative conception of mental life; but the underlying point – that minds are things we infer – is the same.

The Old Testament God seems to sit at the other end of the spectrum. He's got plenty of agency, whether He's sending pestilences, raining sulphur on cities or turning disobedient women into pillars of salt. However, His emotional register is rather limited. Anger and wrath feature pretty highly, but it's difficult to envisage Him weeping even after flooding all the Earth. When people are asked to attribute feelings to Him, they have trouble imagining Him hungry, afraid, embarrassed or in pain.

70 The moral character of what we infer is the most important. See, for example, [72].

71 In this book, we've said that the reason we read others' minds is to model them, to predict their behaviour and to act accordingly. This is a widely held belief among scientists: why else would we do it?

But in truth, it's an assumption. An extremely important assumption that underpins some of the arguments made in this book, but also a vast swathe of social psychology as well as literature and everyday reasoning. Whenever I say things like 'I married Fiona because she is kind,' 'I ran from Bob because he was angry with me and would have hit me,' or 'I forgave my daughter Margaret because she was sorry,' I am making the assumption. I believe that my behaviour changes (I marry, run or don't impose a punishment) because of what I read in somebody else's mind (kindness, anger, intentions, repentance).

Who doubts that you are more likely to steer clear of a big chap you have inferred to be angry with you than one you've inferred is pleased with you? Or that this is *because* you've inferred he is angry?

But proving this scientifically is fearsomely difficult. And because the answer is so widely assumed, perhaps enough effort isn't put into worrying about it. Let's explain.

There are lots of experiments which show how you can manipulate facts in a story or video and change what people infer about the characters within them (i.e. a red face and a scowl are signals from which people infer anger). We therefore know that mindreading happens, and we know much about how it happens.

There are also plenty of experiments which manipulate what a partner is supposed to have done in a game and show that this changes how they actually act towards them (i.e. people run away from a big man with a red face and a scowl). We therefore know that the same inputs that go into mindreading also affect behaviour.

But there's remarkably little that convincingly shows that the two are connected: that it is the properties we infer in the mind that leads to the behavioural change (i.e. that people are more likely to run away from big people who they have inferred to be angry with them than big people they have inferred like them).

Some academics are aware of the point (see, for instance, [5] chapter six). The problem also comes up a lot in animal studies, and this perhaps illustrates why it is so difficult to solve.

When animal researchers propose that e.g. chimps have some social skill that humans do, and claim that this is evidence of mindreading, they face an attack. The attackers point out that there are ways in which chimps could respond like this (i.e. have the social skill) without a mediating step in which a mind is read. Perhaps, for example, chimps have a rule which just says 'run away from scowling chimps' – they don't need to go from scowling to anger to running if they can go directly from scowling to running.

In humans, we can ask, did you run from Bob because you thought he was angry, or just on noticing that he had a red face? But as we've seen, humans confabulate reasons for their behaviour. That they believe it was Bob's anger doesn't mean it was. In theory, at least, Bob's red face could trigger two chains. One goes straight to a fast decision to run (skipping mind inference altogether). And the other goes into the bit of the brain that concocts explanations for why they did what they did.

We might try and concoct an experiment which proves what we want to prove. Perhaps we could create an ambiguous scenario. One in which some participants would infer that the target had particular attributes (e.g. suffering) and others wouldn't. You could then test at once (i) what individuals inferred and (ii) what actions they were willing to undertake (e.g. to alleviate the suffering). If you found that those who inferred suffering were also the ones who gave money, you might think that you'd proved your point.

But I'm not sure you have. If you ask participants whether they think the target was suffering *after* they've given money, it's possible that they inferred from the action of giving that they'd identified suffering. If you ask them *before* they have the chance to donate, it might be the social signal that they've given (saying they have identified the suffering) that influences their decision to donate rather than the mindreading itself.

You might make some progress with autistic children. They fail to infer false beliefs in other people, and also in themselves. They also have social difficulties. But you'd have to prove that the first causes the second, and aren't separate consequences of the condition. If you stab me in the eyes, I won't be able to see and I'll have a pain in my head. But it's not the blindness that causes the pain, and it's not the pain that causes the blindness.

This is probably a bigger problem writ small. How do you ever demonstrate that the contents of consciousness change behaviour? Many psychologists have debated and tested whether you can provoke certain social behaviours unconsciously. In principle, this is easier to prove: if people's behaviour changes, and they can't explain what the manipulation was, then it must have been unconscious. But the elephant in the room is that nobody has ever shown directly that human consciousness changes behaviour (so why chimp researchers think they'll be able to do so in their subjects is beyond me).

The exception to all of this is possibly speech. The act of saying you believe somebody is angry is itself a form of social behaviour. What you say changes how people act towards you. (That, we can prove easily.) And the way we measure mindreading is usually by asking subjects what they believe about somebody. But the claim that the only thing that mindreading does is change what we say is rather less than most researchers would like, and certainly less than I have assumed in this book.

If this were a purely academic tome, I might try and side-step this problem. In describing the theory I've proposed, I might call it something like 'a socially useful and apparently reportable model of ourselves'.

But believing that mind-inferences affect how we behave remains an assumption, however plausible it is, and one that most people don't realise they are taking on trust. Some might think that worrying about this assumption is pernickety, like mathematicians worrying about whether a straight line really is the shortest distance between two points.

Others might think that social psychology won't make concrete progress until they've seriously tackled their foundational assumptions, just as, to make progress, mathematicians had to do the hard work of fathoming out under which circumstances they could prove a straight line really is the shortest distance between two points.

72 At least it's easy now we have the answer. But it took some brilliant minds to conjure up the rules and others to test them: for most of human history it wasn't at all obvious.

73 [210]

74 Purpose isn't everything though. The volunteers reckon that intentional harms are worse than intended but unsuccessful harms, but they also claim there's something at least a little bit immoral when somebody meant no harm but did it accidentally. Children weigh outcomes as more important than goals. People with autism also have greater difficulty making the jump from actions to intentions to moral culpability. [147]

75 [209]

76 [169, 155]. Chimps have very crude strategies for responding to intentions and beliefs, which might not amount to an assessment of them, see e.g. [108, 206, 23, 4].

77 These experiments assume that the subjects not only believe all the facts in the vignettes but also don't question the narrator's motives. In normal discourse, of course, we ask why people are giving us information, what they want us to do with the information and

whether the storyteller is telling the whole truth. The answers we arrive at to these questions also affect what we say and do.

78 [3]

79 These example numbers are from a single study. Of course, it's difficult to calibrate. Were the misdeeds of equal strength to the good deeds? It's hard to know. But given that research usually finds we take greater notice of the bad than the good, and there are strong theoretical reasons to expect this, it's plausible that the direction of travel will be general.

80 https://aiimpacts.org/brain-performance-in-teps

81 [35]

82 [152]

83 [104, 31]. The second paper explores some of the moderators of this effect (and also makes the charitable giving more real). There are circumstances – such as when the transgression is old – that guilt isn't the overriding driver of behaviour. I'm also unsure that the manipulation in Study 2 of the first paper 'used others to get something they wanted' would universally be considered immoral. To get almost anything you want, you have to use other people.

84 See e.g. [34].

85 [33]

86 [138]

87 [143]

88 [168]

89 [57]

90 E.g. https://www.independent.co.uk/arts-entertainment/bochaste-the-truth-about-gandhis-sex-life-1937411.html

91 When people rate films as lowbrow vs highbrow, and as a vice vs virtue, there's a near perfect correspondence between the two scales. I sometimes think that's why modern philosophy is written in such a dry tone: after you've ploughed through the text, you're convinced you must have derived some benefit from the effort. At least until you've tried to work out what exactly it is. Earlier philosophers wrote with wit; I think they were less concerned that their subject might ultimately be empty.

92 [112]
93 The balance of probabilities must be that this was about signal-
    ling. It's unlikely that either group thought that the borrowed
    film would be the last film they ever watched.
94 [193, 192]. See [191] for a broader review.
95 [19, 213, 212, 185]
96 [7, 139, 18]
97 [13]
98 [61]
99 In this chapter, and throughout the rest of this book, I've used
    the term 'self-model'. This isn't a standard phrase, and it's used
    to emphasise a novel idea, so it seems worthwhile briefly
    explaining what is new and how it fits in with other theories for
    those of you who want to explore further. To avoid too much
    repetition with the main text, I have assumed that you've finished
    the book and are coming back to this endnote.

    Something in some ways similar to the self-model in relation
    to attitudes was described by Daryl Bem in the Sixties ([12]). At
    the time, it was considered in opposition to cognitive dissonance.
    He called it 'self-perception theory', and the term is still often
    used. The essential idea in self-perception theory is that many
    statements of attitudes seem to arise as if they were interpersonal
    judgements in which the observer and the observed happen to
    be the same people.

    The historical debate around the mechanism (dissonance reduc-
    tion or self-perception) is academically fascinating (and, from our
    perspective, undisturbing, as we'll explain below). More important
    is the number of experiments that these ideas generated. I've
    included a number in chapters five and six, but there are broader
    compilations (see e.g. [123]). There's very strong evidence that
    people's self-reports of their attitudes and feelings are influenced
    by external cues of the sort that we use in assessing other people's
    attitudes and feelings. Self-reports of goals, emotions, guilt, confi-
    dence, self-esteem: all are formed as if from the outside in.

    Peter Carruthers, a philosopher, expands on such ideas, and

broadens them, in a framework he calls 'interpretive sensory access' (ISA; see [27, 28]). He claims our own mind is a result of interpreting sensations in much the same way that we infer others' minds from what we know of them. It has access to these sensations through a global broadcast of information in the brain.

What is perhaps surprising, given all the sometimes great experimental and theoretical work on the topic, is the relative lack of interest in *why* we should read our own minds from the outside in. It's widely assumed that we infer *other people's* minds to predict and manipulate them better: minds are the way we model other people. As social animals, it seems there's a clear evolutionary benefit to doing so. But predicting our own behaviour, modelling ourselves, might seem an odd thing to do. If it is indeed beneficial to do so, why not just use accurate information about why we do what we do rather than creating a (frequently mistaken) outside-in model of why we do what we do? It certainly requires some convincing explanation.

Some think that perhaps it is accidental. We have mindreading capabilities for reading other people's minds, and it's an inevitable consequence of having these capabilities that we will interpret our own minds. Maybe the information we use to do so is readily available to us as a consequence of a global broadcast of information within the brain that evolved for other purposes. You apply your other mindreading tools to this set of information and – wham – you have a mind of your own.

Others take a different tack. Daniel Wegner was particularly interested in the way that we inferred our intentions and whether we'd done something purposely (see e.g. [203, 204]). He described a 'self-portrait that captures how it *thinks* it operates,' the illusion of 'conscious will'. He believed (as I do) that the evidence is that the self-portrait is 'reached through a process of inference of *apparent mental causation*'. But what did he think we did this for? He thought the aim was to give us a sense of authorship of our actions. The self-portrait allows us to take responsibility for our actions.

This book takes a very different approach. I can't see that having a sense of authorship would, in itself, give many benefits to my ancestors. Accepting responsibility for your actions when you could have gotten away with them seems quixotically anti-evolutionary. To demonstrate a benefit to our ancestors we have to show how they changed our ancestors' *behaviour*: not only what they *felt*. And this change in behaviour has to be to our ancestors' (genes') benefit.

I'm also unconvinced that our self-models are either particularly frugal or could have arisen by accident. Let's give two of the reasons we can reach that conclusion.

First, the types of information that we use in building our self-models aren't all of the type that fit into our models of other people. We've seen that heart rates, nerve impulses that tell us we've been hurt and nerve impulses that tell us what movements we've made and what expressions our face is making, feed into the self-model.

According to our explanation: that modelling ourselves from the outside in enables us to (and evolved to) predict what other people will model about us, this makes sense. When we model other people, most of our information about them (which feeds into our models of them) is visual and auditory. But we can't see ourselves: our eyes are on the front of our head.

I can see whether you're frowning or smiling, whether your face is flushed or white, whether the scratch on your nose is bleeding. You can't see what I'm seeing. So to accurately work out what I'm seeing of you, you have to use information from other sources.

However, the observation that we use input from our nervous system to build our outside-in models strongly points against the idea that our self-model is an accidental consequence of applying our other-models to ourselves. Your model of others isn't designed to take other people's nerve responses into account: you don't have access to them. Some work has had to be done to turn that nervous-system information into something our self-model can work with and to integrate it with the other information. That we do this, and still make the sort of mistakes other people might make (about the source of our smile or whether we're proud, for example) points to an adaptively beneficial use of this self-model. The second reason to doubt that the self-model is an accidental consequence of other-modelling or that it serves an internal psychological purpose is that we can report the outputs of our self-model. We can say 'I am happy', 'I decided to turn my head to look for my slippers' or 'my pain is a seven on a one-to-ten scale'. Indeed, most of the direct evidence for the self-model and our inference of our own minds comes from such self-reports.

But self-reports are fundamentally social. When you say 'I am happy' you are communicating. As we've pointed out in this book, humans are subject to tremendous social selection. What we say and do changes how other people treat us, and that affects the success of our genes. So whatever underlies self-reports, it's been subject to a great deal of evolutionary pressure *from conspecifics* to be what it is. If self-reports are the result of an accident, or merely serve some internal psychological benefit, then we should become creationists: Darwin was wrong.

Instead, this book argues it's more likely that our self-models *did* give an evolutionary benefit to our ancestors. And this benefit was a social benefit: it changed our ancestors' behaviour (what they said and did) in a way that changed conspecifics' behaviour towards them.

What could this benefit have been? Why might we have a flawed model of ourselves? One that makes the sort of mistakes about us that other people make about us? One that is influenced by what we believe others are thinking about us? One that requires, and justifies, the huge brainpower that goes into creating it?

I think the obvious answer to why we'd create a model of ourselves that approximates the model other people make of us is to approximate the model that other people are making of us.

Why would we do this? In order to answer that, we have to understand the very special social pressures that humans are subject to.

Various theories claim that morality (defined in different ways) arose as a result of punishment from other humans. Boyd, Gintis and Bowles ([20]) showed in theoretical models that coordinated punishment can proliferate (i.e. genes for joining in will spread), and that this works better if we assume the cost of punishing decreases as the number of punishers increases. In the main text, we discuss Bingham and his colleagues' work which shows why, in humans, the cost of punishing *does* decrease rapidly as the number of punishers increase: humans alone can kill at a distance. This is a tremendous theoretical observation, but Bingham and his colleagues have also compared the timeline between humans developing throwing ability and evidence that society has changed.

This still leaves us with a practical question. If punishment underpins morality, how do we choose who to trust and who to punish? About a decade ago, Gray, Young and Waytz ([77]) posited that moral judgement is about the (imaginary) minds we infer in other people (moral mind perception). In chapter three, we suggested that this was blindingly obvious. If you take that view, I tend to agree – but nevertheless it is a relatively novel observation academically.

Once we have the theories of moral mind perception and social selection to avoid punishment, it doesn't seem a great leap to hypothesise that we have evolved to manage the minds that others are perceiving in us. I argue that the evidence we have that we model ourselves from the outside in is evidence of a self-model that helps us to do this.

In the latter part of the book, we move onto groups. That humans are groupish, signal their group membership and infer minds in a different way in out-group members is well known. However, I've not seen the connection made that (i) if morality arose to avoid intra-group punishment and (ii) mind inference is the basis of morality, then it's not surprising that our differing treatment of out-group members is mediated proximately by a change in the way we infer minds.

Robert Kurzban and colleagues (e.g. [50]) made a very similar argument to mine that moral judgements can't have evolved to make us altruistic, but seem to do very well at helping us to choose sides in a conflict. He also gave good evolutionary arguments for why this is a beneficial thing to do. This book extends those arguments to the way in which we form alliances in the first place: the commitments we make and which form the basis of our judgements (e.g. Mack judges that Biff is in the wrong because Biff pickets abortion clinics and Mack is committed to the view that 'preventing abortions is immoral') are group-membership signals.

It is, of course, elegant that moral commitments lead us to judge bad intentions in people who hold differing views, and that our moral beliefs seem to be a major part, if not the most important part, of who we think we are. It brings us back to our starting point: we infer minds in others to judge them, we infer our own minds to work out how we will be perceived, and group decisions underpin the evolution of morality.

I mentioned above that the debate between self-perception theory and cognitive dissonance shouldn't perturb us. I don't think we have space to go into detail here (this is already an extraordinarily long endnote), but it might be worth outlining the big differences.

Self-perception theory says that we observe ourselves from the outside in. Cognitive dissonance claims that we observe differences between our attitudes and our behaviour, which causes an uncomfortable sensation (dissonance), and we act to reduce this dissonance, frequently by changing our views.

Often, these two theories make the same prediction. If we observe ourselves telling somebody else we enjoy our work, do we simply infer from that we enjoyed the work? Or do we notice an inconsistency with an earlier observation (we were hunched over the work with a frown on our face) and our new experience of dissonance, and change our view to get rid of that experience by claiming that we enjoyed the work after all? But it is possible to tease the two apart, and it seems likely that there is sometimes a dissonance step.

However, the self-model's purpose isn't merely to infer things about us, *it's to change our behaviour in a way that brings us social benefits*. It is plausible that we trust people better whose actions and commitments are consistent. So it's not unreasonable that, once we have perceived that our views and actions are inconsistent, we think we are in a poor place. (We can call this output of the model 'dissonance'.) If the signals that our self-model gave out didn't frequently lead to us getting out of this poor place, we'd be surprised.

The net result: that we end up with a view of ourselves that is consistent with what other people might have inferred about us, is generally the same. In the main text, I've therefore bunched the two together.

100 Many of the other claims about power-posing (made famous in a TED talk) have failed to replicate. Other researchers couldn't detect any change in hormone levels as a result of power-posing. They didn't see any increase in risk tolerance. Interview results? Unchanged [162, 113]. See also [177] for a statistical review. The various groups that have tried to reproduce Cuddy's work have mostly failed, but they've tested the finding mentioned to destruction and it's still there. After people have posed as Wonder Woman, or unleashed their inner Napoleon, for a couple of minutes, they report feeling more powerful[162, 81, 38].

101 This experiment [188] was also subject to a replication effort that failed [200]. However, Strack identified an important difference between his original experiment and the replication: the use of cameras to record the subjects [187]. When a group tried the experiment both with and without cameras, they failed to find any effect of smiling/frowning when a camera was present, but found one when there wasn't [151]. I've written more about this here: https://www.theguardian.com/science/2018/oct/17/smiling-does-make-you-happier-under-carefully-controlled-conditions

102 [184]

103 [64]. See [123] for a readable overview of self-perception theory and many further examples.

104 This is still true even if you smile alone in a locked room. We have evolved to signal to other people, but that doesn't mean our behaviours are switched off when we think there's nobody else around.

105 [109, 157]

106 [32]

107 The missing link is the impact of obedience and social pressure. We underestimate its effect on behaviour when we judge what other people say and do, and we also underestimate it when working out the causes of what we say and do ourselves.

108 [82]. Study 1 (volunteering) is horrifically designed. The volunteering scenario is for a research study that aimed at 'revealing' the negative consequences of discrimination against gays and lesbians. Not everybody would have perceived volunteering for this as an ethical action. Indeed, if the reason we're more moral when we're frightened is because we're more groupish, for some a higher heart rate might be the signal NOT to sign up. However, given that other studies show most (but not all) students are liberal-leaning, the dependent variable *probably* offered *most* of the students the chance to do something they believed was ethical (and conservatives would presumably have said no either way, but it would have been nice to see this as a control).

109 You can't usually hear your own pulse, so even if your heart rate is an input into your decision making then you must have some other way of detecting it. Whatever that mechanism is presumably continues operating whatever you hear.

110 [194]

111 [195]

112 You might note that when listening to thump-thump music, or watching a film with a heart-beat track, we don't necessarily attribute the noise to our own heart. And yet our mood changes, and quite possibly our behaviour. I agree. This is an important loose end that hasn't been tied up in the literature yet. Tying it up promises to be an interesting line of research linking social psychology, self-inference, emotions and music, which isn't a well-understood psychological phenomenon. What *is* the benefit of

humans enjoying listening to certain combinations of sounds; why does it bind us socially and change our emotional state? Nobody really knows.

However, on our main topic, some sort of misattribution does seem to be occurring. This is best shown in the erotic images study. Not only did the men rate the images higher when the rate was faster, they still preferred the images several weeks later when asked to choose some to take home (!) and without the presence of the sounds.

113 [55]

114 [22]

115 These type of manipulations work because we vastly underestimate how likely we are to do something because we're asked to do so, especially when our peers are doing it. Real knowledge of human behaviour is far harder to come by than imagined knowledge.

You might contrast the 'foot-in-the-door' experiments of this section with the 'moral licensing' sections we saw earlier (when doing good led people to be bad later). Mostly the difference seems to be whether you infer from your initial action that you believe in something (i.e. you learn you have a value) or that you have displayed your moral worth (i.e. you have learnt a different type of thing/displayed a different type of thing about yourself in the first step). If you plan to use these techniques, an interesting review of the differences is [149].

116 [83]

117 [24]

118 Indeed, the second group are *less* likely to offer their time after agreeing to the first request, perhaps reasoning that they've already done their bit. We might hypothesis that giving signals one way and then doing something else makes it harder to settle on a single view of themselves – or for other people to form a view and interact with them, unsure what they might do next. It is perhaps not surprising that they suffer for this capriciousness.

119 [87]

120 The same group of psychologists have done other magic tricks.

They've swapped jams and teas in consumer tests. They've switched pictures of women that men had rated. In general, they've gotten away with it [88, 99]. But entering those experiments, participants can't have had strong opinions about women they'd never seen or jams they hadn't tasted.

121 This isn't an isolated experiment. In another study, experimenters asked supporters of Schroeder and Stoiber (then competing for the German Chancellorship) whether they agreed with statements the two men had made. The voters tended to agree with the statements that they thought their man had made, even when it was the opposite of their actual position. It seems that we reason that we must support something because we believe in the arguments that are for it, when in fact we believe in the arguments because we believe in the answer [215].

122 Of course, when psychologists describe human behaviour, they too are building models. It's all science is. The physicist has a mathematical model of atoms with electrons, protons and neutrons. The chemist models reactions with double bonds and free electrons. But we should be able to separate science's best model of the causes of human actions and the internal model that we all have of the causes of our actions.

Ideally, we'd use different words. The impetus that makes you give money to the poor wouldn't be called generosity or compassion or duty or piety. You don't seek pleasure, you only infer that you do; you don't avoid pain, seek status or act ethically.

Unfortunately, we don't have such separate terms. This makes psychology seem easier than it is: when we read a result about prejudice, we imagine we know what it is talking about. But in truth, it makes psychology harder than it needs to be: it encourages scientists to imagine they also know, at some deep level, the characteristics they are talking about.

Psychology is behind the other sciences because of, not in spite of, the fact that we all come with rough and ready models of how people behave. The problem with psychologists is that they're humans. And humans think they know how humans work.

123 [48]

124 [172]

125 [75]

126 [2]

127 [135]. There's a link to a video of the experiment if you wonder how this is done in practice.

128 The entire fruit fly brain has been imaged with electron microscopy. Very cool. [214]

129 [87]. The researchers posed the question in many different ways: psychoactive drugs that distort personality and perception, and ensoulment. In each case, it was individuals' morality that was most important, with memory and personality (shy, playful, artistic, etc.) typically coming in as distant runners-up.

130 And if it does, would you like the old naïve person back?

131 [44]

132 Reviewed in e.g. [134]. You'll still be wrong frequently, though. And the reasons you're more often right may not be savoury.

133 Indeed, this happened. The experimenters quizzed the students further. Those who saw poor Hannah thought that the test was easy; those who saw rich Hannah thought the test was harder. They exaggerated which proportion of the questions in each category (easy, moderately difficult and difficult) they thought she got correct.

134 [43]. Other results showing that adding riskiness to the dictator game reduces people's altruism are in [86].

135 Contrast this with mink. One of the successes of the anti-fur movement is convincing shoppers that *all* mink fur is unethically produced (or at least a sufficient proportion of the population in countries such as the UK that wearing it is socially unacceptable). They also ensured that people were aware of their ethical concerns whether they wanted to or not. If instead they'd targeted certain farms with poor standards, I suspect that there'd have been a period in which some shoppers avoided those farms, but in the long run the farmers would have done fine as people chose not to look too closely at the provenance of their garments. It can be productive to be absolutist.

136 [36]

137 [80, 79]

138 [63]

139 What's very curious is that participants who were asked what *other* people would do underestimated this. We might have expected the arms race between manipulator and manipulated to have ironed these errors out. People speak to change your behaviour, and you try to correct for their biases and create accurate models of them. One possibility is that the volunteers were signalling their own intentions. If they say that other people would be less willing to shock when it was real, they are flaunting their own empathy and their willingness to believe in the goodness of others. It would be interesting to re-run the experiment with money and shocks on the table for the predictors too. Perhaps they could place bets on what people would answer in real and hypothetical scenarios. If their hand is placed on the table when somebody else is making a choice whether to give up money or give a shock, how confident are they really? One paradigm to do this would be to give the predictor the opportunity to give up some of their own money to reduce any shocks that they are given (unbeknown to the chooser). If they are really confident that other people would not give shocks for money, they would keep their money (and have their hand fried). The control group would presumably have accurate statistical information on what choosers did. In fact, it would be nice to have a sequence of 'control' groups who had different 'facts' about what people really did to investigate (a) whether they believed the manipulation, and (b) how they respond to perceived risk of shocks. But that's a lot of scorched skin.

140 [40]

141 Tajfel summarised his experiments in a *Scientific American* article: [179]. Asking subjects to estimate the number of dots in a cluster, and telling some that they are 'overestimators' and others that they are 'underestimators' works just as well.

142 Indeed, his set-up relied on the teens' total lack of interest in

abstract painters: in truth, he split the children at random, which-ever paintings they preferred, and none realised they'd been hoodwinked.

143   [54]; see also [52]. There are some interesting subtleties around how out-group members react to in-group members that we don't have space to go into. However, the pattern that even young children score the same as adults is replicated.

144   Much of the basic mind inference that we've been discussing in this book is new to them. [207]

145   [53]. Intriguingly, as a bi-product, they were able to measure boys and girls preference for their own sex. Girls have considerably more in-gender preference. This apparently replicates a large body of research on the topic. In fact, the main result is also driven by the girls showing much more preference for other children in the same colour group as they are in. The children who were rated/received coins were actually photos of children wearing red or blue clothing.

146   They can see what is coming. The consequences of us being how we are, are inevitably at odds with how we'd like to be.

147   If you think racism is genetically caused yet distinct from more general groupishness, it seems you might subscribe to one of two hypotheses.

The first is that the genes for racism belong to our earliest common ancestors. Implicit racism exists in infants of all groups that have been studied (from Africans to Europeans to Asians) because the group that gave birth to them had that gene. But this doesn't hold much water because the earliest common ances-tors didn't have races. Races must have come after this, once we'd colonised the world and become cut off from each other. What possible good could a racism gene have done to the common ancestor before there were races to discriminate against?

The second is that racism developed independently in each race once they'd formed. It was useful in some way. But this isn't plausible either because intra-race contact (or at least breeding) was low. If it wasn't, the races wouldn't exist.

148 E.g. [175].

149 [8]

150 Or at least won't spread with better than random chance, and this seems unlikely to be what happened in the case of the complicated mechanics behind racism or being nice to your twin.

151 Strictly speaking, it's not the number of genes that we share that matters. We share most of our genes with mice. What matters is the probability a member of the population shares the gene when the gene is spreading, or when a competing allele is spreading. It's the scenario *if there were* variation that's important – even when there is no variation. The details are beyond the scope of this book, but the point once grasped is profoundly satisfying. John Maynard Smith's book is the best I know of [182]. It requires a little maths, but it's a mathematical topic.

152 Even salmon are more aggressive when they're hungry. [150]

153 [127]

154 [145]

155 [14]. Importantly, attitudes of Whites to other Whites didn't change. It wasn't a generic cooling to all people, any of whom could be competitors, it was a cooling only to out-group members.

156 [91]

157 [120]. Of 71 participants in Study 1, 67 self-identified as White, one as Asian and three as Latino. In Study 2, all self-identified as White.

158 In this section, we find that ordinarily we can tell the difference between a fake and a real smile. But in an earlier section, we included evidence that holding a pen between your lips changes how funny you find cartoons. I think there is an explanation needed to bridge the two. To my knowledge, it isn't an inconsistency that has been resolved.

159 [67]

160 [110]. This experiment doesn't quite, in itself, demonstrate the link that emotional inference is impaired in experimentally created out-groups, but see [211] which does (though in a different way).

161 At least one test-seller explains that their product is (scientifically) valid because their research shows that a majority of participants

agree with the tests' findings. This is no great shakes. The tests are of self-perception; it would be a shock if they couldn't find a label that matched participants' self-perception.

Imagine I gave you a series of statements to score. 'I feel my energy levels rising in the evening,' 'I take a while to come round in the morning,' 'I like vampires better than larks', and so on. On the basis of your scoring, I declare that you're a Morning Person, A Night Owl, or A Good All-rounder. I then ask you whether you agree with the tests' results. If I can't get most people to say that the test is valid, then I've really messed up. Getting a high 'validity' score doesn't mean that my test is predictive of behaviour, or that taking the test (and sharing their results with colleagues) will improve workers' performance.

(Similarly, finding that the scores on almost synonymous questions correlate well isn't proof that the test is useful: just that you have a thesaurus. It's hidden in technical language, but the 'scientific confirmation' that some tests give amount to saying that most people who say they prefer mornings also say that they like evenings less. If they didn't, the test is clearly a dud, but the fact that they do isn't much to crow about.)

Another reason to shy away from such tests is that they might create, or emphasise, the extreme behaviour types. Giving personality test feedback (even false feedback) changes people's actions, and not necessarily for the better (e.g. [11]).

162 [202]. The Palestinians did measurably attribute other Palestinians' support of rocket firing to love for Palestinians above hatred for Israelis. But the difference was very small. (The belief that Israelis were motivated by hatred for Palestinians rather than love of their own was substantial, as were the differences in Israelis' beliefs on both measures.)

163 Logically, it's also possible that the Israelis are right on both counts and the Palestinians wrong on both counts or vice-versa.

164 [48]

165 2 Maccabees

166 One of the barbarian things that my British ancestors did in the time of Caesar was to drink milk. [92]

167 [156]

168 [26]

169 [89]

170 https://www.bbc.com/news/world-us-canada-47892747

171 https://www.telegraph.co.uk/women/womens-life/11308082/ Azealia-Banks-Vs-Iggy-Azalea-White-people-shouldnt-steal-hip-hop.html Think how absurd it would sound if somebody told Azealia that men had invented hip-hop and therefore women shouldn't write or perform it. There's a reason for this difference.

172 [71]

173 An expansion of some of these arguments (and a very interesting read) is: [50]. That paper focuses more on deciding which side to take in individual disputes; the current chapter suggests that moral judgement serves a broader function of determining groups. But the theoretical background is quite similar.

174 [179]

175 https://www.pewforum.org/2018/08/29/politics-and-policy-2/#highly-religious-groups-more-likely-than-others-to-morally-oppose-abortion-homosexual-behavior-and-drinking-alcohol Not considering it a moral issue doesn't mean that they are indifferent to whether it is legal or not. A moralist might think that eating bananas is neither moral nor immoral, but believe that banning people from eating bananas is wrong. It's also possible to believe that something is immoral, but still believe that the state shouldn't prohibit it. A liberal might think that gambling or taking crack is wrong, but still believe that individuals should make that choice rather than the state. As such, a majority of Americans are against overturning Roe vs Wade, at least in its entirety. https://www.pewresearch.org/politics/2019/0829/u-s-public-continues-to-favor-legal-abortion-oppose-overturning-roe-v-wade/#most-americans-oppose-overturning-roe-v-wade.

What isn't clear from these quizzes though is the strength of feeling on each side. If pro-lifers think that abortion is the killing of a person, we might expect them to be more strongly against it than pro-choicers are for it. If the ethical principle is really group signalling then you'll see equally strong reactions from both sides. In a completely unscientific (and surely biased) scouting for videos of pro-choice and pro-life rallies, I'd say that both sides are equally fanatical.

The abortion debate is fascinating for students of morality. There's the issue of backwards reasoning. It seems that some pro-choicers believe that unborn children aren't living humans. The academic, philosophical arguments in favour of legal abortion don't go there: it's quite hard to draw a line that makes the unborn anything other than (dependent) human individuals. What's probably happening is that pro-choice advocates (unknowingly so) are trying to square off 'killing is wrong' and 'abortion is OK'. How they do this should be studied a lot harder than it is.

Secondly, there's the question of how one side might convince the other side. Mostly, the debate seems (from across the pond) to be the type that we'd expect from group signalling, that is, with theoretical, philosophical and religious arguments. To a neutral moralist, the pro-choicers will win because the group membership stuff will go over their heads and it's easier to empathise with a woman facing the end of her career dreams than a clump of cells.

If I was fighting the pro-life battle, I'd emphasise the minds: foetus videos can be quite cute. Foetus movements lead us to infer minds. Indeed, minds of the right sort: vulnerable ones. (Pictures don't do it for me: they look like aliens.) As with all mind inference, that doesn't necessarily mean there's any such thing there. But contrast with conservation campaigners: they know they aren't going to win their battles by telling us that genetic diversity is a good thing for scientists in the future, or for the survival of a population. They don't get into the thorny question of whether the death of the last kind of a species is any more painful than the death of any other individual – they have panda mascots!

176 [174]. The prejudice scoring was an explicit measure. Irritatingly, there was no control that tested how far participants with various

scores would have sat from European American confederates. Do the less-prejudiced European Americans who believe that their group is also less prejudiced sit closer to African Americans to signal their group membership, or is there some conflict between this signalling and implicit prejudices? We don't know. We also can't rule out from this experiment the possibility that racists are antisocial types who'd sit further away from other people whoever they were. However, none of this detracts from the important effect for our purposes. The manipulation (made by the experimenters) of whether participants thought that prejudices were widely held was properly controlled and affected seating distance, which shows that seating distance is, at least in part, a group signalling effect.

177 One could make a case that economic changes, household appliances and easily available contraception have changed our attitudes to sex and the workplace. They have removed impediments to behaviour that was formerly inefficient or dangerous. Yet it's not at all clear that these are morally relevant changes.

178 [122]. I've simplified the dilemma a bit. See the supplementary information of [78] for the full thing (and other vignettes used in the study).

179 [215]

180 [93] Even when strongly moralised, only a minority are willing to have their opinions published. Most people are shy and wouldn't have their names in the student newspaper under an essay that said the Earth orbited the Sun, or a photo of them saying boo to a goose. Experimentally, the interesting thing is the direction of travel caused by the manipulation. People are considerably more willing to speak out about moral issues than non-moral issues, and they're indifferent to the norms of peers. The latter cuts across a huge body of scientific research on non-moral topics. Even on objective issues, such as which line is the longest (or, indeed, which beer tastes best!), people's attitudes move towards that of people like themselves [6]. Moral commitments really are strong.

181 [128]

182 But there are risks. People are willing to accept democracy, the

courts and compromise as ways of settling non-moral issues. Once they believe an ethical principle is at stake, the process doesn't matter, only the answer [180, 167]. And the only answer that's acceptable is the one that you and your group have claimed.

Political institutions, like money and morality, are imaginary: they have an effect because people believe in them. Morality is the stronger set of beliefs; when political issues are moralised, it's the political process that people stop believing in.

This matters because political institutions and morals are natural antagonists. Morals create stubborn, conflicting groups.

183 https://www.nytimes.com/2004/10/05/nyregion/study-finds-citys-muslims-growing-closer-since-911.html http://www.columbia.edu/cu/news/04/09/muslims.html

184 What you shouldn't do is what the Church of England do. They've steadily moved towards the common ethics outside the church with things like women bishops. They've installed a helter skelter in one cathedral and a pitch and putt golf course in another. No joke; look them up. I'm sure these are well-meaning attempts to increase the accessibility of their churches. But congregations aren't great, as we would predict.

Compare this with the tithing churches in the US. They demand members of the congregation give a percentage of their income to their pastors. The pastors drive swanky cars and live in mansions. This dual cost: giving up money and enduring ridicule for the non-Christian behaviours of the men skimming them help explain (rather than acting as obstacles to) their huge congregations.

185 [124]. See [58] chapter nine for many other experiments in the same vein.

186 [126]

187 E.g. [95, 107]

188 https://www.theguardian.com/world/2018/oct/10/germanys-afd-leader-alexander-gauland-accused-of-echoing-hitler-in-newspaper-article

189 https://www.theguardian.com/lifeandstyle/2017/sep/10/great-british-bake-off-presenter-paul-hollywood-pictured-wearing-fancy-dress-nazi-uniform

190 https://www.wistv.com/story/2805045/britains-prince-harry-criticized-for-wearing-nazi-uniform-to-costume-party/

191 In Britain, the outrage around swastika-wearing is about anti-Semitism. In the stories on Prince Harry and Paul Hollywood, you'll find references to the opinions of the Israeli foreign minister, holocaust survivors, the Board of Deputies of British Jews, the Holocaust Education Trust and the Reform Synagogues of Great Britain. There's comparatively little from non-Jewish veterans of the war. There aren't quotes from leaders of countries which were invaded. They weren't the story. See, for example, https://www.theguardian.com/media/2005/jan/13/roy; https://www.telegraph.co.uk/news/uknews/1481148/Prince-Harry-faces-outcry-at-Nazi-outfit.html

    Anti-Semitism is a live topic in the UK. As I write, one of the two large political parties is getting itself in a mess over the topic. There are tensions in the Middle East which, for historic and economic reasons, the UK still has a role in. Anti-Semitic incidents, from violence to name-calling to property damage are increasing steadily. https://www.bbc.com/news/uk-politics-45030552 https://www.theguardian.com/news/2019/feb/07/antisemitic-incidents-uk-record-high-third-year-in-row-community-security-trust

192 But I doubt this. When we dislike an argument, we imagine it might harm more feeble-minded types. We, of course, are too intelligent to be fooled.

193 [74]

194 [141]

195 There is an opposing view that purity and harm are distinct moral judgements. The main arguments of this chapter are agnostic to the ultimate answer (why should a signal be interpreted as harmful; we don't infer an old school tie is anything but a sign).But I think that the weight of evidence *at the moment* suggests that harm is the primary inference in negative moral judgements.

Even in the endnotes, there's not space to go into this controversy, or why I've reached the conclusions that I have. For the intrigued and diligent reader, some starting places are [84, 68, 165, 170, 190]. One thing to be wary of is dismissing claims of harm as 'post hoc justifications'. Nearly all social reasoning is a post hoc justification of one form or another (even if it's an internal testing of the social acceptability of a proposed action).

The controversy is also bound up with another: is morality reasoned or intuitive? But you can take different answers to the two. You can believe that the evidence is for intuitive moral decisions, yet think that people will ultimately construct reasons for these decisions that are mostly based on harm. One must also remember that morality's a communal thing: one might believe that the answer is certain and that the reasoning can be obtained, but also believe that the detailed reasoning could only be provided by somebody else. There's no inconsistency between a Catholic saying that the Trinity exists, that it's based on certain knowledge and infallible reasoning, but also that they haven't the foggiest what that reasoning is. I know that the heart is controlled by electrical impulses, but I couldn't give you a scrap of evidence for it: I put my trust in the knowledge of my community.

One also doesn't have to accept dyadic completion to accept the evidence gathered in support of the theory. It seems to me that this theory still suffers from a problem of punishment. The general idea in dyadic completion is that in immoral acts we see a victim and a perpetrator. The perpetrator is heavy in agency and the victim in experience. You lose one aspect of mind as you gain the other. Yet punishment is based (at least within our minds) on the idea that the perpetrator is capable of suffering. If a pederast gets hold of one of my daughters, I will do terrible things to him not because he can't feel, but because he can. If you can't explain punishment satisfactorily, it seems to me that you are missing the heart of morality.

But it's also worth reading a bit on motivated moral reasoning [121, 51]. Also on the biased searches that people make of information for and against their moral views (e.g. [125]), and the belief that people on both sides have that a report on a topic they care about is biased against them (e.g. [196]). These are all consistent with the view that people imagine that reasoning is important to their moral commitments. (As is the whole of moral philosophy.) And reasoning doesn't stop with 'it's impure and therefore it's wrong'.

On both a short time scale and after lengthier reasoning, on an implicit basis and a reportable one, harm of various forms seems to be at the root of people's moral commitments. Of course, this nicely ties groupish morality to the in-group morality of the earlier chapters.

196 Think back to the experiment which showed that people accepted their guilt when their confession was apparently unforced.

197 This isn't a unique position. Nobody really *gets* quantum mechanics or general relativity. They can do the maths behind them, and make and test the models' predictions. But the physical sciences don't demand of anybody that they change a fundamental part of themselves. This is the reason that social psychology is the hardest of all the sciences. And why we imagine it is the softest: because we already think we know how we work.

198 A truly excellent book on the numbers, and on what sorts of things make a difference (and don't) to carbon dioxide levels is [130]. I own up to some bias: David MacKay was one of my better lecturers as an undergraduate (though the topic was information theory rather than sustainable energy).

199 See https://crowtherlab.pageflow.io/cities-of-the-future-visualizing-climate-change-to-inspire-action

200 [21]

201 See https://www.epa.gov/climate-indicators/climate-change-indicators-atmospheric-concentrations-greenhouse-gases

202 [137] briefly reviews a number of reasons that climate change doesn't efficiently engage people's moral facilities.

203 You might counter that there have been storms, some flooding

and even droughts that might have been caused by (made more likely by) global warming. However, nothing has yet happened on a scale that would motivate the kind of changes that will need to be made to reduce carbon emissions meaningfully.

204 See e.g. [142] for a nuanced review of the effects of various perceived distances on willingness to act.

205 E.g. [114, 181]. Intriguingly, education isn't the key. When you tell people about the effect, they donate less to the named individual rather than more to the group.

206 [10]

207 [1]

208 [201]

209 Something rather less than 0.1 per cent by weight. https://phys.org/news/2018-04-science-amount-straws-plastic-pollution.html

210 [97]

211 [130]. His italics. He spoke with at least as many italics as he used in his writing.

212 [69]

213 If activists miraculously convinced naysayers of the scientific consensus, it would be the rationalisation that changed not the moral. They'd claim that it was impossible to stop global warming while China was polluting, for example. That the boffins will invent a carbon sink, or that they will engineer drought-resistant crops. It's not their problem to fix. It seems much less likely that they'd switch teams.

214 Buy yours here: https://shop.donaldjtrump.com/products/trump-straws

215 [186]

216 From burning fossil fuels [21].

217 See, for example, https://www.scmp.com/news/china/society/article/3030293/cool-reception-china-greta-thunbergs-global-warming-message http://www.globaltimes.cn/content/1173682.shtml The quote is in: https://www.ft.com/content/be1250c6-0c4d-11ea-b2d6-9bf4d1957a67

218 [130]

219 [96]

220 There has been some success when framing global warming as a conservative issue [65]

221 She might be a little less impressed by my casual conversion of correlation into causation. But if the tests made weren't tests of an explicit prediction, they should have been: that moral behaviour is a social signal ought to be an obvious hypothesis. (And already has plenty of experimental support as outlined in earlier parts of the book.) Within the paper, the researchers do a separate test that attempts to prove the direction of causation. But it's a hypothetical test with Amazon Mechanical Turk participants and isn't nearly as exciting as the main event. The headline is real behaviour with real money and real reputations at stake in a real-life setting and with vast data-sets.

222 I've since confirmed they actually do this. They even have an infographic, which I should also have predicted. 20TWH is the number they claim, which is apparently enough to power Spain for a month or toast 5,700 billion slices of bread.

Incidentally, Oracle cite savings of 1.5 to 2.5 percent 'with Opower Energy Efficiency (EE)' https://www.oracle.com/industries/utilities/products/opower-energy-efficiency-cloud-service/

223 People even engage in moral licensing within a single product choice. [60]. Because a single product has many environmental facets – it might be organic, low-carbon, or without single-use plastic – they are happy to purchase a product that is good on one dimension but poor on others.

224 I used four different online calculators. Three gave answers in this range, two at the top end, and the fourth gave an answer of half this (that calculator put a premium ticket in the range quoted). The per capita emissions of 4.8 tonnes is from [198].

225 [30]

226 https://ec.europa.eu/eurostat/statistics-explained/index.php/Air_transport_statistics

227 Mercedes' shareholders don't fund a Formula One team out of the goodness of their hearts. You might think that Mr Hamilton

is simply stupid. But if morals are to change people's behaviour for the better, they have to change the behaviour of the less intelligent portion of the population too. Indeed, most of the criticism of Hamilton was aimed at his personal carbon footprint and that of his team and sport rather than the demand they create for the high-performance petrol engines that his team sells. But surely the latter have a larger impact in aggregate.

228 UBS, the bank, estimated in 2019 that the number of flights within the EU would in the future increase by 1.5 per cent a year; half the rate than expected by Airbus (https://www.bbc.com/news/business49890057). Of course, the Covid-19 pandemic will have changed the figure somewhat.

229 But not as much as you might expect. Gasoline's notoriously price inelastic, at least in the short-term: the cost at the pump has to go up a lot before people stop going to work or school.

230 [119]

231 Walmart employs 2.2 million people (page 13, Annual Report 2019). The approximate date comes from assuming exponential growth using the data in Appendix C of [119].

REFERENCES

[1]   H-K. Ahn, H. J. Kim, and P. Aggarwal. Helping fellow beings: Anthropomorphized social causes and the role of anticipatory guilt. *Psychological Science*, 25(1):224–229, 2014.

[2]   E. Ambler. *The dark frontier*. Hodder, 1936.

[3]   D. R. Ames and G. V. Johar. I'll know what you're like when I see how you feel: How and when affective displays influence behavior-based impressions. *Psychological Science*, 20(5):586–593, 2009.

[4]   K. Andrews. Apes track false beliefs but might not understand them. *Learning & behavior*, 46(1):3–4, 2018.

[5]   I. Apperly. *Mindreaders: the cognitive basis of 'theory of mind'*. Psychology Press, 2010.

[6]   S. E. Asch. Opinions and social pressure. *Scientific American*, 193(5):31–35, 1955.

[7]   C. C. Ballew and A. Todorov. Predicting political elections from rapid and unreflective face judgements. *Proceedings of the National Academy of Sciences*, 104(46):17948–17953, 2007.

[8]   D. P. Barash. *The whisperings within*. Penguin, 1979.

[9]   P. Barclay. Altruism as a courtship display: Some effects of third-party generosity on audience perceptions. *British Journal of Psychology*, 101(1):123–135, 2010.

[10] J. Baron. Cognitive biases. In R. Goodman, D. Jinks, and A. K. Woods, editors, *In Understanding social action, promoting human rights*, page 203. OUP, 2012.

[11] R. F. Baumeister, J. M. Twenge, and C. K. Nuss. Effects of social exclusion on cognitive processes: Anticipated aloneness

reduces intelligent thought. *Journal of Personality and Social Psychology*, 83:817–827, 2002.

[12] D. J. Bem. Self-perception: an alternative interpretation of cognitive dissonance phenomena. *Psychological Review*, 74(3):183–200, 1967.

[13] J. Berg, J. Dickhaut, and K. McCabe. Trust, reciprocity, and social history. *Games and economic behavior*, 10(1):122– 142, 1995.

[14] E. C. Bianchi, E. V. Hall, and S. Lee. Reexamining the link between economic downturns and racial antipathy: Evidence that prejudice against blacks rises during recessions. *Psychological science*, 29(10):1584–1597, 2018.

[15] P. M. Bingham. Human uniqueness: A general theory. *The Quarterly Review of Biology*, 74(2):133–169, 1999.

[16] P. M. Bingham and J. Souza. *Death from a distance and the birth of a humane universe*. BookSurge, 2009.

[17] S. Blackburn. *Spreading the word: groundings in the philosophy of language*. OUP, 1984.

[18] I. V. Blair, C. M. Judd, and K. M. Chapleau. The influence of afro-centric facial features in criminal sentencing. *Psychological science*, 15(10):674–679, 2004.

[19] C. F. Bond, D. S. Berry, and A. Omar. The kernel of truth in judgements of deceptiveness. *Basic and Applied Social Psychology*, 15(4):523–534, 1994.

[20] R. Boyd, H. Gintis, and S. Bowles. Coordinated punishment of defectors sustains cooperation and can proliferate when rare. *Science*, 328(5978):617–620, 2010.

[21] BP. Statistical review of world energy. 2019.

[22] J. M. Burger and R. E. Guadagno. Self-concept clarity and the foot-in-the-door procedure. *Basic and Applied Social Psychology*, 25(1):79–86, 2003.

[23] D. Buttelmann, F. Buttelmann, M. Carpenter, J. Call, and M. Tomasello. Great apes distinguish true from false beliefs in an interactive helping task. *PLoS One*, 12(4):e0173793, 2017.

[24]   J. D. Campbell, P. D. Trapnell, S. J. Heine, I. M. Katz, L. F.
       Lavallee, and D. R. Lehman. Self-concept clarity:
       Measurement, personality correlates, and cultural boundaries.
       Journal of personality and social psychology, 70(1):141–156,
       1996.

[25]   K. M. Carlsmith, J. M. Darley, and P. H. Robinson. Why do
       we punish? Deterrence and just deserts as motives for punish-
       ment. *Journal of personality and social psychology*, 83(2):284,
       2002.

[26]   G. Carrus, A. Nenci, and P. Caddeo. The role of ethnic iden-
       tity and perceived ethnic norms in the purchase of ethnical
       food products. *Appetite*, 52(1):65–71, 2009.

[27]   P. Carruthers. How we know our own minds: the relationship
       between mindreading and metacognition. *Behavioral and
       Brain Sciences*, 32(2):121–182, 2009.

[28]   P. Carruthers. *The opacity of mind: An integrative theory of
       self-knowledge*. OUP, 2011.

[29]   E. Chen and K. A. Matthews. Cognitive appraisal biases: An
       approach to understanding the relation between socioeco-
       nomic status and cardiovascular reactivity in children. *Annals
       of Behavioral Medicine*, 23(2):101–111, 2001.

[30]   European Commission. *Special Eurobarometer 490: Climate
       Change*. 2019.

[31]   P. Conway and J. Peetz. When does feeling moral actually
       make you a better person? Conceptual abstraction moderates
       whether past moral deeds motivate consistency or compensa-
       tory behavior. *Personality and Social Psychology Bulletin*,
       38(7):907–919, 2012.

[32]   J. Cooper. Confessing to an immoral act. In J. P. Forgs, L.
       Jussim, and P. A. M. van Lange, editors, *The social
       psychology of morality*, pages 139–151. Routledge, 2016.

[33]   J. Cotte, R. A. Coulter, and M. Moore. Enhancing or
       disrupting guilt: The role of ad credibility and perceived
       manipulative intent. *Journal of Business Research*, 58(3):361–
       368, 2005.

[34] R. A. Coulter and M. B. Pinto. Guilt appeals in advertising: what are their effects? *Journal of applied Psychology*, 80(6):697, 1995.

[35] C. R. Critcher, Y. Inbar, and D. A. Pizarro. How quick decisions illuminate moral character. *Social Psychological and Personality Science*, 4(3):308–315, 2013.

[36] M. J. Crockett, Z. Kurth-Nelson, J. Z. Siegel, P. Dayan, and R. J. Dolan. Harm to others outweighs harm to self in moral decision making. *Proceedings of the National Academy of Sciences*, 111(48):17320–17325, 2014.

[37] R. Croson and U. Gneezy. Gender differences in preferences. *Journal of economic literature*, 47(2):448–74, 2009.

[38] A. Cuddy, S. J. Schultz, and N. E. Fosse. P-curving a more comprehensive body of research on postural feedback reveals clear evidential value for power-posing effects: Reply to Simmons and Simonsohn (2017). *Psychological Science*, 29(4):656–666, 2018.

[39] O. S. Curry, D. A. Mullins, and H. Whitehouse. Is it good to cooperate? *Current Anthropology*, 60(1):47–69, 2019.

[40] M. R. Dadds, C. Whiting, and D. J. Hawes. Associations among cruelty to animals, family conflict, and psychopathic traits in childhood. *Journal of interpersonal violence*, 21(3):411–429, 2006.

[41] M. Daly and M. Wilson. Child abuse and other risks of not living with both parents. *Ethology and sociobiology*, 6(4):197–210, 1985.

[42] M. Daly and M. Wilson. *Homicide*. Aldine Transaction, 1988.

[43] J. Dana, R. A. Weber, and J. Xi Kuang. Exploiting moral wiggle room: Experiments demonstrating an illusory preference for fairness. *Economic Theory*, 33(1):67–80, 2007.

[44] J. M. Darley and P. H. Gross. A hypothesis-confirming bias in labeling effects. *Journal of Personality and Social Psychology*, 44(1):20–33, 1983.

[45] J. M. Darley and T. S. Pittman. The psychology of compensatory

and retributive justice. *Personality and Social Psychology Review*, 7(4):324–336, 2003.

[46] P. J. Darlington. Group selection, altruism, reinforcement, and throwing in human evolution. *Proceedings of the National Academy of Sciences*, 72(9):3748–3752, 1975.

[47] S. Davidai and T. Gilovich. The ideal road not taken: The self-discrepancies involved in peoples most enduring regrets. *Emotion*, 18(3):439–452, 2018.

[48] J. M. R. Delgado. *Physical control of the mind: Toward a psycho-civilized society*. Harper and Row, 1969.

[49] S. Desai and A. Dubey. Caste in 21st century India: Competing narratives. *Economic and political weekly*, 46(11):40–49, 2012.

[50] P. DeScioli and R. Kurzban. Morality is for choosing sides. In K. Gray and J. Graham, editors, *Atlas of moral psychology*, pages 177–185. The Guilford Press, 2018.

[51] P. H. Ditto, D. A. Pizarro, and D. Tannenbaum. Motivated moral reasoning. *Psychology of learning and motivation*, 50:307–338, 2009.

[52] Y. Dunham, A. S. Baron, and M. R. Banaji. The development of implicit intergroup cognition. *Trends in cognitive sciences*, 12(7):248– 253, 2008.

[53] Y. Dunham, A. S. Baron, and S. Carey. Consequences of minimal group affiliations in children. *Child development*, 82(3):793–811, 2011.

[54] Y. Dunham, E. E. Chen, and M. R. Banaji. Two signatures of implicit intergroup attitudes: Developmental invariance and early enculturation. *Psychological Science*, 24(6):860–868, 2013.

[55] D. G. Dutton and A. P. Aron. Some evidence for heightened sexual attraction under conditions of high anxiety. *Journal of Personality and Social Psychology*, 30:510–517, 1974.

[56] R. Dworkin. Objectivity and truth: You'd better believe it. *Philosophy & Public Affairs*, 25(2):87–139, 1996.

[57] D. A. Effron, J. S. Cameron, and B. Monin. Endorsing Obama licenses favoring whites. *Journal of experimental social psychology*, 45(3):590–593, 2009.

[58] N. Ellemers. *Morality and the regulation of social behavior.* Routledge, 2017.

[59] N. Emler, S. Renwick, and B. Malone. The relationship between moral reasoning and political orientation. *Journal of Personality and Social Psychology,* 45(5):1073, 1983.

[60] J. Engel and N. Szech. A little good is good enough: Ethical consumption, cheap excuses, and moral self-licensing. *PloS One,* 15(1):e0227036, 2020.

[61] J. A. C. Everett, N. S. Faber, Julian Savulescu, and M. J. Crockett. The costs of being consequentialist: Social inference from instrumental harm and impartial beneficence. *Journal of Experimental Social Psychology,* 79:200–216, 2018.

[62] S. Fazel and J. Danesh. Serious mental disorder in 23000 prisoners: a systematic review of 62 surveys. *The Lancet,* 359(9306):545–550, 2002.

[63] O. Feldman-Hall, D. Mobbs, D. Evans, et al. What we say and what we do: The relationship between real and hypothetical moral choices. *Cognition,* 123(3):434–441, 2012.

[64] L. Festinger and J. M. Carlsmith. Cognitive consequences of forced compliance. *The Journal of Abnormal and Social Psychology,* 58(2):203–210, 1959.

[65] I. Feygina, J. T. Jost, and R. E. Goldsmith. System justification, the denial of global warming, and the possibility of "system-sanctioned change". *Personality and social psychology bulletin,* 36(3):326–338, 2010.

[66] R. A. Fisher. *The genetical theory of natural selection.* OUP, 1930/ 1958.

[67] J. P. Friesen, K. Kawakami, L. Vingilis-Jaremko, et al. Perceiving happiness in an intergroup context: The role of race and attention to the eyes in differentiating between true and false smiles. *Journal of personality and social psychology,* 116(3):375–395, 2019.

[68] J. A. Frimer, C. E. Tell, and J. Haidt. Liberals condemn sacrilege too: The harmless desecration of Cerro Torre. *Social Psychological and Personality Science,* 6(8):878–886, 2015.

[69] C. Funk and M. Hefferon. *U.S. Public Views on Climate and Energy*. Pew Research Centre, 2019.

[70] F. Gino and D. Ariely. The dark side of creativity: Original thinkers can be more dishonest. *Journal of personality and social psychology*, 102(3):445–459, 2012.

[71] H. Gintis, C. van Schaik, and C. Boehm. Zoon politikon: The evolutionary origins of human socio-political systems. *Behavioural processes*, 161:17–30, 2019.

[72] G. P. Goodwin, J. Piazza, and P. Rozin. Moral character predominates in person perception and evaluation. *Journal of personality and social psychology*, 106(1):148–168, 2014.

[73] H. M. Gray, K. Gray, and D. M. Wegner. Dimensions of mind perception. *Science*, 315(5812):619–619, 2007.

[74] K. Gray, C. Schein, and A. F. Ward. The myth of harmless wrongs in moral cognition: Automatic dyadic completion from sin to suffering. *Journal of Experimental Psychology: General*, 143(4):1600– 1615, 2014.

[75] K. Gray and D. M. Wegner. The sting of intentional pain. *Psychological Science*, 19(12):1260–1262, 2008.

[76] K. Gray and D. M. Wegner. Moral typecasting: Divergent perceptions of moral agents and moral patients. *Journal of personality and social psychology*, 96(3):505, 2009.

[77] K. Gray, L. Young, and A. Waytz. Mind perception is the essence of morality. *Psychological inquiry*, 23(2):101–124, 2012.

[78] J. D. Greene, S. A. Morelli, K. Lowenberg, L. E. Nystrom, and J. D. Cohen. Cognitive load selectively interferes with utilitarian moral judgement. *Cognition*, 107(3):1144–1154, 2008.

[79] J. D. Greene, L. E. Nystrom, A. D. Engell, J. M. Darley, and J. D. Cohen. The neural bases of cognitive conflict and control in moral judgement. *Neuron*, 44(2):389–400, 2004.

[80] J. D. Greene, R. B. Sommerville, L. E. Nystrom, J. M. Darley, and J. D. Cohen. An fMRI investigation of emotional engagement in moral judgement. *Science*, 293:2105–2108, 2001.

[81] Q. F. Gronau, S. Van Erp, D. W. Heck, J. Cesario, K. J. Jonas, and E. Wagenmakers. A Bayesian model-averaged meta-analysis of the power pose effect with informed and default priors: The case of felt power. *Comprehensive Results in Social Psychology*, 2(1):123–138, 2017.

[82] J. Gu, C-B. Zhong, and E. Page-Gould. Listen to your heart: When false somatic feedback shapes moral behavior. *Journal of Experimental Psychology: General*, 142(2):307–312, 2013.

[83] R. E. Guadagno and J. M. Burger. Self-concept clarity and responsiveness to false feedback. *Social Influence*, 2(3):159–177, 2007.

[84] J. Haidt. The emotional dog and its rational tail: A social intuitionist approach to moral judgement. *Psychological review*, 108(4):814, 2001.

[85] J. Haidt, S. H. Koller, and M. G. Dias. Affect, culture, and morality, or is it wrong to eat your dog? *Journal of personality and social psychology*, 65(4):613, 1993.

[86] E. C. Haisley and R. A. Weber. Self-serving interpretations of ambiguity in other-regarding behavior. *Games and Economic Behavior*, 68(2):614–625, 2010.

[87] L. Hall, P. Johansson, and T. Strandberg. Lifting the veil of morality: Choice blindness and attitude reversals on a self-transforming survey. *PloS One*, 7(9):e45457, 2012.

[88] L. Hall, P. Johansson, B. Tärning, S. Sikström, and T. Deutgen. Magic at the marketplace: Choice blindness for the taste of jam and the smell of tea. *Cognition*, 117(1):54–61, 2010.

[89] C. M. Harmeling, R. W. Palmatier, E. Fang, and D. Wang. Group marketing: Theory, mechanisms, and dynamics. *Journal of Marketing*, 81(4):1–24, 2017.

[90] J. Heffner and O. Feldman-Hall. Why we don't always punish: Preferences for non-punitive responses to moral violations. *Scientific reports*, 9(1):1–13, 2019.

[91] J. T. Hepworth and S. G. West. Lynchings and the economy: A time-series reanalysis of Hovland and Sears (1940). *Journal of Personality and Social Psychology*, 55(2):239–247, 1988.

[92] T. Holland. *Rubicon*. Hachette UK, 2011.

[93] M. J. Hornsey, J. R. Smith, and D. Begg. Effects of norms among those with moral conviction: Counter-conformity emerges on intentions but not behaviors. *Social Influence*, 2(4):244–268, 2007.

[94] J. Howland, R. Hingson, T. W. Mangione, et al. Why are most drowning victims men? Sex differences in aquatic skills and behaviors. *American journal of public health*, 86(1):93–96, 1996.

[95] Y. Inbar and J. Lammers. Political diversity in social and personality psychology. *Perspectives on Psychological Science*, 7(5):496–503, 2012.

[96] J. M. Jachimowicz, O. P. Hauser, J. D. OBrien, E. Sherman, and A. D. Galinsky. The critical role of second-order normative beliefs in predicting energy conservation. *Nature Human Behaviour*, 2(10):757–769, 2018.

[97] J. R. Jambeck, R. Geyer, and C. Wilcox and others. Plastic waste inputs from land into the ocean. *Science*, 347(6223):768–771, 2015.

[98] S. A. Jelbert, A. H. Taylor, L. G. Cheke, N. S. Clayton, and R. D. Gray. Using the Aesop's fable paradigm to investigate causal understanding of water displacement by New Caledonian crows. *PloS One*, 9(3):e92895, 2014.

[99] P. Johansson, L. Hall, S. Sikstrom, and A. Olsson. Failure to detect mismatches between intention and outcome in a simple decision task. *Science*, 310:116–119, 2005.

[100] J. J. Jordan, M. Hoffman, P. Bloom, and D. G. Rand. Third-party punishment as a costly signal of trustworthiness. *Nature*, 530(7591):473, 2016.

[101] J. J. Jordan and D. G. Rand. Signaling when no one is watching:
A reputation heuristics account of outrage and punishment in one-shot anonymous interactions. *Journal of personality and social psychology*, 118(1):57, 2020.

[102] J. J. Jordan, R. Sommers, P. Bloom, and D. G. Rand. Why do

we hate hypocrites? Evidence for a theory of false signaling. *Psychological science*, 28(3):356–368, 2017.

[103] J. Jordan, E. Mullen, and J. Keith Murnighan. Striving for the moral self: The effects of recalling past moral actions on future moral behavior. *Personality and Social Psychology Bulletin*, 37(5):701–713, 2011.

[104] R. Joyce. *The myth of morality*. CUP, 2001.

[105] R. Joyce. Moral fictionalism. In M. E. Kalderon, editor, *Fictionalism in metaphysics*, pages 287–313. OUP, 2005.

[106] R. Joyce. *The evolution of morality*. MIT press, 2007.

[107] L. Jussim. Liberal privilege in academic psychology and the social sciences: Commentary on Inbar & Lammers (2012). *Perspectives on Psychological Science*, 7(5):504–507, 2012.

[108] K. Karg, M. Schmelz, J. Call, and M. Tomasello. Differing views: Can chimpanzees do level 2 perspective-taking? *Animal Cognition*, 19(3):555–564, 2016.

[109] S. M. Kassin and K. L. Kiechel. The social psychology of false confessions: Compliance, internalization, and confabulation. *Psychological science*, 7(3):125–128, 1996.

[110] K. Kawakami, A. Williams, D. Sidhu, et al. An eye for the I: Preferential attention to the eyes of ingroup members. *Journal of Personality and Social Psychology*, 107(1):1–20, 2014.

[111] S. Kelly and R. I. M. Dunbar. Who dares, wins. *Human Nature*, 12(2):89–105, 2001.

[112] U. Khan and R. Dhar. Where there is a way, is there a will? The effect of future choices on self-control. *Journal of Experimental Psychology: General*, 136(2):277, 2007.

[113] L. Klaschinski, K. Schnabel, and M. Schröder-Abé. Benefits of power posing: Effects on dominance and social sensitivity. *Comprehensive Results in Social Psychology*, 2(1):55–67, 2017.

[114] T. Kogut and I. Ritov. The 'identified victim' effect: an identified group, or just a single individual? *Journal of Behavioral Decision Making*, 18(3):157–167, 2005.

[115] L. Kohlberg. Continuities in childhood and adult moral development revisited. In P. B. Baltes and K. W. Schaie, *Life-span developmental psychology*, pages 179–204. Elsevier, 1973.

[116] M. W. Kraus, S. Côté, and D. Keltner. Social class, contextualism, and empathic accuracy. *Psychological science*, 21(11):1716–1723, 2010.

[117] M. W. Kraus and D. Keltner. Social class rank, essentialism, and punitive judgement. *Journal of personality and social psychology*, 105(2):247, 2013.

[118] M. W. Kraus, P. K. Piff, R. Mendoza-Denton, M. L. Rheinschmidt, and D. Keltner. Social class, solipsism, and contextualism: how the rich are different from the poor. *Psychological review*, 119(3):546, 2012.

[119] M. Kremer. Population growth and technological change: One million BC to 1990. *The Quarterly Journal of Economics*, 108(3):681–716, 1993.

[120] A. R. Krosch and D. M. Amodio. Scarcity disrupts the neural encoding of black faces: A socioperceptual pathway to discrimination. *Journal of personality and social psychology*, 117(5):859, 2019.

[121] Z. Kunda. The case for motivated reasoning. *Psychological Bulletin*, 108(3):480–498, 1990.

[122] P. Kundu and D. D. Cummins. Morality and conformity: The Asch paradigm applied to moral decisions. *Social Influence*, 8(4):268–279, 2013.

[123] J. D. Laird. *Feelings: The perception of self*. Oxford University Press, 2007.

[124] C. W. Leach, N. Ellemers, and M. Barreto. Group virtue: the importance of morality (vs. competence and sociability) in the positive evaluation of in-groups. *Journal of personality and social psychology*, 93(2):234–249, 2007.

[125] C. G. Lord, L. Ross, and M. R. Lepper. Biased assimilation and attitude polarization: the effects of prior theories on subsequently considered evidence. *Journal of Personality and Social Psychology*, 37:2098–2109, 1979.

[126] J. G. Lu, J. Quoidbachi, F. Gino, A. Chakroff, W. W. Maddux, and A. D. Galinsky. The dark side of going abroad: How broad foreign experiences increase immoral behavior. *Journal of personality and social psychology*, 112(1-16):1, 2017.

[127] D. Lukas and E. Huchard. The evolution of infanticide by females in mammals. *Philosophical Transactions of the Royal Society of London. Series B, Biological Sciences*, 2020.

[128] A. Luttrell, R. E. Petty, P. Briñol, and B. C. Wagner. Making it moral: Merely labeling an attitude as moral increases its strength. *Journal of Experimental Social Psychology*, 65:82–93, 2016.

[129] Machiavelli. *The Prince*. CUP, 2019.

[130] D. MacKay. *Sustainable Energy – without the hot air*. UIT Cambridge, 2008.

[131] J. L. Mackie. *Ethics: Inventing right and wrong*. Pelican, 1977.

[132] A. Maden, M. Swinton, and J. Gunn. A survey of pre-arrest drug use in sentenced prisoners. *British journal of addiction*, 87(1):27–33, 1992.

[133] R. Mahalingam. Essentialism, power, and the representation of social categories: A folk sociology perspective. *Human Development*, 50(6):300–319, 2007.

[134] C. K. Malecki and M. K. Demaray. Social support as a buffer in the relationship between socioeconomic status and academic performance. *School Psychology Quarterly*, 21(4):375–395, 2006.

[135] B. R. Malik and J. J. L. Hodge. Drosophila adult olfactory shock learning. *JoVE (Journal of Visualized Experiments)*, (90):e50107, 2014.

[136] J. Mann, B. L. Sargeant, J. J. Watson-Capps, et al. Why do dolphins carry sponges? *PloS One*, 3(12):e3868, 2008.

[137] E. M. Markowitz and A. F. Shariff. Climate change and moral judgement. *Nature Climate Change*, 2(4):243–247, 2012.

[138] N. Mazar and C-B. Zhong. Do green products make us better people? *Psychological science*, 21(4):494–498, 2010.

[139] A. Mazur, J. Mazur, and C. Keating. Military rank attainment

of a west point class: Effects of cadets' physical features. *American Journal of Science*, 90:125–150, 1984.

[140] K. McAuliffe, J. J. Jordan, and F. Warneken. Costly third-party punishment in young children. *Cognition*, 134:1–10, 2015.

[141] A. McCoy. *An intelligent person's guide to Catholicism.* Continuum, 2005.

[142] R. I. McDonald, H. Y. Chai, and B. R. Newell. Personal experience and the psychological distance of climate change: An integrative review. *Journal of Environmental Psychology*, 44:109–118, 2015.

[143] A. C. Merritt, D. A. Effron, and B. Monin. Moral self-licensing: When being good frees us to be bad. *Social and personality psychology compass*, 4(5):344–357, 2010.

[144] A. Miller. *Contemporary metaethics: an introduction* (2nd edition). Polity, 2013.

[145] B. Miller. Exploring the economic determinants of immigration attitudes. *Poverty & Public Policy*, 4(2):1–19, 2012.

[146] L. Molleman, F. Kölle, C. Starmer, and S. Gächter. People prefer coordinated punishment in cooperative interactions. *Nature human behaviour*, 3(11):1145–1153, 2019.

[147] J. M. Moran, L. L. Young, R. Saxe, S. M. Lee, D. O'Young, P. L. Mavros, and J. D. Gabrieli. Impaired theory of mind for moral judgement in high-functioning autism. *Proceedings of the National Academy of Sciences*, 108(7):2688–2692, 2011.

[148] Y. Mu, S. Kitayama, S. Han, and M. J. Gelfand. How culture gets embrained: Cultural differences in event-related potentials of social norm violations. *Proceedings of the National Academy of Sciences*, 112(50):15348–15353, 2015.

[149] E. Mullen and B. Monin. Consistency versus licensing effects of past moral behavior. *Annual review of psychology*, 67:363–385, 2016.

[150] A. G. Nicieza and N. B. Metcalfe. Growth compensation in juvenile Atlantic salmon: Responses to depressed temperature and food availability. *Ecology*, 78(8):2385–2400, 1997.

[151] T. Noah, Y. Schul, and R. Mayo. When both the original study and its failed replication are correct: Feeling observed eliminates the facial-feedback effect. *Journal of personality and social psychology*, 114(5):657–664, 2018.

[152] G. Nunner-Winkler and B. Sodian. Children's understanding of moral emotions. *Child development*, 59(5): 1323–1338, 1988.

[153] D. Okada and P. M. Bingham. Human uniqueness-self-interest and social cooperation. *Journal of theoretical biology*, 253(2):261–270, 2008.

[154] K. Okanoya, N. Tokimoto, N. Kumazawa, S. Hihara, and A. Iriki. Tool-use training in a species of rodent: The emergence of an optimal motor strategy and functional understanding. *PloS One*, 3(3):e1860, 2008.

[155] G. H. Patel, D. Yang, E. Jamerson, L. H. Snyder, M. Corbetta, and V. P. Ferrera. Functional evolution of new and expanded attention networks in humans. *Proceedings of the National Academy of Sciences*, 112(30):9454–9459, 2015.

[156] J. E. Pelletier, D. J. Graham, and M. N. Laska. Social norms and dietary behaviors among young adults. *American journal of health behavior*, 38(1):144–152, 2014.

[157] J. T. Perillo and S. M. Kassin. Inside interrogation: The lie, the bluff, and false confessions. *Law and Human Behavior*, 35(4):327–337, 2011.

[158] P. K. Piff, M. W. Kraus, S. Côté, B. H. Cheng, and D. Keltner. Having less, giving more: the influence of social class on prosocial behavior. *Journal of personality and social psychology*, 99(5):771–784, 2010.

[159] P. K. Piff, D. M. Stancato, S. Côté, R. Mendoza-Denton, and D. Keltner. Higher social class predicts increased unethical behavior. *Proceedings of the National Academy of Sciences*, 109(11):4086–4091, 2012.

[160] Plato. *The Republic*. CUP, 2000.

[161] Plato. *The Laws*. CUP, 2016.

[162] E. Ranehill, A. Dreber, M. Johannesson, S. Leiberg, S. Sul, and R. A. Weber. Assessing the robustness of power posing: No

effect on hormones and risk tolerance in a large sample of men and women. *Psychological science*, 26(5):653–656, 2015.

[163] M. Rendall, C. Couer, T. Lappegard, et al. First births by age and education in Britain, France and Norway. *Population Trends*, 121:27–34, 2005.

[164] N. T. Roach, M. Venkadesan, M. J. Rainbow, and D. E. Lieberman. Elastic energy storage in the shoulder and the evolution of high-speed throwing in Homo. *Nature*, 498(7455):483–486, 2013.

[165] E. B. Royzman, K. Kim, and R. F. Leeman. The curious tale of Julie and Mark: unraveling the moral dumbfounding effect. *Judgement & Decision Making*, 10(4):296–313, 2015.

[166] B. Russell. *History of Western philosophy*. Simon & Schuster, 1945.

[167] T. J. Ryan. No compromise: Political consequences of moralized attitudes. *American Journal of Political Science*, 61(2):409–423, 2017.

[168] S. Sachdeva, R. Iliev, and D. L. Medin. Sinning saints and saintly sinners: The paradox of moral self-regulation. *Psychological science*, 20(4):523–528, 2009.

[169] R. Saxe. Uniquely human social cognition. *Current opinion in neurobiology*, 16(2):235–239, 2006.

[170] C. Schein and K. Gray. The theory of dyadic morality: Reinventing moral judgement by redefining harm. *Personality and Social Psychology Review*, 22(1):32–70, 2018.

[171] D. Schkade, Cass R. Sunstein, and D. Kahneman. Deliberating about dollars: The severity shift. *Colum. L. Rev.*, 100:1139, 2000.

[172] A. Schweiger and A. Parducci. Nocebo: The psychologic induction of pain. *The Pavlovian journal of biological science*, 16(3):140–143, 1981.

[173] E. Schwitzgebel. Do ethicists steal more books? *Philosophical Psychology*, 22(6):711–725, 2009.

[174] G. B. Sechrist and C. Stangor. Perceived consensus influences intergroup behavior and stereotype accessibility. *Journal of personality and social psychology*, 80(4):645–654, 2001.

[175] N. L. Segal and S. L. Hershberger. Cooperation and competition between twins: Findings from a prisoners dilemma game. *Evolution and Human Behavior*, 20(1):29–51, 1999.

[176] R. Shafer-Landau and T. Cuneo. *Foundations of ethics: an anthology*. Blackwell, 2007.

[177] J. P. Simmons and U. Simonsohn. Power posing: P-curving the evidence. *Psychological science*, 28(5):687–693, 2017.

[178] T. Singer, B. Seymour, J. P. O'Doherty, K. E. Stephan, R. J. Dolan, and C. D. Frith. Empathic neural responses are modulated by the perceived fairness of others. *Nature*, 439:466–469, 2006.

[179] L. J. Skitka, C. W. Bauman, and E. G. Sargis. Moral conviction: Another contributor to attitude strength or something more? *Journal of personality and social psychology*, 88(6):895–917, 2005.

[180] L. J. Skitka and G. S. Morgan. The social and political implications of moral conviction. *Political psychology*, 35:95–110, 2014.

[181] D. A. Small, G. Loewenstein, and P. Slovic. Sympathy and callousness: The impact of deliberative thought on donations to identifiable and statistical victims. *Organizational Behavior and Human Decision Processes*, 102(2):143–153, 2007.

[182] J. Maynard Smith. *Evolutionary genetics*. Oxford University Press, 1998.

[183] J-Y. Son, A. Bhandari, and O. Feldman-Hall. Crowdsourcing punishment: Individuals reference group preferences to inform their own punitive decisions. *Scientific reports*, 9(1):1–15, 2019.

[184] S. Stepper and F. Strack. Proprioceptive determinants of emotional and nonemotional feelings. *Journal of Personality and Social Psychology*, 64:211–211, 1993.

[185] M. Stirrat and D. I. Perrett. Valid facial cues to cooperation and trust: Male facial width and trustworthiness. *Psychological science*, 21(3):349–354, 2010.

[186] B. Stokes, R. Wike, J. Carle, et al. *Global Concern about Climate Change, Broad Support for Limiting Emissions*. Pew Research Centre, 2015.

[187] F. Strack. Reflection on the smiling registered replication report. *Perspectives on Psychological Science*, 11(6):929–930, 2016.

[188] F. Strack, L. L. Martin, and S. Stepper. Inhibiting and facilitating conditions of the human smile: A nonobtrusive test of the facial feedback hypothesis. *Journal of Personality and Social Psychology*, 54(5):768–777, 1988.

[189] H. Tajfel. Experiments in intergroup discrimination. *Scientific American*, 223(5):96–103, 1970.

[190] B. Tepe and A. Aydinli-Karakulak. Beyond harmfulness and impurity: Moral wrongness as a violation of relational motivations. *Journal of personality and social psychology*, 117(2):310–337, 2019.

[191] A. Todorov, C. Y. Olivola, R. Dotsch, and P. Mende-Siedlecki. Social attributions from faces: Determinants, consequences, accuracy, and functional significance. *Annual review of psychology*, 66:519–545, 2015.

[192] A. Todorov, M. Pakrashi, and N. N. Oosterhof. Evaluating faces on trustworthiness after minimal time exposure. *Social Cognition*, 27(6):813–833, 2009.

[193] A. Todorov, C. P. Said, A. D. Engell, and N. N. Oosterhof. Understanding evaluation of faces on social dimensions. *Trends in cognitive sciences*, 12(12):455–460, 2008.

[194] S. Valins. Cognitive effects of false heart rate feedback. *Journal of personality and social psychology*, 4(4):400–408, 1966.

[195] S. Valins and A. A. Ray. Effects of cognitive desensitization on avoidance behavior. *Journal of Personality and Social Psychology*, 7(4):345–350, 1967.

[196] R. P. Vallone, L. Ross, and M. R. Lepper. The hostile media phenomenon: Biased perception and perceptions of media bias in coverage of the Beirut massacre. *Journal of Personality and Social Psychology*, 49:577–585, 1985.

[197] M. Van der Veen, A. R. Hall, and J. May. Woad and the Britons painted blue. *Oxford Journal of Archaeology*, 12(3):367–371, 1993.

[198] Various. Time to act: special edition on climate change. *Nature*, 573(7774):303–456, 2019.

[199] M. Virkkunen, J. De Jong, J. Bartko, F. K. Goodwin, and M. Linnola. Relationship of psychobiological variables to recidivism in violent offenders and impulsive fire setters: a follow-up study. *Archives of General Psychiatry*, 46(7):600, 1989.

[200] E-J. Wagenmakers, T. Beek, L. Dijkhoff, et al. Registered replication report: Strack, Martin, & Stepper (1988). *Perspectives on Psychological Science*, 11(6):917–928, 2016.

[201] Waitrose. *Food and drink report 2018-2019*. 2019.

[202] A. Waytz, L. L. Young, and J. Ginges. Motive attribution asymmetry for love vs. hate drives intractable conflict. *Proceedings of the National Academy of Sciences*, 111(44):15687–15692, 2014.

[203] D. M. Wegner. *The illusion of conscious will*. MIT press, 2002.

[204] D. M. Wegner. The minds self-portrait. *Annals of the New York Academy of Sciences*, 1001:1–14, 2003.

[205] K. Weisman, C. S. Dweck, and E. M. Markman. Rethinking peoples conceptions of mental life. *Proceedings of the National Academy of Sciences*, 114(43):11374–11379, 2017.

[206] H. M. Wellman and A. C. Brandone. Early intention understandings that are common to primates predict children's later theory of mind. *Current opinion in neurobiology*, 19(1):57–62, 2009.

[207] H. M. Wellman and D. Liu. Scaling of theory-of-mind tasks. *Child development*, 75(2):523–541, 2004.

[208] P. Wühr, B. P. Lange, and S. Schwarz. Tears or fears? Comparing gender stereotypes about movie preferences to actual preferences. *Frontiers in psychology*, 8:428, 2017.

[209] L. Young, J. A. Camprodon, M. Hauser, A. Pascual-Leone,

and R. Saxe. Disruption of the right temporoparietal junction with transcranial magnetic stimulation reduces the role of beliefs in moral judgements. *Proceedings of the National Academy of Sciences*, 107(15):6753–6758, 2010.

[210] L. Young, F. Cushman, M. Hauser, and R. Saxe. The neural basis of the interaction between theory of mind and moral judgement. *Proceedings of the National Academy of Sciences*, 104(20):8235–8240, 2007.

[211] S. G. Young and K. Hugenberg. Mere social categorization modulates identification of facial expressions of emotion. *Journal of Personality and Social Psychology*, 99(6):964–977, 2010.

[212] L. A. Zebrowitz, C. Andreoletti, M. Collins, S. Lee, and J. Blumenthal. Bright, bad, babyfaced boys: Appearance stereotypes do not always yield self-fulfilling prophecy effects. *Journal of personality and social psychology*, 75(5):1300–1320, 1998.

[213] L. A. Zebrowitz, L. Voinescu, and M. A. Collins. 'wide-eyed' and 'crooked-faced': Determinants of perceived and real honesty across the life span. *Personality and social psychology bulletin*, 22(12):1258– 1269, 1996.

[214] Z. Zheng, J. S. Lauritzen, E. Perlman, et al. A complete electron microscopy volume of the brain of adult Drosophila melanogaster. *Cell*, 174(3):730–743, 2018.

[215] R. Ziegler and M. Diehl. Is politician A or politician B more persuasive? Recipients' source preference and the direction of biased message processing. *European Journal of Social Psychology*, 33:623– 637, 2003.